ABORIGINAL PEOPLES AND ELECTORAL REFORM IN CANADA

~

*This is Volume 9 in a series of studies
commissioned as part of the research program
of the Royal Commission on Electoral Reform
and Party Financing*

ABORIGINAL PEOPLES AND ELECTORAL REFORM IN CANADA

~

Robert A. Milen
Editor

Volume 9 of the Research Studies

ROYAL COMMISSION ON ELECTORAL REFORM
AND PARTY FINANCING
AND CANADA COMMUNICATION GROUP –
PUBLISHING, SUPPLY AND SERVICES CANADA

DUNDURN PRESS
TORONTO AND OXFORD

ISBN 1-55002-105-2
ISSN 1188-2743
Catalogue No. Z1-1989/2-41-9E

Published by Dundurn Press Limited in cooperation with the Royal
Commission on Electoral Reform and Party Financing and Canada
Communication Group – Publishing, Supply and Services Canada.

Canadian Cataloguing in Publication Data

Main entry under title:
Aboriginal peoples and electoral reform in Canada

(Research studies ; 9)
Issued also in French under title: Les Peuples autochtones et la réforme
  électorale au Canada.
ISBN 1-55002-105-2

  1. Indians of North America – Canada – Politics and government.
2. Elections – Canada. I. Milen, Robert A. (Robert Alexander), 1948–   .
II. Canada. Royal Commission on Electoral Reform and Party Financing.
III. Series: Research studies (Canada. Royal Commission on Electoral Reform
and Party Financing) ; 9.

E78.C2A26 1991   323.1′197071   C91-090521-5

Dundurn Press Limited
2181 Queen Street East
Suite 301
Toronto, Canada
M4E 1E5

Dundurn Distribution
73 Lime Walk
Headington
Oxford, England
OX3 7AD

CONTENTS

FIGURES

3. ABORIGINAL PEOPLES AND CAMPAIGN COVERAGE IN THE NORTH

TABLES

3. ABORIGINAL PEOPLES AND CAMPAIGN COVERAGE IN THE NORTH

4. ELECTORAL REFORM AND CANADA'S ABORIGINAL POPULATION: AN ASSESSMENT OF ABORIGINAL ELECTORAL DISTRICTS

FOREWORD

~

THE ROYAL COMMISSION on Electoral Reform and Party Financing
was established in November 1989. Our mandate was to inquire into
and report on the appropriate principles and process that should gov-
ern the election of members of the House of Commons and the financing of political parties and candidates' campaigns. To conduct such a
comprehensive examination of Canada's electoral system, we held
extensive public consultations and developed a research program
designed to ensure that our recommendations would be guided by an
independent foundation of empirical inquiry and analysis.

The Commission's in-depth review of the electoral system was the
first of its kind in Canada's history of electoral democracy. It was dictated largely by the major constitutional, social and technological
changes of the past several decades, which have transformed Canadian
society, and their concomitant influence on Canadians' expectations
of the political process itself. In particular, the adoption in 1982 of the
Canadian Charter of Rights and Freedoms has heightened Canadians'
awareness of their democratic and political rights and of the way they
are served by the electoral system.

The importance of electoral reform cannot be overemphasized. As
the Commission's work proceeded, Canadians became increasingly
preoccupied with constitutional issues that have the potential to change
the nature of Confederation. No matter what their beliefs or political
allegiances in this continuing debate, Canadians agree that constitutional
change must be achieved in the context of fair and democratic processes. We cannot complacently assume that our current electoral
process will always meet this standard or that it leaves no room for
improvement. Parliament and the national government must be seen
as legitimate; electoral reform can both enhance the stature of national

political institutions and reinforce their ability to define the future of our country in ways that command Canadians' respect and confidence and promote the national interest.

In carrying out our mandate, we remained mindful of the importance of protecting our democratic heritage, while at the same time balancing it against the emerging values that are injecting a new dynamic into the electoral system. If our system is to reflect the realities of Canadian political life, then reform requires more than mere tinkering with electoral laws and practices.

Our broad mandate challenged us to explore a full range of options. We commissioned more than 100 research studies, to be published in a 23-volume collection. In the belief that our electoral laws must measure up to the very best contemporary practice, we examined election-related laws and processes in all of our provinces and territories and studied comparable legislation and processes in established democracies around the world. This unprecedented array of empirical study and expert opinion made a vital contribution to our deliberations. We made every effort to ensure that the research was both intellectually rigorous and of practical value. All studies were subjected to peer review, and many of the authors discussed their preliminary findings with members of the political and academic communities at national symposiums on major aspects of the electoral system.

The Commission placed the research program under the able and inspired direction of Dr. Peter Aucoin, Professor of Political Science and Public Administration at Dalhousie University. We are confident that the efforts of Dr. Aucoin, together with those of the research coordinators and scholars whose work appears in this and other volumes, will continue to be of value to historians, political scientists, parliamentarians and policy makers, as well as to thoughtful Canadians and the international community.

Along with the other Commissioners, I extend my sincere gratitude to the entire Commission staff for their dedication and commitment. I also wish to thank the many people who participated in our symposiums for their valuable contributions, as well as the members of the research and practitioners' advisory groups whose counsel significantly aided our undertaking.

Pierre Lortie
Chairman

INTRODUCTION

~

THE ROYAL COMMISSION'S research program constituted a comprehensive and detailed examination of the Canadian electoral process. The scope of the research, undertaken to assist Commissioners in their deliberations, was dictated by the broad mandate given to the Commission.

The objective of the research program was to provide Commissioners with a full account of the factors that have shaped our electoral democracy. This dictated, first and foremost, a focus on federal electoral law, but our inquiries also extended to the Canadian constitution, including the institutions of parliamentary government, the practices of political parties, the mass media and nonpartisan political organizations, as well as the decision-making role of the courts with respect to the constitutional rights of citizens. Throughout, our research sought to introduce a historical perspective in order to place the contemporary experience within the Canadian political tradition.

We recognized that neither our consideration of the factors shaping Canadian electoral democracy nor our assessment of reform proposals would be as complete as necessary if we failed to examine the experiences of Canadian provinces and territories and of other democracies. Our research program thus emphasized comparative dimensions in relation to the major subjects of inquiry.

Our research program involved, in addition to the work of the Commission's research coordinators, analysts and support staff, over 200 specialists from 28 universities in Canada, from the private sector and, in a number of cases, from abroad. Specialists in political science constituted the majority of our researchers, but specialists in law, economics, management, computer sciences, ethics, sociology and communications, among other disciplines, were also involved.

In addition to the preparation of research studies for the Commission, our research program included a series of research seminars, symposiums and workshops. These meetings brought together the Commissioners, researchers, representatives from the political parties, media personnel and others with practical experience in political parties, electoral politics and public affairs. These meetings provided not only a forum for discussion of the various subjects of the Commission's mandate, but also an opportunity for our research to be assessed by those with an intimate knowledge of the world of political practice.

These public reviews of our research were complemented by internal and external assessments of each research report by persons qualified in the area; such assessments were completed prior to our decision to publish any study in the series of research volumes.

The Research Branch of the Commission was divided into several areas, with the individual research projects in each area assigned to the research coordinators as follows:

F. Leslie Seidle	Political Party and Election Finance
Herman Bakvis	Political Parties
Kathy Megyery	Women, Ethno-cultural Groups and Youth
David Small	Redistribution; Electoral Boundaries; Voter Registration
Janet Hiebert	Party Ethics
Michael Cassidy	Democratic Rights; Election Administration
Robert A. Milen	Aboriginal Electoral Participation and Representation
Frederick J. Fletcher	Mass Media and Broadcasting in Elections
David Mac Donald (Assistant Research Coordinator)	Direct Democracy

These coordinators identified appropriate specialists to undertake research, managed the projects and prepared them for publication. They also organized the seminars, symposiums and workshops in their research areas and were responsible for preparing presentations and briefings to help the Commission in its deliberations and decision making. Finally, they participated in drafting the Final Report of the Commission.

On behalf of the Commission, I welcome the opportunity to thank the following for their generous assistance in producing these research studies – a project that required the talents of many individuals.

In performing their duties, the research coordinators made a notable contribution to the work of the Commission. Despite the pressures of tight deadlines, they worked with unfailing good humour and the utmost congeniality. I thank all of them for their consistent support and cooperation.

In particular, I wish to express my gratitude to Leslie Seidle, senior research coordinator, who supervised our research analysts and support staff in Ottawa. His diligence, commitment and professionalism not only set high standards, but also proved contagious. I am grateful to Kathy Megyery, who performed a similar function in Montreal with equal aplomb and skill. Her enthusiasm and dedication inspired us all.

On behalf of the research coordinators and myself, I wish to thank our research analysts: Daniel Arsenault, Eric Bertram, Cécile Boucher, Peter Constantinou, Yves Denoncourt, David Docherty, Luc Dumont, Jane Dunlop, Scott Evans, Véronique Garneau, Keith Heintzman, Paul Holmes, Hugh Mellon, Cheryl D. Mitchell, Donald Padget, Alain Pelletier, Dominique Tremblay and Lisa Young. The Research Branch was strengthened by their ability to carry out research in a wide variety of areas, their intellectual curiosity and their team spirit.

The work of the research coordinators and analysts was greatly facilitated by the professional skills and invaluable cooperation of Research Branch staff members: Paulette LeBlanc, who, as administrative assistant, managed the flow of research projects; Hélène Leroux, secretary to the research coordinators, who produced briefing material for the Commissioners and who, with Lori Nazar, assumed responsibility for monitoring the progress of research projects in the latter stages of our work; Kathleen McBride and her assistant Natalie Brose, who created and maintained the database of briefs and hearings transcripts; and Richard Herold and his assistant Susan Dancause, who were responsible for our research library. Jacinthe Séguin and Cathy Tucker also deserve thanks – in addition to their duties as receptionists, they assisted in a variety of ways to help us meet deadlines.

We were extremely fortunate to obtain the research services of first-class specialists from the academic and private sectors. Their contributions are found in this and the other 22 published research volumes. We thank them for the quality of their work and for their willingness to contribute and to meet our tight deadlines.

Our research program also benefited from the counsel of Jean-Marc Hamel, Special Adviser to the Chairman of the Commission and former

Chief Electoral Officer of Canada, whose knowledge and experience proved invaluable.

In addition, numerous specialists assessed our research studies. Their assessments not only improved the quality of our published studies, but also provided us with much-needed advice on many issues. In particular, we wish to single out professors Donald Blake, Janine Brodie, Alan Cairns, Kenneth Carty, John Courtney, Peter Desbarats, Jane Jenson, Richard Johnston, Vincent Lemieux, Terry Morley and Joseph Wearing, as well as Ms. Beth Symes.

Producing such a large number of studies in less than a year requires a mastery of the skills and logistics of publishing. We were fortunate to be able to count on the Commission's Director of Communications, Richard Rochefort, and Assistant Director, Hélène Papineau. They were ably supported by the Communications staff: Patricia Burden, Louise Dagenais, Caroline Field, Claudine Labelle, France Langlois, Lorraine Maheux, Ruth McVeigh, Chantal Morissette, Sylvie Patry, Jacques Poitras and Claudette Rouleau-O'Toole.

To bring the project to fruition, the Commission also called on specialized contractors. We are deeply grateful for the services of Ann McCoomb (references and fact checking); Marthe Lemery, Pierre Chagnon and the staff of Communications Com'ça (French quality control); Norman Bloom, Pamela Riseborough and associates of B&B Editorial Consulting (English adaptation and quality control); and Mado Reid (French production). Al Albania and his staff at Acart Graphics designed the studies and produced some 2 400 tables and figures.

The Commission's research reports constitute Canada's largest publishing project of 1991. Successful completion of the project required close cooperation between the public and private sectors. In the public sector, we especially acknowledge the excellent service of the Privy Council unit of the Translation Bureau, Department of the Secretary of State of Canada, under the direction of Michel Parent, and our contacts Ruth Steele and Terry Denovan of the Canada Communication Group, Department of Supply and Services.

The Commission's co-publisher for the research studies was Dundurn Press of Toronto, whose exceptional service is gratefully acknowledged. Wilson & Lafleur of Montreal, working with the Centre de Documentation Juridique du Québec, did equally admirable work in preparing the French version of the studies.

Teams of editors, copy editors and proofreaders worked diligently under stringent deadlines with the Commission and the publishers to prepare some 20 000 pages of manuscript for design, typesetting and printing. The work of these individuals, whose names are listed elsewhere in this volume, was greatly appreciated.

Our acknowledgements extend to the contributions of the Commission's Executive Director, Guy Goulard, and the administration and executive support teams: Maurice Lacasse, Denis Lafrance and Steve Tremblay (finance); Thérèse Lacasse and Mary Guy-Shea (personnel); Cécile Desforges (assistant to the Executive Director); Marie Dionne (administration); Anna Bevilacqua (records); and support staff members Michelle Bélanger, Roch Langlois, Michel Lauzon, Jean Mathieu, David McKay and Pierrette McMurtie, as well as Denise Miquelon and Christiane Séguin of the Montreal office.

A special debt of gratitude is owed to Marlène Girard, assistant to the Chairman. Her ability to supervise the logistics of the Commission's work amid the tight schedules of the Chairman and Commissioners contributed greatly to the completion of our task.

I also wish to express my deep gratitude to my own secretary, Liette Simard. Her superb administrative skills and great patience brought much-appreciated order to my penchant for the chaotic workstyle of academe. She also assumed responsibility for the administrative coordination of revisions to the final drafts of volumes 1 and 2 of the Commission's Final Report. I owe much to her efforts and assistance.

Finally, on behalf of the research coordinators and myself, I wish to thank the Chairman, Pierre Lortie, the members of the Commission, Pierre Fortier, Robert Gabor, William Knight and Lucie Pépin, and former members Elwood Cowley and Senator Donald Oliver. We are honoured to have worked with such an eminent and thoughtful group of Canadians, and we have benefited immensely from their knowledge and experience. In particular, we wish to acknowledge the creativity, intellectual rigour and energy our Chairman brought to our task. His unparalleled capacity to challenge, to bring out the best in us, was indeed inspiring.

Peter Aucoin
Director of Research

PREFACE

~

P RIME MINISTER John Diefenbaker ardently believed in equality for all Canadians. In 1960, he reformed Canada's electoral system by removing an important legal impediment to Aboriginal electoral participation. This impediment had denied Indian people living on reserves the right to vote in federal elections. Henceforth, all Aboriginal people would share with other Canadians the right to participate in the electoral process.

Could Prime Minister Diefenbaker have foreseen that collective electoral equality could become an issue? Federal electoral legislation recognizes the concept of the "community of interest" that permits geographically concentrated clusters of linguistic and ethnic minorities to be acknowledged in the drawing of electoral boundaries. How does this concept of community of interest apply to a significant segment of the Canadian population – Aboriginal people – whose distinctiveness is recognized in the Constitution, but who, because of their geographic dispersion, do not form a majority in any electoral district south of the 60th parallel? The result has been only three Aboriginal members of Parliament elected in this century from south of the 60th parallel.

This volume of research seeks to address issues of equality in Canada's electoral system that affect Aboriginal people, and what improvements, if any, are needed or should be made to the electoral system to accommodate the Aboriginal community of interest. The four studies in this volume cover the major issues regarding Aboriginal people and efforts to increase their involvement in the federal electoral system.

The first study is one of my own. Tracing the development of Aboriginal political consciousness from the 1970s, I have undertaken a review of the constitutional and electoral aspirations of Aboriginal people as they unfolded through the 1980s. Recent constitutional initiatives are also considered.

Augie Fleras examines the benefits and disadvantages of the system of guaranteed representation for the Maori in New Zealand. He suggests that this system of representation, which has existed since 1867, offers a number of valuable lessons that could assist in the design of Aboriginal electoral districts in Canada.

Valerie Alia examines how the media have treated Aboriginal electoral issues in northern Canada and to what degree media coverage encourages or discourages the electoral participation of Aboriginal people. Through extensive interviews, Professor Alia has sought to describe Aboriginal people's view of the media. She offers pointed and innovative remedies for reform.

Roger Gibbins examines to what extent the electoral process can and should be modified so as to provide for guaranteed Aboriginal representation in the House of Commons. He constructs a model for electoral reform based on Aboriginal electoral districts and assesses its operational features, its impact on the political powers of Aboriginal communities and its linkage with the underlying values embedded in the Canadian political culture. Professor Gibbins concludes that electoral reform does not provide a suitable vehicle through which Aboriginal aspirations might be addressed.

In the end, these four studies provide a range of views about electoral equality for Aboriginal people. Since there is a lack of unanimity among the authors themselves, it will be left to the readers to form their own conclusions about how the objective of electoral equality for Aboriginal people can best be met.

I owe a debt of gratitude to the following individuals: F. Leslie Seidle and Richard Rochefort, both of the Royal Commission, for their patient cooperation, guidance and direction in preparation of this volume and for their assistance in the other responsibilities I undertook for the Royal Commission; Daniel Arsenault for his long hours of research, editing and proofreading of the studies in this volume; Marc LeClair from Senator Len Marchand's office for graciously permitting me unrestricted access to his extensive library and research materials; and Judy Cavanagh, my partner, who stood solidly by me and encouraged me in the completion of my work in Ottawa over the course of several months while she remained in Vancouver.

Robert A. Milen
Research Coordinator

ABORIGINAL PEOPLES AND ELECTORAL REFORM IN CANADA

~

1

ABORIGINAL CONSTITUTIONAL AND ELECTORAL REFORM

~

Robert A. Milen

ABORIGINAL ISSUES AND CONCERNS – such as land claims and self-government – have sparked an interest in the minds of Canadians. The responses of Aboriginal people on such diverse matters as constitutional reform and natural resource extraction on unceded Indian lands have raised questions about the place of Aboriginal people within the fabric of Canadian Confederation.

Yet these issues and concerns have not always been on the minds of Canadians. For many decades Aboriginal people were seen as poverty-stricken wards of the state, confined to unseen, bush-covered reserves or inhabiting the poorest sections of towns and cities. Many questioned whether Aboriginal people had special rights, and if so, whether these rights should be maintained. Policy makers questioned, in particular, whether the group or collective rights of Indian people impeded their assimilation into the "mainstream" of Canadian society.

The search by Aboriginal people for accommodation within Confederation has been a lengthy one. This study will examine part of this search with a special emphasis upon recent efforts to increase the representation of Aboriginal people in the House of Commons.

FEDERAL ABORIGINAL POLICY FROM 1950 TO 1973

At Confederation, the Parliament of Canada acquired the jurisdiction to make laws for "Indians and Lands reserved for the Indians" pursuant to the provisions of section 91¶24 of the *British North America Act, 1867* (renamed in 1982 *Constitution Act, 1867*). Parliament inherited this responsibility from the British Crown. The *Royal Proclamation of 1763* had recognized Indian people as constituting Indian nations separate from the European settlers in British North America and with whom only the British Crown could enter into treaties. This power to enter into treaties with the Indian nations was assumed by Parliament. A number of treaties were entered into after Confederation. Federal responsibility for Indian people and the treaty process confirmed the distinct status of Indian people.

Parliament, however, has chosen to exercise its jurisdiction for Aboriginal people selectively. The result has been differing administrative and legislative histories for Indians, Inuit and Métis – the three Aboriginal peoples of Canada.

Entering the 1950s, federal Aboriginal policy recognized limited rights for status Indian people who were regarded as wards of the state. Status Indian people are persons registered or entitled to be registered as Indians under the federal *Indian Act*. For example, from 1876 to 1951 the *Indian Act* prevented any Indian person in the Province of Manitoba, the Northwest Territories and the District of Keewatin (which later became the provinces of Manitoba, Saskatchewan and Alberta) from acquiring a homestead or Crown land. From 1927 to 1951 the *Indian Act* made it an offence for any person to pursue an Indian land claim without government permission. The Supreme Court of Canada was of the view that "The language of the [*Indian Act*] embodies the accepted view that these aborigines are, in effect wards of the state, whose care and welfare are a political trust of the highest obligation. For that reason, every such dealing with their privileges must bear the imprint of Governmental approval, and it would be beyond the power of the Governor in Council to transfer that responsibility to the Superintendent General" [Minister of Indian Affairs] (*St. Ann's Island* 1950, 232).

The government of Prime Minister Diefenbaker began to reform some of the provisions of the *Indian Act* that most seriously affected the civil rights of Indians. In 1959, provisions requiring Indian people to obtain the permission of the Indian agent prior to leaving the reserve were abolished. Previously, if such permission was not obtained, the Royal Canadian Mounted Police could be called to return a person to the reserve, even against that person's will. In 1960, the *Canada Elections Act* accorded all Indian people the right to vote in federal elections.[1] At that time approximately three in four Indian people were denied the right to vote in federal elections. Of those who could, only six in ten could exercise the franchise without any conditions attached (Hawthorn 1966, 1:259). It has been suggested that the reason for this denial of democratic rights is the same when any aspect of federal and provincial Indian policy is considered: "Over a century ago the Indian people of Canada were legislated into a state of tutelage and dependence in which the Federal government abandoned them" (Bartlett 1980, 163).

Federal Aboriginal policy treated non-status Indian people and their descendants as having the same individual rights accorded to all other Canadians, but having no group or collective rights. Non-status Indian people are those who have lost their entitlement to be registered under the *Indian Act* by either involuntarily or voluntarily renouncing their right to registration. There have never been any impediments to the exercise of the franchise by non-status Indian persons, as such persons are regarded as full citizens of the Canadian state.

The Inuit are a numerically small minority living in Canada's remote north. A 1939 Supreme Court of Canada decision confirmed federal responsibility for the Inuit pursuant to the provisions of section 91¶24 of the *Constitution Act, 1867* (*Reference*, 1939). However, little was done to exercise this jurisdiction. In fact, federal legislation was passed denying the right of the Inuit to vote from 1934 to 1950. It was only in the 1962 federal election that ballot boxes were finally placed in all Inuit communities in the eastern Arctic, thus permitting full exercise of the franchise.

While no judicial decision has been rendered on federal responsibility for the Métis, the admission of Manitoba into Confederation in 1870 recognized the land rights of the Métis within that province's boundaries.[2] After 1879 and early into this century, the federal government dealt with Métis Aboriginal land rights in the Northwest by providing land scrip, and later land or money scrip, to settle Aboriginal title. There were no negotiations or treaties; rather, unilateral federal legislation was used to deal with these land rights. According to federal policy, the provision of scrip extinguished all claims the Métis had, or may have had, to group or collective rights. The Métis were treated as having the same rights as all other Canadians and, thus, there were never any legislative impediments to the exercise of the franchise by the Métis. Present federal Aboriginal policy denies responsibility for the Métis except north of the 60th parallel, where the Métis are involved with Indian people in land claims negotiations.

During the 1960s, more and more Canadians began to become attuned to the circumstances and plight of Indian people. Canadians looked south of the border to the growing civil rights movement and the plight of Black Americans. Questions were raised about the poverty and treatment of Canadian Indian people. In 1966, the results of a federal review of the situation of Indian people rejected integration or assimilation as proper objectives of federal Aboriginal policy (Hawthorn 1966, 1:13). The review concluded that: "Indians should be regarded as 'citizens plus'; in addition to the normal rights and duties of citizenship, Indians possess certain additional rights as charter members of the Canadian community" (ibid.).

The review concluded that the Department of Indian Affairs should be a positive advocate of Indian needs and had: "a special responsibility to see that the 'plus' aspects of Indian citizenship are respected, and that governments and the Canadian people are educated in the acceptance of this existence" (Hawthorn 1966, 1: 13).

By the conclusion of the decade, federal Aboriginal policy had as its objective the removal of perceived barriers and impediments to the fuller participation of Aboriginal people – particularly Indian people – within the mainstream of Canadian society. In 1969, the federal government released a white paper calling for an entirely different approach to federal Aboriginal policy (Canada, Dept of Indian Affairs 1969). The group or collective rights of Indian people were to be abolished. The intent of the policy was egalitarian in nature: Indian people suffered from socio-economic problems unacceptable to Canadians. The proposed solution was to abolish the Department of Indian Affairs and to allow Indian people to move freely into society unrestricted or unfettered by the provisions of a paternalistic *Indian Act*. The provinces would provide and deliver services as they did to all other Canadians.[3]

Many have suggested that this was the flashpoint, the event that ignited Indian self-awareness and led Indian people to seek greater economic and political control over their own lives. "The paper was so provocative, the theory goes, that it set off Indian bands, tribal councils, and provincial as well as national associations in a burst of self-defining energy across the country" (Cassidy and Bish 1989, 11).

Others have suggested that the struggle for Aboriginal autonomy started at a much earlier date (Cassidy and Bish 1989, 11).

THE 1970s – DECADE OF CHANGE

As a result of the reaction by Indian people to the white paper, the federal government retracted it completely by 1973. "Since then, public policy in relation to Aboriginal people has undergone a remarkable shift toward the acceptance of a right to remain distinct within Canadian society" (Morse 1989, 43).

In 1973, federal policy provided core funding to Aboriginal political organizations. In that same year, a Supreme Court of Canada ruling on a case emanating from British Columbia held that Aboriginal title still existed in parts of Canada, even while the federal government had claimed it was dead (*Calder* 1973).

During the 1970s, Aboriginal organizations began to consider their relationship with the Canadian state. They began to do their own research on land claims and on other issues. For example, the Native Council of Canada (NCC), representing Métis and non-status Indian people, put forward its views for guaranteed Aboriginal representation in the House of Commons. A declaration by the NCC on 19 March 1979 stated that Aboriginal people "have the right to guaranteed representation in all legislative assemblies." The NCC later amended its position to provide for *constitutional* guarantees for Aboriginal representation in Parliament and in the legislative and territorial assemblies in proportion to their share of the Canadian population (NCC 1981, 34–40). The NCC stated:

> On the surface the demand for separate and special representation in Parliament appears to run counter to the fundamental principle underlying Canadian democratic institutions, namely, that there be no distinction amongst citizens because of their background; cultural, racial, linguistic or socio-economic. That there be no special privileges granted to individuals is, however, a truism which rests on an assumption of equality, not simply formal equality before the law but equality of condition, of resources and bargaining power. The demands for and grants of constitutional protection for national minorities are a recognition that formal equality for individuals does not automatically protect minorities and their members from the pressures of the dominant group. (NCC 1981, 34)

By the end of the 1970s, the foremost issues on the agenda of Aboriginal people were political autonomy and land. The right to land was expressed in various forms: Aboriginal title, Indian title, Aboriginal rights and land title. The phrase "self-government" was not then used. As Canada began to become more embroiled over the issue of constitutional reform, this debate spilled over into Aboriginal communities. Aboriginal political organizations were beginning to speak out about constitutional protection of their rights as indigenous peoples. The close of the decade also witnessed a growing frustration by Indian people over what they believed was the "under-utilization of the federal legislative power" (NCC 1981, 73). This was coupled with the reality of the expanding role of the provinces, which was seen as threatening the special relationship between Indian people and the federal government (ibid.). These various issues came to the forefront during the drive to patriation in the decade that followed.

PATRIATION

The term "patriation" refers to the process by which Canada sought to complete its independence from Great Britain by obtaining the right to amend all parts of its "Constitution." In 1980, Canada had no single document that could be regarded as a constitution. The closest approximation was the *Constitution Act, 1867*, a British statute (Hogg 1985, 2). The government of Prime Minister Trudeau sought to make the Constitution a Canadian law with a domestic amending formula so that all future amendments could be made exclusively by the Canadian Parliament. The Trudeau government felt compelled to take this action following the results of the 1980 referendum on sovereignty-association in Quebec and the failure of a first ministers conference on the Constitution held in September 1980.

The process leading to the patriation of Canada's Constitution was fuelled in the mid-1970s by two events – the political forces seeking political sovereignty for Quebec and the rising strength of western Canadian economic power that accompanied that region's feeling of economic alienation (Romanow 1985, 73). The search for secure and expanded supplies of energy also led to a period of internal national expansion whereby lands occupied by northern Aboriginal people and not subject to any treaty were explored for energy resources. This search induced the federal government to commence a land claims process in northern Canada to extinguish the Aboriginal interest in the land, a process which remains unresolved today.

Aboriginal people, and particularly Indian people, sought to ensure that their special relationship of trust with the Crown would not be altered by patriation of the Constitution. They were concerned that the Canadian Parliament could unilaterally enact changes that would affect their rights. Indian people, in particular, still had memories of the 1969 white paper. Indian people conducted extensive lobbying efforts in Great Britain, through which they sought to convince British parliamentarians to amend the *Constitution Act, 1867* to protect Indian rights before permitting Canada to control its own Constitution.

On 30 January 1981, members of a Joint Committee of the Senate and the House of Commons on the Constitution agreed with the leaders of the three national Aboriginal organizations on a provision which would recognize and affirm Aboriginal and treaty rights in a new constitutional resolution. This resolution had to be approved by Parliament before being sent to the British Parliament for passage of enacting legislation. The text of the resolution provided that:

35 (1) The Aboriginal and treaty rights of the Aboriginal people of
Canada are hereby recognized and affirmed.

(2) In this Act, "Aboriginal peoples of Canada" includes the Indian,
Inuit and Métis peoples of Canada. (Canada, Minister of Justice
1981)

Since Aboriginal rights were undefined, section 37 of the resolution provided for a constitutional conference of the Prime Minister of
Canada and the provincial premiers which would include an agenda
item respecting constitutional matters that directly affected Aboriginal
people, including the identification and definition of rights to be included
in the Constitution. Representatives of the Aboriginal people were to
be invited by the prime minister to participate in these discussions.

A further section was agreed upon to ensure that the group or
collective rights of Aboriginal people protected in section 35 of the resolution could not be attacked by protections afforded to individual rights
found in the *Canadian Charter of Rights and Freedoms* in Part 1 of the resolution. Section 25 provided that:

25. The guarantee in this Charter of certain rights and freedoms
shall not be construed so as to abrogate or derogate from any
Aboriginal, treaty or other rights or freedoms that pertain to the
Aboriginal peoples of Canada including

(a) any rights or freedoms that have been recognized by the
Royal Proclamation of October 7, 1763; and

(b) any rights or freedoms that may be acquired by the
Aboriginal peoples of Canada by way of land claims settlement. (Canada, Minister of Justice 1981)

Section 25 thus established a class of rights for Aboriginal people
that was shielded from other provisions of the *Canadian Charter of Rights
and Freedoms*. For some, this meant that the equality rights provisions
in the Charter might not extend to women in Aboriginal communities.

The agreement reached was of significant proportions. No other
constitution in the world would protect Aboriginal and treaty rights
to the same degree, or provide for meetings between the highest political leaders in the land and Aboriginal representatives. The recognition that the Métis were an Aboriginal people was an enormous victory
for the Métis. Prior to the agreement of 30 January, many questioned
whether the Métis were an Aboriginal people (Hawkes 1985a, 9–10).
Recognition could help the Métis press their case for settlement of land
claims in western Canada.

The constitutional critic for the Progressive Conservative party observed that, "I say it quite openly ... it is a difficult role very often to convey to other Canadians that if justice is to be done in the country, it must ... be done first to Canada's Aboriginal people" (Valpy 1981, 12).

The celebration was short-lived, as many Indian people questioned the wisdom of their leadership in agreeing to the amendments. Lobbying efforts continued in England during the rest of the year. Some representatives eventually brought an unsuccessful court case to stop the constitutional process unless greater protections for Indian rights were provided for in the Constitution.

Initially supportive of the agreement, the Native Council of Canada (NCC) subsequently came to reverse its position as well, fearing that the rights of its membership might be affected by patriation. However, lobbying efforts by the NCC were nowhere near as intensive as those of the Indian people.

The Inuit continued to support patriation of the Constitution. They were prepared to stick with the agreement of 30 January that their rights would be redressed upon patriation.

In 1981, the Supreme Court of Canada considered a reference as to whether a convention existed demanding a legal requirement for provincial consent before the British Parliament enacted an amendment to the Constitution that could affect provincial powers (*Manitoba (Attorney General)* 1981). The Court ruled there was no legal requirement for such consent: "A majority of the Court held that there was a convention, and that the convention required the federal government to obtain a 'substantial degree' or 'substantial measure' of provincial consent before requesting the requisite legislation from the United Kingdom" (Hogg 1985, 14).[4]

The Supreme Court held that the federal government needed the agreement of more than two provincial governments supporting the federal resolution to give the patriation plan full constitutional legitimacy. To obtain provincial agreement, the prime minister and the premiers held a further round of constitutional discussions in November 1981. After in camera meetings, a constitutional accord was reached between the prime minister and eight anglophone premiers. The ninth anglophone premier had left the conference earlier to attend a provincial election campaign under way in Manitoba. The Manitoba attorney general did sign the constitutional agreement, but affixed a qualification to the document which required the approval of the Manitoba legislature for a provision respecting minority language education rights in the provinces (Canada, Federal-Provincial Conference 1981). Shortly thereafter, the new premier-elect agreed to the removal of this qualification.

The constitutional agreement deleted almost all explicit references to the protection of Aboriginal rights. First ministers did agree to hold a constitutional conference with representatives of Aboriginal people on the terms and conditions agreed to on 30 January as noted above (Canada, Federal-Provincial Conference 1981, 2). Section 25, which shielded Aboriginal rights from other provisions of the Charter also remained.

Aboriginal leaders reacted strongly to the terms of the agreement.[5] The prime minister initially stated that he did not want to amend the agreement reached with the premiers for fear of jeopardizing it (Sheppard 1981a, 1). He later said that if Aboriginal leaders convinced the premiers, he would agree to changes. Later, in November, it was agreed to restore the protections deleted, with one major exception: only "existing" Aboriginal and treaty rights were to be recognized and affirmed. While Aboriginal people were informed that the addition of the word "existing" had no significant effect, the prime minister and the premiers were not prepared to remove it. Aboriginal leaders believed that the addition of this word did in fact have a legal effect. Its purpose was to prevent the possible revival of previously extinguished rights, especially as they affected the Métis, and to prevent any situation where Aboriginal or treaty rights might interfere with the right of the provinces to dispose of natural resources within provincial boundaries (United Kingdom, House of Commons 1982, 785). One year later, Alberta Premier Peter Lougheed explained his position:

> Our difficulty ... was that the force of the Aboriginal rights provision was unclear. The government of Alberta supported and still does fully support, existing Aboriginal and treaty rights. The proposed Aboriginal rights provision was open to interpretation, however, that it would create new Aboriginal rights that were not previously recognized in law. Not having been part of the earlier discussion between the federal government and Indian leaders, the Premiers on November 5th, 1981 were not prepared to include any additional provisions without understanding fully what was being requested and the consequences of such requests. (Lougheed 1983a, 1)

The final text approved by the Parliament of Great Britain stated, in part:

25.   The guarantee in this Charter of certain rights and freedoms shall not be construed so as to abrogate or derogate from any Aboriginal, treaty or other rights or freedoms that pertain to the Aboriginal peoples of Canada including

(*a*) any rights or freedoms that have been recognized by the Royal Proclamation of October 7, 1763; and

(*b*) any rights or freedoms that may be acquired by the Aboriginal peoples of Canada by way of land claims settlement.

PART II

RIGHTS OF THE ABORIGINAL PEOPLES OF CANADA

35. (1) The existing Aboriginal and treaty rights of the Aboriginal peoples of Canada are hereby recognized and affirmed.

(2) In this Act, "Aboriginal peoples of Canada" includes the Indian, Inuit and Métis peoples of Canada.

PART IV

CONSTITUTIONAL CONFERENCE

37. (1) A constitutional conference composed of the Prime Minister of Canada and the first ministers of the provinces shall be convened by the Prime Minister of Canada within one year after this Part comes into force.

(2) The conference convened under subsection (1) shall have included in its agenda an item respecting constitutional matters that directly affect the Aboriginal peoples of Canada, including the identification and definition of the rights of those peoples to be included in the Constitution of Canada, and the Prime Minister of Canada shall invite representatives of those peoples to participate in the discussions on that item.

(3) The Prime Minister of Canada shall invite elected representatives of the governments of the Yukon Territory and the Northwest Territories to participate in the discussions on any item on the agenda of the conference convened under subsection (1) that, in the opinion of the Prime Minister, directly affects the Yukon Territory and the Northwest Territories. (Canada, *Constitution Act, 1982*)

Notwithstanding the gains made, concern was expressed by the Indian and Inuit leadership over the role the provinces would now have. Future conferences dealing with the rights of Aboriginal people would not only involve the provinces, but their consent would be required under the entrenched amending formula before additional changes to the Constitution affecting their rights could be made. Many Aboriginal leaders felt that the provinces, particularly the western provinces, were too concerned with protecting their jurisdictions from possible constitutional encroachment by Aboriginal people. Provincial governments have historically been concerned that the recognition of Aboriginal and treaty rights could interfere with the disposition of natural resources by a province within its boundaries (Hall 1991a, 125; 1991b, 100–101). Some leaders saw the process of patriation and the constitutional conferences as denoting provincial encroachment upon Aboriginal and treaty rights. This conflicted with the fiduciary obligation of the federal government to protect Aboriginal and treaty rights from provincial encroachment (Robinson and Quinney 1985). Yet others believed that government leaders were more preoccupied with Quebec nationalism and western Canadian alienation (Romanow 1985, 80).

The Prairie Métis did not completely object to the involvement of the provinces. While the Métis argued that they came under federal jurisdiction, they were also very much aware that the provinces controlled natural resources. Since both levels of government claimed that the other had legislative responsibility for the Métis, by having both jurisdictions at the table the Métis hoped some agreements could be made.

The federal and provincial governments, on the other hand, were satisfied that they had taken adequate steps to preserve the existing state of the law pertaining to Aboriginal people by entrenching existing Aboriginal and treaty rights, and by providing for a process through which further rights could be identified, defined and possibly entrenched.

A NEW BEGINNING – FIRST CONSTITUTIONAL CONFERENCE (15–16 MARCH 1983)

On 17 April 1982, the *Constitution Act, 1982* was proclaimed. In accordance with its provisions, a constitutional conference with first ministers and representatives of Aboriginal people had to be called within one year of proclamation. The meeting date was eventually set for 15–16 March 1983.

The 1983 conference was preceded by a number of ministerial meetings during which the Native Council of Canada (NCC) raised the issue of parliamentary representation for Aboriginal people (NCC 1982; 1983c). The purpose of these meetings was to agree upon an agenda for the historic meeting of first ministers and Aboriginal leaders and "possibly lay the groundwork for possible agreement by First Ministers" (Schwartz 1985, 19). Federal and provincial officials attended "to obtain an appreciation and understanding of precisely what was meant by the various proposals put forward by the Aboriginal people" (Dalon 1985, 87). Aboriginal people came to negotiate.

Prior to the meeting of first ministers and Aboriginal representatives, dissension erupted within the NCC. Tensions between the Prairie

Métis and the rest of the Indian and Métis membership of the NCC resulted in a schism within the NCC. The Prairie Métis believed both NCC seats should be occupied only by Métis representatives at the first ministers conference. The Prairie Métis differed with the rest of the NCC as to the definition of the term "Métis," and thus as to who was entitled to occupy the seats at the conference.

The Prairie Métis saw themselves as a people of mixed Aboriginal and non-Aboriginal ancestry who developed into a distinct Aboriginal people in a defined geographic area in western Canada and who shared a common history, culture and political consciousness. The NCC used the term "Métis" in a racial sense to denote those persons of mixed Aboriginal and non-Aboriginal ancestry, regardless of geographic location within Canada.

The Prairie Métis broke away from the NCC and launched a court action against the prime minister to compel him to invite their representative organization, the newly formed Métis National Council (MNC), to the first ministers conference. Failing that, the Métis sought an injunction to prevent the prime minister from holding the meeting of first ministers. The federal government and the leadership of the MNC agreed to a political settlement rather than allowing the courts to render a decision. The Prairie Métis would be permitted a seat at the constitutional conference. Subsequently, four national Aboriginal organizations represented Aboriginal people at all ministerial meetings and meetings of first ministers on Aboriginal constitutional matters.

On 15 and 16 March 1983, a constitutional conference was held with first ministers and representatives of the Aboriginal people. Quebec attended as an observer because of its refusal to sign the 1981 constitutional accord.

In his opening speech to first ministers and Aboriginal representatives, Prime Minister Trudeau committed the federal government to accepting the notion of Aboriginal self-government, while rejecting the extremes of assimilation and full sovereignty. He stated that, "The peoples we represent look to us to move as quickly as we can along the paths to a new consensus, one which all Canadians can share with pride and dignity" (Trudeau 1983, 17).

Aboriginal people spoke of their place within Canada. Chief David Ahenakew, Grand Chief of the Assembly of First Nations (AFN), stated that, "I emphasize that we have more invested, and more at stake, in the future of this nation than anyone else. We are committed to strengthening and building Canada – not to dismantling it" (Ahenakew 1983a, 5).

As the conference unfolded, differing positions and perspectives emerged from the seventeen delegations represented around the table – the federal government, ten provincial governments (including Quebec), two territorial governments, and four Aboriginal organizations – each having its own distinct point of view and opinion on what the conference could, and should, accomplish. For example, governments sought to *define* the rights of Aboriginal people, while the AFN sought an *elaboration* and *guarantee* of Aboriginal and treaty rights, to which it added the concept of "Aboriginal title." To the governments, the term "Aboriginal title" had a technical, legal meaning to be discerned from judicial decisions; to the AFN, the term was equated with land ownership. The Métis sought a separate Schedule in the Constitution for Métis rights (Sinclair 1983a, 145), while the Inuit rejected this idea, stating, "We think there should be one set of all-encompassing principles put into the constitution and the specifics worked out through claims negotiations and through treaties" (Gordon 1983, 149).

The MNC sought the provision of a land base for the Métis in order to practise self-government. The memberships of the MNC and the NCC were landless. Indian people had reserve lands or were involved in land claims negotiations while the Inuit were similarly involved in such negotiations.

Both the MNC and the NCC raised the subject of guaranteed representation in Parliament. The MNC pointed out that, "Historically, the Métis wanted provincial status in Confederation to provide them with political autonomy and guaranteed representation in Parliament. Today, the Métis still seek political participation in the larger political system" (MNC 1983a, 14). The NCC stated "that we have the right to guaranteed representation in Parliament and Legislative Assemblies" (NCC 1983b, 6).

The Manitoba government tabled a paper outlining the views of the Manitoba Métis on such matters as parliamentary representation: "The idea of direct Métis representation in Parliament and in the Manitoba Legislature would give us [the Métis] greater recognition and help protect our rights. However, we do not want token seats as an alternative to real self-government" (Manitoba 1983, 11).

No conference participant responded to this issue when it was raised. Both the MNC and the NCC soon dropped their discussion on parliamentary representation and concentrated on the issues of a land base and self-government. However, both organizations continued to support a two-tiered representational structure for their membership – self-government on a land base and self-governing institutions off a land base, along with guaranteed representation in Parliament and the legislatures. Since their respective memberships lacked a land base, representation was sought in the governing structures of non-Aboriginal bodies (Hawkes 1985a, 36). Guaranteed representation allowed:

Aboriginal people living in the larger Canadian society to increase their involvement in the decision-making process of the state if their collective interests are to be protected and promoted. Without governments of their own and without a population concentration which would favor the election of Aboriginal candidates, they have been alienated by the political system and denied effective representation in political institutions. Proposals for guaranteed representation are designed to ensure that Aboriginal people fully participate in the decisions of public institutions such as legislative assemblies and regional governments which impact directly on their collective interests. (Weinstein 1986, 7)

The provinces and the federal government had their own disagreements. Both levels of government differed on the payment of costs for delivery of services for off-reserve Aboriginal people. This was a major concern in western Canada, where Aboriginal people had moved to the inner cores of urban centres in search of economic opportunity. Their lack of success resulted in "rapid social breakdown with all its attendant glaring statistics and ever-greater dependency on the state" (Weinstein 1986, 21). The federal government saw the provinces as having a leading role in the provision and delivery of services. The provincial governments saw this as a federal responsibility. Their position was best summed up by Premier Grant Devine: "For its part, Saskatchewan will emphasize that there is a national responsibility exercisable by the federal government on behalf of the Aboriginal peoples of Canada. There is no need for constitutional change to assert that fact. What is required is the political will and perhaps a change in attitude" (Devine 1983, 81).

The four Aboriginal organizations wanted no part of this intergovernmental debate on service delivery and preferred to concentrate on rights issues such as self-government. Only two of the four Aboriginal organizations – the AFN (Ahenakew 1983b) and the MNC (MNC 1983a) – tabled significant proposals on the content of self-government and the financing of self-government, the principal source of which was to come from public revenues. The Inuit Committee on National Issues (ICNI) tabled no constitutional proposals (ICNI 1983b). These documents, however, did not answer questions such as those posed by Alberta Premier Peter Lougheed: "On the submissions with regard to self-government, to what extent does that mean that they would not be subjected to the responsibilities of meeting the laws of the provinces, presuming they were living obviously within one of the provinces of Canada?" (Lougheed 1983b, 266).

During the course of the conference it became clear that Aboriginal representatives and first ministers held differing views about the rights of Aboriginal people. There was, however, agreement to amend the Constitution to ensure that Aboriginal and treaty rights applied equally to male and female persons. "This amendment marked an important stage in a concerted campaign to eliminate gender discrimination from the Indian Act and from all aspects of Canadian Aboriginal policy" (Hall 1989, 435).

It was also agreed to amend the Constitution to provide that new land claims agreements could be given the same constitutional protections as treaty rights. Section 35 now stated:

> 35. (1) The existing aboriginal and treaty rights of the aboriginal peoples of Canada are hereby recognized and affirmed.
>
> (2) In this Act, "aboriginal peoples of Canada" includes the Indian, Inuit and Métis peoples of Canada.
>
> (3) For greater certainty, in subsection (1) "treaty rights" includes rights that now exist by way of land claims agreements or may be so acquired.
>
> (4) Notwithstanding any other provision of this Act, the aboriginal and treaty rights referred to in subsection (1) are guaranteed equally to male and female persons. (Canada, *Constitution Amendment Proclamation, 1983*)

Subsection (*b*) of section 25 was consequentially amended to harmonize it with the above amendment. The full section now read:

> 25. The guarantee in this Charter of certain rights and freedoms shall not be construed so as to abrogate or derogate from any aboriginal, treaty or other rights or freedoms that pertain to the aboriginal peoples of Canada including:
>
> (a) any rights or freedoms that have been recognized by the Royal Proclamation of October 7, 1763; and
>
> (b) any rights or freedoms that now exist by way of land claims agreements or may be so acquired. (Canada, *Constitution Amendment Proclamation, 1983*)

During the conference, Aboriginal people had sought a veto over future constitutional amendments affecting their rights. First ministers did agree to a provision whereby Aboriginal people would be consulted over constitutional amendments that directly affected them. The final text stated that:

> 35.1 The government of Canada and the provincial governments
> are committed to the principle that, before any amendment is
> made to Class 24 of section 91 of the "*Constitution Act, 1867*",
> to section 25 of this Act or to this Part,
>
>   (*a*) a constitutional conference that includes in its agenda an
> item relating to the proposed amendment, composed of
> the Prime Minister of Canada and the first ministers of the
> provinces, will be convened by the Prime Minister of
> Canada; and
>
>   (*b*) the Prime Minister of Canada will invite representatives
> of the Aboriginal peoples of Canada to participate in the
> discussions on that item. (Canada, *Constitution Proclamation
> Amendment, 1983*)

The conference participants agreed to entrench two further constitutional meetings to be held by 1985 and 1987. A political accord was
signed to hold a further conference in 1984 (Canada, *Constitutional
Accord* 1983). Given the removal of the Aboriginal and treaty rights
protections on 5 November 1981, Aboriginal representatives sought
guarantees that further constitutional conferences would in fact be held.
An answer to their distrust was to entrench such further meetings. Thus
a basic document to enshrine fundamental rights was amended to deal
with process while substance remained outstanding. Nevertheless, the
amendments agreed upon made the conference "a great success"
(Hawkes 1985b, 8). These amendments were reached notwithstanding
the newness of the process, a massive agenda, the shortness of time
and the multiplicity of parties (16, plus Quebec). There were major
differences among the parties themselves: the federal government and
the provinces disagreed over the nature and extent of federal responsibility for Aboriginal people; the MNC and the NCC differed over who
were "Métis"; each Aboriginal people had different rights and aspirations; Aboriginal people and governments disagreed on the nature and
extent of rights that could or should be entrenched.

While the constitutional amendments did not directly deal with the
major agenda items of Aboriginal title and self-government pursued by
Aboriginal representatives,[6] they remain the only constitutional amendments that have been adopted since patriation under the general amending formula. The agreement for future conferences signified that none of the
participants was giving up on the process. The prime minister stated that,
while all goals were not attained: "We've only had our Constitution a
year and I want to say to Aboriginal people that you are doing pretty
well and I hope you will continue to pick up speed" (Sallot 1983, 10).

SENATE REFORM

In 1983, the Special Joint Committee of the Senate and of the House of Commons on Senate Reform was struck. During its public hearings, the NCC and one of its affiliates, the New Brunswick Association of Métis and Non-Status Indians, spoke in support of guaranteed representation in Parliament. According to the NCC: "The NCC sees guaranteed representation of Aboriginal people in both houses of Parliament and in provincial and territorial legislatures as one of the mechanisms, among several others, that will be necessary in the Aboriginal community. That will foster effective participation of all Aboriginal people in the decision-making process that structures daily life in Canada" (NCC 1983a, 51). For the NCC, such representation was seen as an extension of the Aboriginal right to self-government.

Notwithstanding its break from the NCC, the MNC did not abandon historical Métis support for representation in Parliament. During the hearings on Senate reform in 1983 the MNC stated:

> A recurring theme throughout the evolution of the Métis has been our struggle for political autonomy within the Canadian federation. That is because we have never opted for outright sovereignty. We have sought participation in the larger political system as well as self-government within it. Louis Riel's provisional governments in Manitoba in 1869 and in Saskatchewan in 1885 tried to gain self-government through provincial status as well as guaranteed parliamentary representation. Today we are again seeking forms of self-government as well as representation in national political institutions. (MNC 1983b, 4–5)

This position was supported by three MNC affiliates who also appeared before this Committee – the Association of Métis and Non-Status Indians of Saskatchewan, the Métis Association of Alberta and the Louis Riel Métis Association of British Columbia.

While neither the AFN nor any of its affiliates appeared before the Committee, the Inuit Committee on National Issues (ICNI) spoke extensively on this subject:

> Representation of the Aboriginal peoples in the central institutions of Canada is an extension of our right to self-determination within the federation.
>
> It is on this basis that we seek greater representation of Inuit in both Houses of Parliament for our people to be able to speak in the central institutions of the Canadian federation ... Representation is

sorely needed to protect our interests and affect the policies in this country that concern our people. As one of Canada's original peoples, we seek to bring to the national institutions our history, our values, our strength and determination. We believe that in return we are owed basic recognition in the political centres of decision-making in Canada. (ICNI 1983c, 19–20)

The ICNI sought "effective participation in the life" of Canada and noted:

Since the creation of the Nunatsiaq seat in the House of Commons, Inuit have been more able to reach the federal government. Our member of Parliament, Peter Ittinuar, has consistently worked to bring understanding of the ways of government and its benefits to our people while helping us make known in Parliament our concerns and the problems of this part of the world. For our people, this has been a great benefit; for you legislators and southern Canadians generally, it has been a way to ensure that northern peoples felt a part of Canada and planned their destiny within it. In short, Inuit political participation has had, and will continue to have, a useful function of two-way political accommodation. (ICNI 1983c, 20)

The Inuit sought more seats in both Houses of Parliament. They stated that: "We believe effective and increased Aboriginal participation in the affairs of Parliament would go far in enhancing Parliament's authority, as it would go in furthering the contribution of Canada's Aboriginal peoples to the political process in this country" (ICNI 1983c, 20–21). The Inuit also noted:

We have studied the question of how we would have our members appointed, and several options have been put out. One is using the traditional method that was used in realigning electoral boundaries, and the other one is guaranteed native seats. These two options have been studied, but no hard and fast conclusions have been made on either. We see some problems with the question of realigning electoral boundaries. The numbers are never enough, so they always have to engulf in those electoral boundaries great numbers of southerners, and extend our electoral boundaries far south to be able to justify the numerical requirements of ridings, both federal and provincial.

The question of having so many guaranteed native seats in any of these legislatures or in the Senate also presents another problem that we foresee. That would mean that the native members would more or less be isolated from the general politics of the House or the Senate. This is one of our fears; that they would end up being isolated, not being part of the mainstream. By having somebody ... elected out of the general rules of application, we find it enables him to be a more integral part of the political system than if it were simply a guaranteed seat. (ICNI 1983c, 31–32)

In its final report, the Special Joint Committee believed that no action should be taken to establish separate Senate seats for Aboriginal people. The Committee noted that the ongoing process of constitutional conferences with first ministers and Aboriginal representatives would be discussing the issue of the Senate and other constitutional matters affecting Aboriginal people. The Committee further noted that the Special Committee of the House of Commons on Indian Self-Government had recommended against special representation for First Nations in Parliament (Canada, Parliament 1984, 13).

SECOND CONSTITUTIONAL CONFERENCE (8–9 MARCH 1984)

In October 1983, the Standing Committee on Indian Affairs and Northern Development called for recognition of Indian self-government and for the right to self-government to be "explicitly stated and entrenched in the Constitution of Canada" (Canada, House of Commons 1983, 44). However, this Committee had no mandate to consider Inuit or Métis self-government, since the terms of reference were restricted to a study of band governments on Indian reserves. Such entrenchment would replace the only form of Indian government recognized by the federal government – that of the band council system created by the *Indian Act* and imposed on Indian people.

The Committee also examined the concept of guaranteed representation of Indian people in the House of Commons and concluded that: "The Committee believes that the best way to promote Indian rights is through Indian self-government and not by special representation for First Nations in Parliament. Nevertheless, the situation of Indian peoples will change with self-government, and special representation in Parliament might in future offer benefits that cannot now be anticipated" (Canada, House of Commons 1983, 135).

The Committee noted that most interveners were sceptical about the system of guaranteed parliamentary seats established for the Maori people in New Zealand. In 1867, the Maori people were allocated four electoral districts overlaying all general electoral districts in the country. This would ensure that Maori in all regions of the country would be represented in

Parliament. Maori electors could only vote in the Maori electoral district in which they resided. Since 1975, Maori electors have had the option to register on a Maori roll in their region and vote in a Maori electoral district or register and vote in the general electoral district where they live.

The Committee "concluded that the New Zealand model has a number of problems: The Maoris are under-represented in Parliament; the elected representatives exercise little power; and the system has weakened traditional Maori governmental structures" (Canada, House of Commons 1983, 135).

It is of interest to examine the background of the MPs who served on this Committee. Exercising the franchise granted in 1960, Indian voters helped to elect a small group of non-Aboriginal MPs in the 1970s. The latter "came from ridings with substantial numbers of Indian voters. These MPs were relatively knowledgeable about Indian issues; never before had such a group existed in Parliament" (Tennant 1985, 327–28).

The Committee included some of these MPs. They used their particular knowledge to involve Indian people in the Committee's work at levels that had never before applied. In effect "the committee became a vehicle to secure Indian co-operation and to organize and articulate Indian demands" (Weaver 1984, 217). The Committee's report effectively gave the subsequent ministerial meetings, and the 1984 meeting of first ministers, a central focus: that of Aboriginal self-government (Schwartz 1985, 99).

Aboriginal representatives were ready to begin negotiating agreements at the ministerial meetings that preceded the second constitutional conference, while federal and provincial governments came to listen to what Aboriginal people had to say (Hawkes 1985a, 85). As many governments had not yet even formed policy, the ministerial meetings were judged a failure by both Aboriginal people and participating governments (ibid.).

The constitutional conference opened with some observations of the prime minister:

> We started in 1982 by inserting in our Constitution section 35, in which Aboriginal and treaty rights were recognized and affirmed. We were aware at the time that these rights needed to be identified and further defined through a constitutional process. My own view is that the *identification* of rights is well-advanced. On both sides now we have a clearer idea of the subject matters the Aboriginal peoples have in mind when they speak about their rights. However, neither they nor we have the same clarity of ideas when it comes to the *definition* of those rights. And that is not surprising given the complexity of the subjects identified. (Trudeau 1984, 3)

With respect to Aboriginal self-government the prime minister stated:

There is nothing revolutionary or threatening about the prospect of
Aboriginal self-government. Aboriginal communities have rightful
aspirations to have more say in the management of their affairs
and to exercise more responsibility for decisions affecting them.
These functions are normal and essential to the sense of self-worth
that distinguishes individuals in a free society. The Government of
Canada remains committed to the establishment of Aboriginal self-
government, and it is my impression that the provinces are very much
of the same mind. (Trudeau 1984, 9–10)

Aboriginal representatives sought to entrench judicially enforceable rights to self-government, notwithstanding differing approaches
to the content of self-government. The Assembly of First Nations (AFN)
spoke of the sovereignty of First Nations, where sovereignty meant
"full autonomy and self-determination *within* Canada and the Canadian
Constitution" (Ahenakew 1984a, 5). The Assembly tabled extensive
draft constitutional amendments which reduced to legal terms the
detailed proposals tabled at the preceding constitutional conference in
1983. This included "the inherent right of each First Nation to self-
government" (Ahenakew 1984b, 1).

The Métis National Council (MNC) and the Native Council of Canada
(NCC) did not speak of "sovereignty" or "inherent" rights, but of their
right to self-government as Aboriginal people (MNC 1984; NCC 1984).
The MNC wanted a firm agreement on Métis self-identification and
an enumeration process by which the Métis membership would be
established (MNC 1984, 1). The MNC also stated that "with respect to the
process to date, its structure has not served to facilitate discussions.
It is unrealistic to expect the different Aboriginal peoples – with their
distinct identities, cultures, legal situations and aspirations – and
thirteen governments to sit down at the officials' and ministers' tables
and accomplish much" (ibid., 5).

The MNC sought a sectoral forum involving, besides itself, the three
Prairie provinces, British Columbia, Ontario and the Northwest
Territories – all of which cover the Métis homeland. "The sectoral process
... would delineate the boundaries of a Métis land base and identify the
powers and responsibilities of self-government to be entrenched or
delegated on the land base. The process would also deal with special
political arrangements for those Métis choosing to live off a Métis land
base" (MNC 1984, 6).

The Inuit, represented by the Inuit Committee on National Issues
(ICNI), expressed self-government aspirations through the creation of a

nonethnic, public government in a new territory called Nunavut to be established in the eastern part of the Northwest Territories. "A Nunavut government would be elected by all permanent residents of the Territory but because Inuit control the vast majority of our population, the government would be responsive to our needs – our language, culture and ways of doing things" (ICNI 1984, 5).

An Inuit Nunavut government would have jurisdiction over education, social services, local economic development, local government, housing, wildlife management and public works (ICNI 1984, 5). "Self-government is the exercise of effective control by a people over matters directly affecting them," stated Zebedee Nungak (ICNI 1984).

Aboriginal representatives were frustrated by the lack of progress made.[7] As it turned out, only three provinces – Ontario, New Brunswick and Manitoba – supported a federal initiative to include in the Constitution a non-justiciable right of Aboriginal people to self-governing institutions. The federal proposal made the following statement:

2.   The government of Canada and the provincial governments are committed to negotiating with representatives of the Aboriginal peoples of Canada to identify and define the nature, jurisdiction and power of self-governing institutions that will meet the needs of their communities, as well as the financing arrangements relating to those institutions, and to present to Parliament and the provincial legislatures legislation to give effect to the arrangements resulting from the negotiations. (Trudeau 1984, 8)

In opposition to the proposed federal resolution the AFN, the ICNI and the NCC tabled a common resolution which sought a legally enforceable right to self-government. This resolution stated, in part, the following:

2.   The government of Canada and the provincial governments, to the extent that each has jurisdiction, are committed to negotiate treaties respecting self-government with representatives of the Aboriginal peoples of Canada. Such negotiation will include the scope, jurisdiction and powers of self-government, and such related matters as fiscal relationships and lands and resources. Such treaties shall be treaties within the meaning of s. 35(1). (AFN et al. 1984)

An agreement on a constitutional amendment pertaining to Aboriginal self-government was not reached at this conference. The majority of premiers wanted to see the details of self-government before they were prepared to consider entrenching anything. Premier Grant Devine of Saskatchewan stated:

> To achieve further constitutional change, it seems to be essential to us that any draft amendments be fully discussed with the implications fully analyzed, fully understood, and fully agreed upon by all.
>
> An example of a fundamental difference of viewpoint is the position taken by the Aboriginal associations that it is possible to immediately entrench a general right to Aboriginal government in the constitution.
>
> Governments on the other hand take the position that the concepts must be fully defined and understood before entrenchment can be contemplated. (Devine 1984a, 4–5)

The premier called the federal proposal for self-government a "pig in a poke" (Devine 1984b, 279).

The conference concluded without agreement on a future plan of action. According to one observer, the conference "was a failure of colossal proportions" (Hawkes 1985b, 10). All Aboriginal representatives were unanimous in their criticism of the outcome of the conference. Notwithstanding this criticism, it should be noted that for the first time the federal government, along with three provinces, expressed guarded support for the entrenchment of Aboriginal self-government.

Subsequently, Aboriginal representatives subsumed all unresolved Aboriginal issues, including land claims, under the aegis of "self-government."

A NEW PRIME MINISTER FACES ABORIGINAL PEOPLE (2–3 APRIL 1985)

In September 1984, a Progressive Conservative government was elected. Aboriginal representatives hoped a new prime minister might bring a new approach to constitutional discussions. Prime Minister Mulroney recognized this need for a new approach as the third constitutional conference began on 2 April 1985. In his opening remarks the prime minister stated that, having been a labour negotiator, he knew what it was like to have powerful interests on the other side of the table. He said that "the Canada we are building for the twenty-first century must have room for self-governing Aboriginal peoples" (Mulroney 1985a, 30). The prime minister expressed his view that "the key to change is self-government for Aboriginal peoples within the Canadian federation" (ibid., 5). The issue was not whether there should be self-government, but rather how it should be implemented.

Aboriginal representatives remained united in their goal for the entrenchment of a judicially enforceable right of self-government. The Inuit representatives summed up the thrust of this common goal:

One – there must be a basic statement of our right to self-government in the Constitution.

Two – there must be some mechanism for the establishment of institutions of self-government and the implementation of our right to self-government.

Three – there must be some way of ensuring that these agreements on self-government will be constitutionally protected. (ICNI 1985, 4)

The prime minister tabled a proposal which sought to entrench the right to Aboriginal self-government subject to a number of conditions. The nature and extent of the right had to be set out in agreements. Federal and provincial governments would be constitutionally committed to entering into negotiations to conclude self-government agreements. The rights of Aboriginal people contained in these agreements would receive constitutional protection if the parties agreed. These agreements would be negotiated at the community level (Mulroney 1985b). Recognizing the differences that had developed between the majority of the provinces and Aboriginal people, the prime minister noted that: "it appears ... that the real question is how to blend the desire of the Aboriginal people for constitutional entrenchment of the right to self-government with the desire of governments for sufficient definition of those rights" (Canada 1985a, 1).

The prime minister's approach for community-based or "bottom-up" negotiations contrasted with the "top-down" approach at the two earlier conferences wherein Aboriginal people sought constitutional entrenchment of the right to self-government which would be implemented through self-government agreements or, failing that, left to the courts to determine the nature and extent of the right to self-government. To the criticism that further definition of the right to self-government would be required at the conference before anything could be entrenched, federal Minister of Justice John Crosbie stated: "The objection is raised that somehow we are agreeing to an undefined commitment or an undefined right. As I see it, there is not a Constitution in the world that, when it is adopted, you are adopting a whole series of undefined commitments and rights" (Crosbie 1985, 13).

As the conference unfolded, the prime minister found his proposal lacked support from a number of provinces and from all Aboriginal representatives. To build a basis for expanded provincial support, the prime minister tabled a proposed accord which contained provisions designed to be more attractive to the more resistant provinces such as Saskatchewan. The provision to negotiate with Aboriginal people would become legally non-enforceable, instead of being constitutionally entrenched as previously proposed by the federal government. Saskatchewan had objected to "the possibility that courts might be invited to interfere and intervene in the way that commitment is acted upon" (Devine 1985, 9). Saskatchewan also called for a provision whereby any agreements reached could only be entrenched with the consent of Parliament and the province(s). This request was also acceded to by the federal government (Canada 1985b).

Support for this accord grew as seven provinces and two Aboriginal organizations agreed to it, including the Métis National Council and the Native Council of Canada.[8] The support of these two organizations was obtained when the prime minister met privately and separately with leaders from each group. The prime minister promised both groups that he would hold a meeting with them to address Métis concerns, including land – an offer which he repeated publicly at the conference. As the membership of both organizations lacked a land base, representatives of both organizations felt compelled to accept the prime minister's offer. In addition, both groups found attractive the idea of community-based negotiations to conclude self-government agreements and to deal with the priorities of their membership living off a land base. "Tripartite negotiations appeared to offer a concrete and pragmatic method of concluding regional agreements outside the unwieldy forum of the section 37 process" (Weinstein 1986, 18).

The Assembly of First Nations did not support the federal accord and indicated it could accept no less than the entrenchment of the inherent right to self-government, a position it had maintained from the outset of the conference (Ahenakew 1985; AFN 1985). Their representatives could not accept any commitment to negotiate agreements unless that commitment was entrenched and could be enforced by the courts. The Inuit Committee on National Issues required more time to debate and discuss the federal accord. Their representatives indicated that they were afraid that accepting a flawed proposal could split Inuit groups (Platiel and Sallot 1985, 2). Both organizations did not agree with the provincial ratification of agreements requirement, as they believed this amounted to a "provincial veto" (Weinstein 1986, 18).

The parties became deadlocked. After it became clear that the discussions were not advancing during the intense meetings that followed, the prime minister adjourned the conference. On 5 and 6 June, conference participants, excluding first ministers, convened again. The federal proposal died on the table after two days of fruitless discussions.

Provincial governments – particularly the three western ones – remained opposed to entrenching an undefined, enforceable right to self-government. They would not agree to entrenching self-government unless the details were clearly spelled out. By offering to consider entrenching a non-justiciable right to Aboriginal self-government, the provinces sought a shield to ensure that nothing would be left to judicial chance.[9]

No consensus was built toward entrenching a provision acceptable to all four Aboriginal organizations. Rather, a rift developed among the four Aboriginal organizations.

LAST CONSTITUTIONAL CONFERENCE (26–27 MARCH 1987)

The prime minister opened the 1987 conference, stating that "What we are seeking to do is make self-government a practical reality for Canada's Aboriginal peoples" (Mulroney 1987b, 1). Grand Chief Georges Erasmus of the AFN stated that "Nothing short of Aboriginal self-government will achieve our aspirations for survival as distinct peoples" (Erasmus 1987b, 4). The other Aboriginal organizations were of the same view.[10] At the close of the first day of the conference no progress had been made. Only three provinces – Ontario, New Brunswick and Manitoba – supported constitutional language that had a "remote hope of coming close" to the position of the Aboriginal people (Platiel and Fraser 1987, 1). The prime minister concluded the day, noting that "there is a need for [a] constitutionally-provided process of negotiations to undertake the definition of rights" (Mulroney 1987c, 2).

As the final day of the conference began, the federal government tabled a proposed, legally non-enforceable political accord that called for the right to Aboriginal self-government to be entrenched subject to a number of conditions. The jurisdiction, legislative powers and rights of self-government were to be determined and defined through agreements. Governments would commit themselves to discussing the schedule, scope and nature of agreements with representatives of Aboriginal people. Governments would also commit themselves to negotiating agreements. Agreements concluded could be entrenched, provided Parliament and the legislature of the province that made the agreement so approved. There would be a further first ministers conference in 10 years to review progress (Mulroney 1987a).

The proposed accord was rejected by British Columbia, Alberta, Saskatchewan and Newfoundland, who had all hardened their positions against entrenchment. Alberta Premier Don Getty stated:

> Entrenchment of the principle of Aboriginal self-government without
> prior adequate definition could be a reversal of our traditional demo-
> cratic process, and would also be inconsistent with Canada's historic
> development and our democratic process. Surely we have to be able
> to accept that people elected to Parliament, to our legislatures, working
> with our Aboriginal people, have the responsibility to clearly define
> self-government. It is our responsibility; otherwise, we merely invite
> confusion and uncertainty and then we will leave it to the courts to
> do our job; we will leave it to the courts to interpret the meaning of
> self-government. (Getty 1987, 86)

The Aboriginal representatives also rejected the federal proposal.
However, the four national Aboriginal organizations, determined to
demonstrate solidarity and to deal with concerns that Aboriginal self-
government was unspecified in the proposal, tabled a joint proposal
which called for the entrenchment of the "inherent" right to self-
government (AFN et al. 1987). The Aboriginal proposal was not discussed
before the prime minister adjourned the meeting. The conference
concluded without an agreement, leaving Aboriginal representatives to
express great bitterness and anger (Fraser 1987, A4).

While Aboriginal people were frustrated by the outcome of the
four conferences, progress had been made. Aboriginal self-government
was now being openly debated. For many, the issue was not whether
there should be self-government; rather, the issue was how to implement it.

There was room for argument on this score. While the issue was
indeed being debated there were profound and seemingly unbridge-
able differences among the parties around the constitutional table.
Governments saw Aboriginal self-government as a created right, one
which was dependent upon a constitutional amendment for its existence. Aboriginal representatives saw it as an inherent right existing independently of the constitutional process and before Canada itself existed.

AFTERMATH – THE MEECH LAKE ACCORD

On 30 April 1987, one month after the failure of the 1987 constitutional
conference, first ministers met and all reached an agreement in principle
on the constitutional means by which Quebec would accept the 1982
Constitution Act. The linchpin of the agreement was a clause recognizing Quebec as a "distinct society."

For Aboriginal people this agreement created mixed feelings, which
came to be expressed during the hearings of the Special Joint Committee
of the Senate and the House of Commons on the Meech Lake Accord.

In testimony before the Committee in August 1987, Aboriginal representatives expressed their support for "Quebec's aspirations to be a
functioning partner in Confederation" (Erasmus 1987a, 49).[11] Their
support, however, was conditional upon the Aboriginal contribution to
Canada's constitutional order also being entrenched (Bruyère 1987a,
96; Gordon 1987, 26).

A number of concerns were expressed by representatives from all
four Aboriginal organizations about both the content of the Accord and
the political process itself. With respect to the latter, Aboriginal representatives expressed concerns that a double standard applied. It was
inconsistent to reject entrenchment of a justiciable right to Aboriginal
self-government in the Constitution after several ministerial meetings
and four constitutional conferences over five years, while agreeing,
after a shorter period of negotiations, to entrench the "distinct society"
clause, which the courts could review. Aboriginal people wondered
why their distinct societies could not also be recognized. Their representatives were concerned that:

> To make Quebec the one and only society in Canada that could be
> defined in the constitution as "distinct" seemed like a distortion of
> history and a misrepresentation of present realities. Aboriginal people,
> some of whom still speak Aboriginal languages that are often uniquely
> distinct to this country, felt themselves once again pushed aside by
> Euro-Canadian politicians whose respect for cultural pluralism seemed
> to begin and end with acknowledgment of their own major linguistic
> division. The fact that the accord would entrench the French and
> English languages as the exclusive expression of "the fundamental
> characteristic of Canada" added weight to Aboriginal peoples'
> contention that the Meech Lake accord symbolically confirmed their
> exclusion from the key theatres of Canadian public life. The exclu-
> sion was one that might eventually find strong reflection in the course
> of Canadian jurisprudence and in the institutional design of Canadian
> self-government. (Hall 1989, 441)

Aboriginal representatives expressed concerns about completing
the agreed-upon agenda from the 1983 first ministers conference on
Aboriginal Constitutional Matters. The Native Council of Canada
expressed the view that the unanimity provisions of the Accord relating
to the amending formula meant that matters such as Aboriginal representation in the House of Commons and the legislatures would never
be considered (Bruyère 1987a, 107). Aboriginal representatives expressed
concerns that the terms of the Accord itself could impair constitutional

objectives. The Accord failed to guarantee Aboriginal participation at conferences of first ministers on matters that affected them. Aboriginal representatives feared that this would permit the premiers to infringe upon their group or collective rights. The AFN stated that their support for the Accord was contingent upon, among other things, recognition that any federal-provincial agreements would not prejudice the rights of Aboriginal people (Erasmus 1987a, 49–50).

Various Aboriginal representatives listed a number of other areas of concern about the terms of the Accord, such as: the opting-out provisions, wherein provinces could disengage themselves from national programs and which might prevent Aboriginal people from accessing such national programs (Erasmus 1987a, 52–53); Quebec's control over cultural matters (Gordon 1987, 26); the unanimity provisions regarding the admission of new provinces;[12] and the method by which new appointments would be made to the Supreme Court of Canada and the Senate. The terms of the Accord provided that only the provinces would submit the names of Supreme Court and Senate nominees to the federal government. The substantial Aboriginal population in the Northwest and Yukon Territories would not be part of this process.

Aboriginal representatives expressed their views about the process leading up to the Accord and the content of the Accord itself in very harsh terms.[13]

CHAREST COMMITTEE, 1990

After nearly three years of public debate, concerns by New Brunswick about the content of the Meech Lake Accord led its premier, the Hon. Frank McKenna, to prepare the proposed Companion Resolution to the Meech Lake Accord in April 1990. Subsequently, hearings were conducted by a special joint committee of the Senate and the House of Commons. This committee came to be called the Charest Committee after its chair, the Hon. Jean Charest.

In his appearance before the Committee Premier McKenna observed that:

> The Meech Lake Accord was not designed to deal with the interests of the Aboriginal people of Canada. I think we can all have sympathy for the frustration they must feel at not being able to get a process identified so that their legitimate concerns can be brought to the first minister's level. That really represents the approach we have tried to adopt in this companion resolution. We do not think the process of Canadian constitutional reform is going to be complete until justice

and appropriate recognition are assured for our first people. It cannot be obtained by adding a few words or phrases to the Meech Lake Accord. We know that. We know that it is going to require long and laborious and elaborate negotiations, involving the Aboriginal people. What our recommendations have done is point us in the direction of that consultative process.

I believe all Legislatures, and Canadians in general, should readily accept to include, in the future constitutional agenda, matters directly affecting the Aboriginal peoples. The New Brunswick resolution makes such a provision and further requires that representatives of the Aboriginal peoples and the territories be invited to participate in these discussions. (McKenna 1990, 24)[14]

Three of the four national Aboriginal organizations – the Assembly of First Nations, the Native Council of Canada and the Inuit Committee on National Issues – appeared before the Committee and stated that the Companion Resolution still did not meet basic Aboriginal concerns (AFN 1990; Amagoalik 1990; McCormick 1990). One representative stated that, to address Aboriginal concerns at least four elements had to be included in a companion accord: "One, [a] recognition of Aboriginal peoples as a distinct and fundamental part of Canada; two, a clear and ongoing process for constitutional reform appropriate to our needs; three, the return to the normal rules for provincehood in the north; and four, [the] reinstatement of equality in northern representation in national institutions" (Amagoalik 1990, 37).

Despite these objections, there was Aboriginal support for Quebec's aspirations: "Collective rights and collective needs are a reality in Canada. We must accommodate them. This is one reason why we understand and are not opposed to the Meech Lake accord's recognition of Québec's distinctiveness within Canada. It is not productive to either ignore or repress our collective realities. The failure of Canada to come to grips with Aboriginal issues is compelling testimony to the tragedy of that route" (McCormick 1990, 32–33).

Aboriginal representatives were again critical of the process leading to the Accord as well as its content.[15] The NCC pointed out that: "One of the major hurdles confronting Meech Lake is the Senate. It is the position of the Native Council of Canada that Aboriginal people should have guaranteed representation in the Senate in this country. To be not allowed to participate in discussions at the first ministers' conference would be to never see this come to a reality in this country" (McCormick 1990, 45).

Aboriginal representatives rejected the notion that Aboriginal rights could only be dealt with after the Meech Lake Accord was adopted, and that the failure of adoption would mean that Aboriginal rights would not be dealt with until the next century. A significant positional shift came from the Métis National Council, which had reversed its strong opposition and now supported passage of the Accord with or without the Companion Resolution. The MNC was now of the view that Aboriginal rights could and would only be dealt with after Quebec's demands had been met. The MNC representative stated that: "I believe the demise of the Meech Lake accord means we will never be able to return to the negotiating table to discuss our constitutional issues" (Dumont 1990, 176).

Except for the support of the MNC, Premier McKenna's proposed Companion Resolution did not receive endorsement from any Aboriginal intervener who appeared before the Charest Committee. Aboriginal representatives expressed their belief that the Companion Resolution failed to address the issues that concerned them most. The political will and initiative of Premier McKenna was certainly praised, but many representatives felt that the Companion Resolution was a classic case of too little, too late.

In June 1990, the Meech Lake process came to an end. A meeting of the first ministers agreed on 9 June 1990 to pass the Meech Lake Accord without amendments. This required the provinces that had not ratified the Accord – New Brunswick, Manitoba and Newfoundland – to do so within a short, prescribed period of time. Under the amending formula in the *Constitution Act, 1982*, the 1987 Meech Lake Accord had to be ratified within three years. The Accord failed to receive the required unanimous consent of all provinces when Aboriginal MLA Elijah Harper blocked its passage in the Manitoba legislature and the Accord did not come to a vote in Newfoundland. Resolution of Aboriginal issues remained stalled with no further initiatives contemplated by governments.

RECENT EVENTS

Two separate events regarding Aboriginal people came to capture the public's attention in 1990. On the one hand there was Manitoba MLA Elijah Harper, standing tall and proud, eagle feather clutched firmly in hand, saying "No, Mr. Speaker," thereby blocking passage of the Meech Lake Accord in the Manitoba legislature. A powerful symbol of the impact of electing Aboriginal legislators, this scene contrasted strongly with events at Oka, Quebec.

Unresolved conflicts over land immediately adjacent to the Municipality of Oka go back to the year 1717 (Canada, House of Commons 1991b, 7). In recent years, the municipality sought to permit the expansion of a private golf club on lands claimed by the Mohawks of Kanesatake. As events escalated in the spring of 1990, the Sûreté du Québec was called in to remove armed Mohawk Warriors barricaded on the disputed lands (The Pines). This resulted in an exchange of gunfire leaving one police officer dead. It also resulted in the blocking of the Mercier Bridge to Montreal, a major traffic artery, by armed Mohawks from nearby Kahnawake.

The events at Oka mesmerized Canadians. They were transfixed by the televised confrontation of Oka Warriors and Canadian army regulars. For the first time since the Northwest Resistance of 1885, the Canadian army was requested to ensure law, order and civil rights in an area controlled by armed Aboriginal people.

The Standing Committee on Aboriginal Affairs, chaired by MP Ken Hughes, stated in its fifth report:

> There is a deep well of public support for First Nations people on the issues of land rights and self-government. There is an equally deep commitment to the principle of non-violent social and political change. ... Canadians want to see justice achieved for Aboriginal people in Canada but will not accept any side of the negotiating table resorting to the use of arms as a negotiating technique. In a world of competing interests and often conflicting perspectives and values, peaceful conflict resolution is the only real guarantee of human rights and good government. (Canada, House of Commons 1991b, 29)

Acts of Indian defiance grew across the country during and following the events at Oka.[16] Whether such defiance presages future violence is another matter. The first warning of Aboriginal violence was issued in 1967 by Dr. Howard Adams, then president of the Métis Society of Saskatchewan. Educated at Berkeley during the height of the student activism of the period, he brought his idea of American-style radicalism back to his homeland. While warnings of violence seem to be an everyday occurrence now, his statement, reported as a national news story, caused a sensation at the time.

The former Grand Chief of the AFN, Georges Erasmus, stated that frustration can lead to violence: "The internal violence has been contained for a long time. It cannot be contained forever" (Turner 1990, A1). Nevertheless, all six candidates who ran to succeed Grand Chief Erasmus as head of the AFN in June 1991 condemned the use of violence to achieve results (Henton 1991, A23). At the same time Canadians continued to receive disturbing news about the terrible and worsening economic and social conditions of Aboriginal people. In a major federal-provincial study of the justice system in Alberta, the Task Force on the

Criminal Justice System and its Impact on the Indian and Métis Peoples of Alberta examined the role of Aboriginal people in the justice system and found that: "Aboriginals are often at the receiving end of what appears to be a foreign system of justice delivered to a large extent by non-Aboriginals" (Alberta, Task Force 1991, 1:1).

The Task Force also found that "the imposition of the majority's justice system on the Aboriginal minority results frequently in unfairness and inequity" (Alberta, Task Force 1991, 1:2). The findings of the Task Force, named the Cawsey Commission after its chair, led one newspaper to comment that Cawsey had found evidence of cruel apathy, and racism, at all levels of Alberta society and that Canadians would condemn it as an abuse of human rights if they found it in another country.

The Report of the Aboriginal Justice Inquiry, in its examination of the justice system in Manitoba, stated:

> The justice system has failed Manitoba's Aboriginal people on a massive scale. It is not merely that the justice system has failed Aboriginal people; justice also has been denied to them. For more than a century the rights of Aboriginal people have been ignored and eroded. The result of this denial has been injustice of the most profound kind. Poverty and powerlessness have been the Canadian legacy to a people who once governed their own affairs in full self-sufficiency. (Manitoba, Public Inquiry 1991, 1:1)

The Report concluded that: "Canada's treatment of its first citizens has been an international disgrace" (Manitoba, Public Inquiry 1991, 1:674).

The Canadian Human Rights Commission has noted that, while progress has been made in the last quarter century, the gains of Aboriginal people have not kept pace with Canada's international obligations (Canadian Human Rights Commission 1990, 2). The Interim Report of the Citizens' Forum (Spicer Commission) found almost unanimous consensus amongst Canadians "that Aboriginal peoples in Canada have been unfairly treated, that this has besmirched our international reputation, and that it offends our collective principles of caring and fairness" (Canada, Citizens' Forum 1991a, 4).

The concept of Aboriginal self-government is one which more and more Canadians are seriously examining. The Royal Commission on the Economic Union and Development Prospects for Canada (Macdonald Commission) noted that: "Aboriginal claims for self-government are an understandable response to social, economic and historical circumstances and are in accord with the political awakening evident in Aboriginal populations around the world" (Canada, Royal Commission 1985, 3:365–66).

However, the Commission found the concept of self-government to be ambiguous and doubted whether it was the surest means of achieving all Aboriginal goals. Commissioners were concerned "that the single-minded pursuit of self-government might unwittingly delay the massive effort which is needed to solve the major social and economic problems of Aboriginal communities" (Canada, Royal Commission 1985, 3:366).

The Canadian Bar Association has stated that: "It is widely recognized that the right of self-determination through self-government is a fundamental human right of all peoples" (Canadian Bar Association 1988, 31).

During 1991 some progress on outstanding issues has been made. In an address to the First Nations Congress in Victoria, BC in April 1991, Prime Minister Mulroney noted that the "friendship and reasonableness" of Aboriginal people has not always been reciprocated by other Canadians. The prime minister stated that Aboriginal people "too often have been treated insensitively, unfairly and even illegally" (Mulroney 1991, 2). To redress outstanding issues, the prime minister promised a number of significant initiatives including "a Royal Commission to examine the economic, social and cultural situation" of Aboriginal people; a quadrupling of resources on specific land claims; agreement to consider pre-Confederation land claims; initiatives to improve economic and social conditions on Indian reserves; and a major review of Indian housing options (ibid., 2–4).[17] The prime minister also agreed to launch an Indian Claims Commission, which he did during the summer. On 27 August 1991, the prime minister announced the formation of the Royal Commission on Aboriginal Peoples. In so doing he stated: "Anybody with an eye to see who has ever walked across an Indian reserve knows that these are Third World conditions that we would deplore anywhere else" (Speirs 1991, A4).

Some provinces have also undertaken some initiatives. British Columbia has agreed to discuss Indian land claims in that province after denying the legitimacy of such claims for over a century. Ontario has recognized the inherent right of Aboriginal people to self-government. Nova Scotia and New Brunswick are each considering the establishment of one Aboriginal electoral district to ensure representation in their provincial legislative assemblies (*Ottawa Citizen* 1991, 8; *Globe and Mail* 1991, A1). Quebec is considering an electoral district in northern Quebec for the Inuit (*Gazette* 1991, 12). There is recognition that Aboriginal people must have their input into any new process to bring about constitutional change (Gougeon 1991, 2). In August 1991, nine premiers were addressed on Aboriginal self-government by the leaders of the four national Aboriginal organizations. The premier of Quebec was absent, declining to attend any meetings of premiers because of the failure to ratify the Meech Lake Accord. This invitation to meet the premiers was unprecedented. British Columbia Premier Rita Johnson later stated that the premiers agreed to accept the concept of self-government (Cernetig et al. 1991, A1; Simpson 1991, A8).

The report of the Special Joint Committee of the Senate and the House of Commons on the Process for Amending the Constitution of Canada (the Beaudoin-Edwards Committee) in June 1991 recommended that any constitutional amendment directly affecting Aboriginal people have their consent, that Aboriginal people be invited to participate in all future constitutional conferences, and that constitutional conferences be called biennially to address the rights of Aboriginal people (Canada, Parliament 1991, 17). As well, Constitutional Affairs Minister Joe Clark agreed in July with the AFN to involve Indian people in a new national unity plan. To deal with Aboriginal issues, Aboriginal people would be involved in their own "parallel process." However, the four national Aboriginal organizations have not come to an agreement on how to participate in this parallel process (Cernetig 1991, A1; *Winnipeg Free Press* 1991, 6; *Toronto Star* 1991, A8).

In September 1991, Prime Minister Mulroney announced proposals for major constitutional reform. The prime minister underlined the importance of recognizing the significance of Aboriginal people in the fabric of Canadian society. He noted that: "the prominent roles aboriginal peoples have played in Canada's history represent a vital part of Canada's identity. Increasingly, the sharing of different perspectives which stem from the contact between aboriginal and non-aboriginal people is seen as a source of richness to be valued, celebrated and preserved in a spirit of mutual respect" (Canada 1991, 6).

For the first time the Government of Canada committed itself to a provision that would constitutionally entrench a justiciable right to Aboriginal self-government. This would not be an inherent right to self-government, but one which would be exercised within the Canadian constitutional framework and subject to the *Canadian Charter of Rights and Freedoms* and to many federal and provincial laws of general application (Canada 1991, 7). The right to self-government could not be enforced for a 10-year period during which there would be "regularly scheduled First Ministers conferences" to deal with outstanding Aboriginal issues and to monitor progress on the negotiation of self-government agreements (ibid., 8). The prime minister further proposed to entrench "a commitment by governments to negotiate self-government agreements with the aboriginal peoples" (ibid.).

Other initiatives included a commitment to include Aboriginal people in current constitutional deliberations and guaranteed representation in a reformed Senate (Canada 1991, 11). The prime minister also proposed to entrench a "Canada clause" "to affirm the identity and aspirations of the people of Canada" (ibid., 9). A number of "characteristics and values" of Canadians were to be stated in the "Canada clause" including the: "recognition that the aboriginal peoples were historically self-governing, and recognition of their rights within Canada" (ibid.).

ABORIGINAL ELECTORAL REFORM
Improved Aboriginal representation in the House of Commons was identified as an important objective by Aboriginal representatives at the public hearings of the Royal Commission on Electoral Reform and Party Financing in 1990. During these hearings, representatives of Aboriginal people proposed the creation of special electoral districts based on their proportionate share of the Canadian population.

Native Council of Canada
In its appearance before the Royal Commission, the NCC called for guaranteed representation in Parliament. The NCC stated its view that such participation is critical to involving Aboriginal people in the decision-making processes that affect them. The NCC stated that "self-government can mean little if it is not reflected in national institutions" (NCC 1990a, 6). This position was supported by two NCC affiliates who also appeared before the Commission – the New Brunswick Aboriginal Peoples Council and the Native Council of Nova Scotia.

One affiliate representative stated that "the Aboriginal people of this country not only have the collective right, but also a need, socially, economically and politically, to participate in the Canadian political process, the very process that elects governments, that governs this land, that makes laws that impact upon all citizens, and that has for far too long treaded upon the rights of Aboriginal people" (Gould 1990b, 11244).

Another representative questioned: "Is it responsible and fair government to not have a minority of people represented in the House of Commons, when legislation affecting this people, is debated and passed?" (Robinson 1990b, 11213).

In dealing with legislation before the House of Commons, Dr. Robinson stated: "Only an Aboriginal person and only an Aboriginal representative can speak about whether the proposed legislation is justifiable in light of what it will do or what its effect on the Aboriginal people of Canada will be" (Robinson 1990b, 11216).

Métis National Council

Only one brief was received by the Royal Commission on behalf of the Prairie Métis. The Métis Society of Saskatchewan (MSS) supported the creation of guaranteed seats in Parliament for Aboriginal people, but also suggested the creation of a new seat in northern Saskatchewan with an Aboriginal majority. The MSS noted that there is no conflict between the goals of self-government and representation in Parliament: "Constitutional recognition of Aboriginal self-government, as a third order of government, will not detract from Aboriginal involvement in Federal and Provincial orders of government. In fact, it would make it more necessary to accommodate Aboriginal representation in those two orders. Providing for guaranteed representation in Parliament and the senate is one method of doing this" (Morin 1990, 143–44).

Inuit Tapirisat of Canada

The Inuit representatives continued to support greater representation of their people in Parliament, as they had done in the past. They noted that they had more influence in Parliament since the federal constituency of Nunatsiaq was created in 1975. As in the 1983 Senate reform hearings, discussed above, the Inuit representatives again expressed the desire for additional representation for the Inuit in northern Quebec and Labrador. The Inuit admitted that they had not changed their views about the efficacy of guaranteed representation in Parliament. While they found the idea of guaranteed seats based on the New Zealand precedent worth studying, they preferred that a new riding be created in northern Quebec covering Inuit communities. This would ensure that the Inuit constituted a majority in that constituency (Nungak 1990, 13238–39). As one representative noted: "I think that it has been previously said by other speakers that we never see any candidates during election time. We have never even seen their pictures. So people, if they do vote at all, are basically voting blind" (ibid., 13225).

The creation of a new constituency in northern Quebec for all Aboriginal people was supported by the member of Parliament for the area. "The process for self-government for the Inuits (sic) and other native populations should include representation by a native person in the House of Commons. I find it extremely difficult to represent and defend the interests of the native populations for a score of reasons ranging from cultural differences, languages and distances" (Langlois 1990, 1–2).

A private member's bill was also introduced by the Hon. Warren Allmand in the House of Commons to create a new constituency in northern Quebec identical to the area covered by the James Bay and

Northern Quebec Agreement of 1975 (Canada, House of Commons 1990, 15682).

Assembly of First Nations

On national issues such as Aboriginal electoral reform, the AFN allows its members to express their own points of view. A number of them did so before the Royal Commission. Grand Chief Matthew Coon Come of the Grand Council of the Crees of Quebec stated: "I am here today to testify before this Royal Commission because I am an Indian and, as an Indian, my vote does not count. I cannot vote for a candidate of my choice, I have never seen the name of the person who represents my People or myself on a ballot and I am effectively disenfranchised" (Coon Come 1990, 622).

He also maintained that: "Although we now have the right to vote, the social attitudes and political policies which stood in the way of our right to participate in the political process for more than one hundred years still dominate the electoral process in this country and still prevent our free participation in government" (Coon Come 1990, 623).

The Crees of Quebec considered options such as a system of representation based upon the New Zealand experience or a separate electoral district for themselves (Crees of Quebec 1990, 18–21). The Manitoba Keewatinowi Okimakanak Inc. called for greater representation in the House of Commons so that their vote would matter. They stated:

> We need members of Parliament who do not have to be taught who we are, what we want, and why we are important to this country. We need our people in Parliament in greater numbers than is possible under the power or influence that our votes are reduced to ... In other words to perpetuate the current electoral system is in effect to make a mockery of our right to vote and to condemn our people to the politics of the majority. To be effective, we have to have the capacity to elect our own representatives to the House of Commons. (Manitoba Keewatinowi Okimakanak 1990, 133–34)

The Siksika Nation noted the "need to get into the House of Commons instead of drumming on the steps of the House of Commons and being ignored" (Favel 1990). Their solution was the creation of electoral districts based on treaty areas throughout Canada in which only Indian candidates and Indian voters would be allowed. Representation based on the New Zealand experience was also considered.

While other submissions generally reflected the view that there was a need for improved representation in the House of Commons, questions were also raised about the likelihood that the Royal Commission would deal seriously with the issue. The Assembly of Manitoba Chiefs stated that "we are uncertain whether our views and our concerns would be taken seriously by the Commission. We've had experience in the last while that would suggest to us that what Aboriginal people have to say is really unimportant to the people that make all of the decisions that affect all Canadians" (Fontaine 1990b, 9587). Their representative also expressed the following view:

> So when we come to a forum such as this one, we're of course concerned and really uncertain whether our views and our concerns will be taken seriously. And whether this particular forum has invited representatives – Aboriginal representatives in effect to legitimize this process, that will in the end, once again, deny us our proper place in this country and will deny us a real role in the institutions that give expression to your peoples, and we hope, of course, that will not be the case. (Fontaine 1990b, 9590)

The representative of the Dakota-Ojibway Tribal Council stated: "Elected officials to Parliament have no sensitivity – I should say some [of them] – have no sensitivity or understanding of Indian issues, never mind the Treaties or the articles of the Treaties" (Dakota-Ojibway 1990). The Tribal Council suggested that it was a contradiction to have a formal, Indian government-to-government relationship with Canada and then to elect Indian people to Parliament.

Ovide Mercredi, then Vice-Chief of the Manitoba Region of the AFN stated that "our faith in Canada is weakening. We have, as individuals and collectively as a people, a deep sense of alienation and rejection. There is a growing opinion amongst our leaders that we are wasting our energy and resources trying to find acceptance and friendship in a home that does not want Indians" (Mercredi 1990, 179).

He also maintained: "We recognize that we can and do participate in the political life of our country. However, we do not do so to denounce or to diminish our ancient and inherent rights of self-government. We do participate in the electoral process with the expectation and antici- pation that we may be able to influence the better treatment of our people and the full enjoyment of our collective rights and freedoms" (Mercredi 1990, 182).

The issue of Aboriginal self-government was frequently raised during the Royal Commission hearings. Most saw self-government and improved representation in the House of Commons as being comple- mentary. However, self-government remained the priority. Georges

Erasmus, then Grand Chief of the AFN, stated that he believed electoral reform did not conflict with Aboriginal sovereignty and self-government issues (Platiel 1991, A5), but that Aboriginal electoral districts were not a substitute for self-government (Richardson 1991).

Other interveners also spoke on improving Aboriginal representation in Parliament. The first Indian person elected to Parliament, Senator Len Marchand, stated that:

> I have always believed that the electoral system is the fundamental bridge binding citizens and legislatures. Its legitimacy and hence Parliament's rests upon its ability to ensure that all Canadians have an opportunity to participate on an equal footing.
>
> Today, Commissioners, I find that Aboriginal people do not participate in the electoral process on an equal footing with other Canadians, nor as a result do Aboriginal peoples have the opportunity to participate in the parliamentary process on an equal footing with other Canadians.
>
> As it stands today, Parliament is the exclusive domain of the settler, a reflection, no doubt, of the fact the electoral system was designed by settlers for settlers and historically developed to exclude Aboriginal peoples ... For the vast majority of Aboriginal Canadians Parliament is seen in the distance but there is no trail to get there. The trails that do exist are made for the workboots of the settlers. The path has been too sharp and barnacled for the moccasins of our people. (Marchand 1990, 661–63)

The above-mentioned submissions to the Royal Commission were supplemented by a series of consultations held with Aboriginal leaders across Canada in January 1991. Led by Senator Marchand, the findings of this process reinforced what was heard during the public hearings. These consultations revealed general support for measures to effectively improve the representation of Aboriginal people in the House of Commons. Aboriginal people noted that their own members of Parliament could pursue priority agenda items with great vigour, as opposed to the situation faced by some current Aboriginal MPs who could not act without "fear of alienating their non-Aboriginal constituents" (LeClair et al. 1991, 4). But not all leaders consulted favoured the creation of Aboriginal electoral districts; some identified other priority agenda items such as self-government. "However, most leaders believe Aboriginal Parliamentary representation can complement self-government and would be helpful in supporting self-governing institutions" (ibid.).

Others were not prepared to commit themselves to the idea of distinct Aboriginal electoral districts at that time. However, all indicated they would not oppose the creation of Aboriginal electoral districts if other Aboriginal people wanted them.

In May 1991, the Committee for Aboriginal Electoral Reform was formed to undertake more extensive consultations on the concept of Aboriginal electoral districts. Chaired by Senator Len Marchand, the Committee was composed of five former and current MPs.[18] They stated:

> There has been a general feeling among Aboriginal people that the electoral system is so stacked against them that [Aboriginal electoral districts] are the only way they can gain representation in Parliament in proportion to their numbers.
>
> Direct representation of Aboriginal people would help to overcome long-standing concerns that the electoral process has not accommodated the Aboriginal community of interest and identity. Aboriginal electors would elect Members of Parliament who would represent them and be directly accountable to them at regular intervals. MPs from [Aboriginal electoral districts] would understand their Aboriginal constituents, their rights, interests, and perspectives on the full range of national public policy issues. (Committee 1991b, 14)

The Committee found strong support for the creation of Aboriginal electoral districts, noting that such a concept is complementary to self-government and would not abrogate or derogate from existing Aboriginal, treaty or other rights or freedoms. The Committee stated:

> The absence of Aboriginal voices in the House of Commons undermines the Canadian commitment to pluralism and forces Aboriginal concerns and opinions onto the lawns of the Parliament buildings where more often than not they are heard but not heeded. Aboriginal views will continue to be expressed by Aboriginal leaders and their organizations and through Aboriginal governments. But Aboriginal people are also citizens of Canada and have as much right as any other citizen to participate freely in the parliamentary process on an equal footing with other Canadians.
>
> If Canadians are serious about building bridges with the Aboriginal community, the electoral process must be designed to ensure that Aboriginal people not only have the opportunity to participate, but also the right to participate effectively. (Committee 1991b, 43)

TOWARD ABORIGINAL SELF-GOVERNMENT AND ELECTORAL REFORM

Aboriginal people enjoy a special position within the fabric of the Canadian constitutional order, in which their distinctiveness as Aboriginal people has had additional recognition since Confederation. The land rights of the Métis were recognized within the original boundaries of the Province of Manitoba in the *Constitution Act, 1871.* When the Prairie provinces entered Confederation, ownership and control of natural resources within provincial boundaries remained vested in the federal government. The *Constitution Act, 1930* transferred the resources to each of these provinces. The Act protected the rights of Indian people in each province with respect to the unfulfilled land provisions of the treaties as well as certain hunting, fishing and trapping rights. In 1939, the Supreme Court of Canada ruled that the Inuit were a federal responsibility pursuant to Section 91¶24 of the *Constitution Act, 1867.*

Recognition of the distinctiveness of Aboriginal people continued with the *Constitution Act, 1982,* which recognized and affirmed the existing Aboriginal and treaty rights of the three Aboriginal peoples of Canada. The Act referentially incorporated into the Constitution the *Royal Proclamation of 1763,* a document which predated the existence of Canada by 104 years. This Act protected the rights and freedoms accorded to the Indian nations in the Proclamation. Provision was made for one constitutional conference of first ministers and Aboriginal representatives. In fact, four such conferences were held in the early 1980s.

Aboriginal representatives brought to these conferences their vision of a Canada in which their place had been constitutionally secured. These historic conferences, unique to the world, witnessed Aboriginal representatives expressing the rights of their people in their own political and legal terms.

The expression of these rights and how to protect them were at odds with approaches taken by governments who participated at these conferences. Aboriginal representatives sought a constitutional guarantee of their Aboriginal and treaty rights. Governments sought to identify, define and, perhaps, entrench further rights. Indian representatives equated "Aboriginal title" with land ownership, while governments expressed a narrow, technical, legal meaning of the term to be discerned through judicial decisions.

It was agreed at the first conference to amend the *Constitution Act, 1982* to ensure that Aboriginal and treaty rights applied equally to male and female persons, to recognize modern-day land claims agreements as treaties and to provide that no amendments could be made to section 91¶24 of the *Constitution Act, 1867* and to sections 25 and 35 of the

Constitution Act, 1982 without consulting Aboriginal people at a constitutional conference.

At these conferences, self-government emerged as the dominant issue. For Aboriginal people, self-government is the inherent right of a community to control its own land base and to make decisions pertaining to the cultural, social, financial, educational and political institutions which shape that community, including membership (or citizenship) in that community and economic development on that land base. The right to self-government is considered inherent, on the basis that it existed prior to Confederation, has never been surrendered and continues today. For the most part, governments saw self-government as a contingent or created right depending upon a constitutional amendment for its recognition. The constitutional conferences floundered on this fundamental difference.

Throughout the Meech Lake process Aboriginal people opposed measures that they believed were detrimental to them. Their representatives lobbied for recognition of their rights through a new constitutional process in which they would participate. Recent events indicate movement toward recognition of self-government rights. The 1991 constitutional proposals advanced by the federal government would entrench a justiciable right to Aboriginal self-government, but with some substantial limitations which do not satisfy Aboriginal representatives. Among these limitations is a failure to recognize self-government as an inherent right. However, the minister responsible for constitutional affairs, the Rt. Hon. Joe Clark, made the following statement during a meeting with chiefs from the Assembly of First Nations:

> I am encouraged by what I have seen as an emerging practice among Aboriginal leaders – that they are talking about the inherent rights within the context of Canadian federation. I think this is an approach very much worth discussing with the Special Joint Parliamentary Committee and I would encourage you to do so. If this is pursued and commands support from the Special Joint Parliamentary Committee, then certainly I believe our Government would not stand in the way. (Clark 1991, 4)

The most significant positional change comes from Ontario, which early in the summer of 1991 recognized the inherent right of Aboriginal people to self-government.

Self-government presumes the existence of a land base which eludes the Métis and non-status Indians. Their political representatives have sought to promote and protect their collective interests through self-governing institutions off a land base and through representation in

Parliament and in the legislatures. Through representation in such political institutions, these Aboriginal people seek participation in the decisions that directly affect their collective rights and freedoms. The Métis National Council and the Native Council of Canada raised the issue of representation in Parliament and in the legislatures at the first constitutional conference in 1983. They subsequently postponed further discussion of this issue in favour of a united front with the AFN and the ICNI on the self-government issue.

Inuit representatives support enhanced Inuit electoral participation in Parliament. They point to the increase of influence they have had in Parliament since the federal electoral district of Nunatsiaq was created in 1975.[19] The Inuit in northern Quebec seek a similar accommodation.

While the Committee for Aboriginal Electoral Reform found strong support for the concept of creating Aboriginal electoral districts, there was some opposition. Due to legislative impediments to the exercise of the federal franchise, traditions of political participation did not develop in Indian communities as in the rest of Canadian society. Even when the franchise was fully extended to Indian people in 1960, many Indian people objected:

> The basic fear of many was that the vote was the beginning of an attack on their treaty rights. Spokesmen for Indians pointed out that since Indians had been told for decades that the franchise was incompatible with their Indian status, it was scarcely surprising that they were suspicious of a sudden reversal of federal policy which implied their complete compatibility. (Hawthorn 1966, 1:260; see also Dempsey 1986, 174–76; Hall 1991b, 92–94)

These concerns brought a personal commitment in 1960 from Prime Minister Diefenbaker that extension of the franchise would not interfere with their treaty rights:

> I say this to those of the Indian race, that in bringing forward this legislation the Minister of Citizenship and Immigration (Mrs. Fairclough) will reassure, as she has reassured to date, that existing rights and treaties, traditional or otherwise, possessed by the Indians shall not in any way be abrogated or diminished in consequence of having the right to vote. That is one of the things that throughout the years has caused suspicion in the minds of many Indians who have conceived the granting of the franchise as a step in the direction of denying them their ancient rights. (Canada, House of Commons 1960, 67)

Traditions of electoral participation also did not develop because of differing Indian views about their own sovereignty. While the Committee for Aboriginal Electoral Reform asserts that Indians are citizens of Canada, this view is not consistently held within the Indian community. Most Indian people see themselves as citizens of their own sovereign nations who enjoy a nation-to-nation relationship with the federal government (Cassidy and Bish 1989, 55–57). The focus of their efforts toward constitutional reform has been to seek constitutional confirmation of their inherent right to self-government, while continuing to develop in the future as distinct people with collective rights and freedoms (Mercredi 1988).

Such a view does not necessarily rule out participation in the federal electoral system. Many Indian people reside off-reserve and will continue to do so. The recognition of self-government will not necessarily stem the flow of off-reserve migration. Migration decisions may be beyond the control of Aboriginal governments and can be influenced by such factors as enhanced economic opportunities in nearby urban centres (Gerber 1984). People in this situation might benefit from representation in the House of Commons in order to participate in the decisions which might impact on their collective rights and freedoms outside a reserve land base.

The Committee for Aboriginal Electoral Reform is of the view that "Aboriginal parliamentary representation [in the House of Commons] can complement self-government and would be helpful in supporting Aboriginal self-governing institutions" (Committee 1991b, 26). In a consultation paper, the Committee drew "an analogy with the European community where strong sovereign governments have believed it proper and effective to give their people the ability to elect representatives to the European Parliament. Elected representatives from each member country are thus in a position to advance their common interests and to deal effectively with issues that cut across their individual boundaries" (ibid.).

The Committee also maintained that "Aboriginal people would benefit if Aboriginal MPs were more numerous. They would be in a position to complement and strengthen self-government, as well as to promote the Aboriginal position on issues that go beyond the boundaries of Aboriginal lands but have a particular impact on Aboriginal people" (Committee 1991a, 1).

Aboriginal representatives would not be representing Aboriginal governments, "but they would be the pivot point between the Aboriginal government and the overall self-government of Canada" (Hall 1991b, 104; 1986a, 204). Professor Tony Hall also maintained:

> Parliamentarians representing Aboriginal constituencies would not be leaders of Aboriginal governments. The task of choosing those leaders must take place within an institutional framework of Aboriginal people's own making. But Parliamentarians representing federal Aboriginal ridings would be well placed to act as intermediaries who could help smooth the relationship between Aboriginal governments and the federal government. Certainly they would be in a better position to perform that function than the individual who presently holds that responsibility, the minister of Indian Affairs. (Hall 1991a, 135)

Within the Canadian system of electoral democracy and representative government, Aboriginal people constitute a special community of interest and identity which has not been reflected in the House of Commons. Only 12 self-identified Aboriginal MPs have been elected since Confederation out of a total of 10 966 available seats. The failure of the House of Commons to reflect in its make-up the uniqueness and importance of the Aboriginal community of interest calls into question the legitimacy of Parliament itself. Redrawing electoral district boundaries is unlikely to reflect this special community of interest due to numbers and geographic dispersion. The concept of Aboriginal electoral districts offers an alternative which can be enacted by Parliament alone, pursuant to its powers under section 44 of the *Constitution Act, 1982*.

The concept of group representation is not a departure from Canadian electoral experience. The provision for Maori electoral districts in New Zealand demonstrates that the concept of electoral districts for a distinct, indigenous people is a recognized and compatible part of the parliamentary system of democracy.[20] As noted, the *Constitution Act, 1982* provides that Aboriginal people have a right to participate at constitutional conferences with respect to certain provisions of the Constitution which directly affect them. Is it not now time to consider extending an invitation to Aboriginal people to participate in the Parliament of Canada, which has exclusive jurisdiction for them and makes decisions which affect their collective rights and freedoms?

The creation of Aboriginal electoral districts would ensure that long-overlooked Aboriginal issues would have a fairer chance of redress in the House of Commons. Aboriginal people believe that Canadians would also benefit from a House of Commons to which they would bring their values and perspectives. Aboriginal people have demonstrated their willingness to participate in the central political institutions of Canada. The level of Aboriginal participation in federal (and territorial) elections north of the 60th parallel testifies to that fact. The creation of Aboriginal electoral districts could help encourage a greater and more effective participation in the electoral process on the part of Aboriginal people. Aboriginal electoral districts could meet the challenge of meaningful electoral reform consistent with Canada's recognition of the distinctiveness of Aboriginal people and consistent with their own rights and freedoms, goals and aspirations.

ABBREVIATIONS

c.	chapter
D.L.R.	Dominion Law Reports
R.S.C.	Revised Statutes of Canada
s(s).	section(s)
S.C.	Statutes of Canada
S.C.C.	Supreme Court of Canada
S.C.R.	Supreme Court Reports

NOTES

This study was completed 4 December 1991.

I wish to thank five individuals for their contribution to this study. I have benefited greatly from the constructive criticism of two of my professional colleagues who graciously consented to do a peer review. I owe sincere thanks for the penetrating evaluation and incisive commentary of F. Leslie Seidle, the Senior Research Coordinator at the Royal Commission. I would especially like to thank my willing assistant, Daniel Arsenault, also of the Royal Commission. His tireless work contributed substantially to the quality of this study. I appreciate his hours of dedicated service ranging from research to editing and proofreading. I also wish to express great appreciation to my partner Judy Cavanagh, for her ongoing support and encouragement.

1. Quebec was the last province to grant the franchise to Indian people in 1969.

2. *The Manitoba Act, 1870* was constitutionalized by virtue of the *Constitution Act, 1871.*

3. Prime Minister Pierre E. Trudeau would come to explain the rationale for this proposed course of action at the First Ministers Conference on Aboriginal Rights on 15 March 1983. The prime minister stated that "It seemed clear enough to me that the Aboriginal peoples were culturally unique and were being treated differently by governments, but largely in a negative way, by being pushed aside from the mainstream of Canadian evolution, left behind in remote or out of the way places. They were not always left alone, however, because of the relentless pressures along our expanding frontiers, first for settlement, later for resource development."

Upon taking office, the prime minister called for a comprehensive review of the situation of Aboriginal people. This review culminated in a 1969 white paper. See Trudeau (1983, 13).

4. See *Manitoba (Attorney General v. Canada (Attorney General)* (1981, 905)).

5. See *Globe and Mail* (1981, 11). In Canada's North, schools were closed in protest (Sheppard 1981a, 10).

6. This has led some observers to remark that the conference was only partially successful. See Schwartz (1985, 29) and Platiel (1983, 10).

7. See Inuit Committee on National Issues (1984). Grand Chief David Ahenakew of the AFN stated that "We wanted a harmonious accommodation with the Canadian Confederation," but noted that "We have often felt treated, in the process, like colonized and subjugated peoples who are some sort of social problem needing the 'therapy' which officials seem to think assimilation would provide. Federal and provincial participants often appear more preoccupied with process than with substantive issues" (Ahenakew 1984a). Harry W. Daniels, vice-president of the Native Council of Canada said: "Far too often much of the dialogue at these meetings was more concerned with whether or not rights should be entrenched rather than how they should be entrenched. Technical and bureaucratic apprehension over jurisdictional responsibility too frequently obscured the simple fact that we are trying to assume our rightful place in the Constitution as the Aboriginal people of Canada" (NCC 1984, 7–8).

8. The provinces that held out were Alberta and British Columbia. Quebec was not a hold-out, but declined to make any agreements in a constitutional conference when it did not recognize the legitimacy of the Constitution patriated in 1982.

9. The Aboriginal people noted that individuals and groups could go to court to seek the protection of their Charter rights. However, when Aboriginal people sought similar protection, the provinces objected.

10. See, for example, Bruyère (1987b, 12). Mr. Bruyère stated that the Constitution must be amended to provide an explicit and non-contingent statement of recognition of the right to self-government. See also Nungak (1987b, 2). Mr. Nungak stated that "Aboriginal self-government is a necessary concept in the political culture of Confederation."

11. See also Métis National Council (1987, 46). The Inuit stated that they did not object to "the principle of Quebec being included or being a full partner in the Constitution of Canada" (Gordon 1987, 26).

12. The fear was that the Yukon and the Northwest Territories, populated by a majority of Aboriginal peoples in each case, might never be admitted into Confederation. The door would again be closed to the aspirations of Aboriginal people.

13. As one leader stated: "It hurts us very much when political leaders like the prime minister continue to say that the two founding nations of this country are the French and the English" (Amagoalik 1987, 28). Others stated that it was "offensive and insulting not to recognize the Aboriginal contribution to Canadian society" (Gordon 1987, 26).

The Métis National Council strongly expressed the view that they were not appearing "as Canadians," but as people who were "outside of Canada, outside of Confederation" (Sinclair 1987, 29–30).

Aboriginal representatives noted that after four failed constitutional conferences, "we are beginning to feel that the doors are slamming and we are being left out in the cold" (Gordon 1987, 40). Another questioned: "What motivation will we have to follow the regulations and laws of a country that refuses at least to acknowledge that we have unfinished business and therefore deserve some attention" (Nungak 1987a, 31).

14. The specific wording advanced by Premier McKenna follows:

50(1)(a.1) Annual Constitutional Conferences

The companion resolution would add to the agenda of the annual conferences on the Constitution guaranteed by the Meech Lake Accord the following item: "constitutional matters that directly affect the Aboriginal peoples of Canada, including the identification and definition of the rights of those peoples".

... (4) The Prime Minister of Canada shall invite representatives of the Aboriginal peoples of Canada, and elected representatives of the governments of the Yukon Territory and the Northwest Territories to participate in the discussion on the matters referred to in paragraph (2)(a.1) at the conference convened under subsection (1). (Canada, Federal-Provincial Relations Office 1990, 21–22)

15. Aboriginal people were quick to point out that no hearings to deal with Aboriginal concerns were contemplated or considered when they voiced concerns about the Accord. One representative reminded the Committee that Aboriginal people were given a "solemn promise" that after patriation the identification and definition of their rights would be Canada's first priority. Another noted that: "History has been very cruel to those Aboriginal people who have accepted unenforceable promises" (Amagoalik 1990, 38). Another stated that "we do not have enough faith in political promises that have been made to us in the past" (Gould 1990a, 107).

When it was suggested that Aboriginal rights could only be dealt with after passage of Meech Lake one representative stated: "We are being asked to pay a ransom with no assurance we will ever get released. We are asked to accept Meech Lake in exchange for a potential package of potential amendments that might some day be passed into law. We cannot and will not accept this. Based on solid precedent, we fear that if we pay this ransom it will be taken and we will be left where we are now, as hostages. The only difference is that most of Canada will join us and also become hostage" (Erasmus 1990, 37).

Two other representatives raised the spectre of Aboriginal people being held as hostages to the Meech Lake process (George 1990, 100; Robinson 1990a, 98). Another stated that Indian people need something "etched in stone" because of broken promises. They could no longer "go on the basis of trust" (Fontaine 1990a, 93–94). Another stated that federal and provincial governments had no commitment to resolving Aboriginal agenda items at the first ministers conferences called to identify and define their rights: "The reality is that there was no desire whatsoever to make a commit-ment. There is the hypocrisy of the standards that seem to be applied: one for Quebec because it has MPS; one for the other people because they have the strength; and then one for Aboriginal people because somehow they are not good enough. It disgusts me" (Wilson 1990, 9).

One representative stated that if rights are continually denied then their people "are denied entrance into Canada" (Robinson 1990a, 117). Another stated that his people have never accepted Confederation (Matchewan 1990, 19). According to another: "We are not talking that we dislike Canada; we are not even part of it, you know, and I want to get in. I want to belong to this country. I do not want to be a boat person. I do not want to be just a Prairie person. I want to be a Canadian" (Sinclair 1990, 122).

Chief Joe Norton of the Mohawk Council said that he was neither a Canadian nor a Quebecker (Norton 1990, 20).

16. These acts of defiance have expressed themselves in many ways. Rail lines were blocked in northern Ontario. The Trans-Canada highway was briefly blocked outside of Regina. Logging roads and highways have been blockaded in British Columbia. Indian people in northern Quebec threat-ened to shoot at helicopters involved in hydroelectric power develop-ment, block roads, bring down power lines and sabotage new hydro installations. One prominent Indian leader in Alberta was sentenced to a jail term in connection with the discharge of a weapon over the building of a dam on the Old Man River in southern Alberta. In northern Alberta, the decade-long struggle of the Lubicon Lake Indian people continues to drag on, with its struggle being taken to international forums. One Indian leader has even called for the creation of an army by Indian people (Aubry 1990, A1).

17. In meeting the challenge of resolving outstanding issues it is of interest to consider the following statements made by both the prime minister and by the Citizens' Forum on Canada's Future. Prime Minister Mulroney observed that "Over the past two centuries, native and non-native people have come together to build a great nation. Now we must come together again and chart a new direction for our country, one that will correct past

mistakes and build a future that is based on mutual respect, trust and understanding" (Mulroney 1991, 6).

In its *Report to the People and Government of Canada,* the Citizens' Forum on Canada's Future noted that "Ghandi said that you can judge a civilization by the way it treats its poorest citizens. The forceful moral dimensions of the challenge presented by Aboriginal people give [their] issues a special place. How we resolve them will decide our future as a country that can stand in the world with pride" (Canada, Citizens' Forum 1991b, 120–21).

18. The other Committee members are: Jack Anawak, MP for Nunatsiaq, Ethel Blondin, MP for Western Arctic, Wilton Littlechild, MP for Wetaskiwin, and Gene Rheaume, former MP for Northwest Territories.

19. About 85 percent of the Inuit population live within this electoral district.

20. While assessments of the New Zealand model vary, the proposals by the Committee for Aboriginal Electoral Reform address its most serious deficiency – the number of Maori electoral districts, permanently fixed at four since 1867, and incapable of expansion to reflect increasing population growth. On the other hand, the number of general electoral districts has risen from 72 in 1867 to 97. In 1986, the four Maori seats "represented" a total Maori population of 404 775, while the 97 general ridings were answerable to approximately three million non-Maori (Fleras 1991).

REFERENCES

Ahenakew, David. Assembly of First Nations. 1983a. "Opening Remarks for Presentation by Dr. David Ahenakew, National Chief, Assembly of First Nations, to the First Ministers Conference on Aboriginal Constitutional Matters." 15 March. Ottawa. CICS Document 800-17/028.

———. 1983b. "Proposals for Amendments and Additions to the *Constitution Act, 1982.*" 15 March. Ottawa. CICS Document 800-17/013.

———. 1984a. "Opening Remarks for Presentation by Dr. David Ahenakew, National Chief, Assembly of First Nations, to the First Ministers Conference on Aboriginal Rights." 8 March. Ottawa. CICS Document 800-18/026.

———. 1984b. "Draft Amendments." First Ministers Conference on Aboriginal Rights. 8–9 March. Ottawa. CICS Document 800-18/024.

———. 1985. "Speaking Notes for National Chief." First Ministers Conference on Aboriginal Rights. 2–3 April. Ottawa. CICS Document 800-20/019.

Alberta. Task Force on the Criminal Justice System and Its Impact on the Indian and Métis People of Alberta. 1991. *Justice on Trial.* Vol. 1, *Main Report.* Edmonton.

Amagoalik, John. Inuit Committee on National Issues. 1987. "Minutes of Proceedings and Evidence of the Special Joint Committee of the Senate and the House of Commons on the 1987 Constitutional Accord." 5 August.

————. Inuit Tapirisat of Canada. 1990. "Minutes of Proceedings and Evidence of the Special Committee of the House of Commons to Study the Proposed Companion Resolution to the Meech Lake Accord." 12 April.

Assembly of First Nations. 1985. "The Case for Indian Self-Government." First Ministers Conference on Aboriginal Constitutional Matters. 2–3 April. Ottawa. CICS Document 800-20/007.

————. 1990. "Minutes of Proceedings and Evidence of the Special Committee of the House of Commons to Study the Proposed Companion Resolution to the Meech Lake Accord." 12 April.

Assembly of First Nations, Inuit Committee on National Issues and Native Council of Canada. 1984. "Proposed 1984 Constitutional Accord on the Rights of the Aboriginal Peoples of Canada." Ottawa. CICS Document 800-18/046.

Assembly of First Nations, Native Council of Canada, Métis National Council and Inuit Committee on National Issues. 1987. "Joint Aboriginal Proposal for Self-Government." First Ministers Conference on Aboriginal Constitutional Matters. 26–27 March. Ottawa. CICS Document 800-23/030.

Association of Métis and Non-Status Indians of Saskatchewan. 1983. "Minutes of Proceedings and Evidence of the Special Joint Committee of the Senate and of the House of Commons on Senate Reform." 5 October.

Aubry, Jack. 1990. "Ontario Chief Says Natives Need Their Own Army." *Ottawa Citizen*, 13 December.

Bartlett, Richard H. 1980. "Citizens Minus: Indians and the Right to Vote." *Saskatchewan Law Review* 44:163–94.

Bruyère, Louis. Native Council of Canada. 1987a. "Minutes of Proceedings and Evidence of the Special Joint Committee of the Senate and the House of Commons on the 1987 Constitutional Accord." 25 August.

————. 1987b. "Opening Remarks to the First Ministers Conference on Aboriginal Constitutional Matters." 26 March. Ottawa. CICS Document 800-23/012.

Calder v. British Columbia (Attorney General), [1973] S.C.R. 313.

Canada. *Canada Elections Act*, S.C. 1960, c. 39.

————. *Canadian Charter of Rights and Freedoms*, Part I of the *Constitution Act, 1982*, being Schedule B of the *Canada Act 1982* (U.K.), 1982, c. 11.

————. *Constitution Act, 1982*, ss. 25, 35, 35.1, 37, being Schedule B of the *Canada Act 1982* (U.K.), 1982, c. 11.

————. *Constitution Amendment Proclamation, 1983*, SI/84-102.

————. *Constitutional Accord on Aboriginal Rights, 1983.* 1983. First Ministers Conference on Aboriginal Constitutional Matters. 15–16 March. Ottawa. CICS Document 800-17/041.

————. *Indian Act*, S.C. 1876, c. 18.

————. *Indian Act*, R.S.C. 1906, c. 81.

————. *Indian Act*, R.S.C. 1927, c. 98.

————. *Indian Act*, S.C. 1951, c. 29.

————. *Manitoba Act, 1870*, S.C. 1870, c. 3.

————. *Royal Proclamation of 1763.* 7 October 1763 [R.S.C. 1985, Appendix I].

Canada. 1985a. *Self-Government for the Aboriginal Peoples – Lead Statement.* First Ministers Conference on Aboriginal Constitutional Matters. 2–3 April. Ottawa. CICS Document 800-20/009.

————. 1985b. *Proposed 1985 Accord Relating to the Aboriginal Peoples of Canada.* First Ministers Conference on Aboriginal Constitutional Matters. 2–3 April. Ottawa. CICS Document 800-20/041.

————. 1991. *Shaping Canada's Future Together: Proposals.* Ottawa: Minister of Supply and Services Canada.

Canada. Citizen's Forum on Canada's Future. 1991a. *Theme Report: A Working Paper.* Ottawa: Minister of Supply and Services Canada.

————. 1991b. *Report to the People and Government of Canada.* Ottawa: Minister of Supply and Services Canada.

Canada. Department of Indian Affairs and Northern Development. 1969. *Statement of the Government of Canada on Indian Policy.* Ottawa.

Canada. Federal-Provincial Conference of First Ministers on the Constitution. 1981. *First Ministers' Agreement on the Constitution.* 5 November. Ottawa. CICS Document 800-15/021.

Canada. Federal-Provincial Relations Office. 1990. *A Companion Resolution to the Meech Lake Accord.* March. Ottawa.

Canada. House of Commons. 1960. *Debates.* 18 January.

————. 1990. *Debates.* 23 November.

Canada. House of Commons. Special Committee on Indian Self-Government. 1983. *Indian Self-Government in Canada.* Ottawa: Minister of Supply and Services Canada.

Canada. House of Commons. Standing Committee on Aboriginal Affairs. 1991a. "Minutes of Proceedings and Evidence of the Standing Committee on Aboriginal Affairs." April.

———. 1991b. *The Summer of 1990*. Fifth Report of the Standing Committee. Ottawa.

Canada. Indian and Northern Affairs Canada. 1990. *Highlights of Aboriginal Conditions: 1981–2001: Part I Demographic Trends*. Ottawa.

Canada. Minister of Justice. 1981. *Consolidation of proposed resolution. And Section 91(24) of the Constitution Act, 1867*. 13 February 1981 with amendments approved by the House of Commons 23 April 1981 and by the Senate 24 April 1981.

Canada. Parliament. Special Joint Committee of the Senate and the House of Commons on the Process for Amending the Constitution of Canada. 1991. "Minutes of Proceedings and Evidence of the Special Joint Committee of the Senate and the House of Commons on the Process for Amending the Constitution of Canada." June.

Canada. Parliament. Special Joint Committee of the Senate and of the House of Commons on Senate Reform. 1984. *Report*. Ottawa: Minister of Supply and Services Canada.

Canada. Royal Commission on the Economic Union and Development Prospects for Canada. 1985. *Report*. Vol. 3. Ottawa. Minister of Supply and Services Canada.

Canada. Statistics Canada. 1990. *Population Projections for Canada, Provinces and Territories 1989–2011*. Ottawa.

Canadian Bar Association. 1988. *Report of the Canadian Bar Association Committee on Aboriginal Rights in Canada: An Agenda for Action*. Ottawa.

Canadian Human Rights Commission. 1990. *A New Commitment: Statement of the Canadian Human Rights Commission on Federal Aboriginal Policy*. Ottawa.

Cassidy, Frank, and Robert L. Bish. 1989. *Indian Government: Its Meaning in Practice*. Halifax: Institute for Research on Public Policy.

Cernetig, Miro. 1991. "Indians Threaten Boycott of Talks." *Globe and Mail*, 19 August.

Cernetig, Miro, Susan Delacourt and Deborah Wilson. 1991. "Native Self-government Accepted by Premiers." *Globe and Mail*, 27 August.

Chronicle-Herald (Halifax). 1991. "Democracy Trumps Geography." 24 April.

Clark, Joseph. 1991. "Notes for a Speech by The Right Honourable Joe Clark, P.C., M.P., President of the Privy Council and Minister Responsible for Constitutional Affairs to the All Chiefs Constitutional Assembly of the Assembly of First Nations." 27 November. Ottawa: Federal-Provincial Relations Office.

Committee for Aboriginal Electoral Reform. 1991a. *Aboriginal Electoral Districts: The Path to Electoral Equality*. Ottawa.

———. 1991b. *The Path to Electoral Equality*. Reprinted in Royal Commission on Electoral Reform and Party Financing. *Report*. Vol. 4. Ottawa: Minister of Supply and Services Canada.

Coon Come, Matthew. Crees of Quebec and the Grand Council of the Crees (of Quebec). 1990. Testimony before the Royal Commission on Electoral Reform and Party Financing. 13 March. Ottawa.

Crees of Quebec and the Grand Council of the Crees (of Quebec). 1990. Testimony before the Royal Commission on Electoral Reform and Party Financing. 13 March. Ottawa.

Crosbie, John. 1985. "Transcript of Proceedings of the First Ministers Conference on Aboriginal Constitutional Matters." 2–3 April. Ottawa.

Dakota–Ojibway Tribal Council. 1990. Testimony before the Royal Commission on Electoral Reform and Party Financing. 19 April. Winnipeg.

Dalon, Richard. 1985. "An Alberta Perspective on Aboriginal Peoples and the Constitution." In *The Quest for Justice: Aboriginal Peoples and Aboriginal Rights*, ed. Manno Boldt and J. Anthony Long. Toronto: University of Toronto Press.

Delacourt, Susan, and Deborah Wilson. 1991. "Natives Promised Role if PM Convenes Premiers." *Globe and Mail*, 30 August.

Dempsey, Hugh A. 1986. *The Gentle Persuader: A Biography of James Gladstone, Indian Senator*. Saskatoon: Western Producer Prairie Books.

Devine, Grant. 1983. "Transcript of Proceedings of the First Ministers Conference on Aboriginal Constitutional Matters." 15–16 March. Ottawa.

———. 1984a. "Opening Remarks by the Hon. Grant Devine." First Ministers Conference on Aboriginal Rights. 8 March. Ottawa. CICS Document 800-18/039.

———. 1984b. "Transcript of Proceedings of the First Ministers Conference on Aboriginal Rights." 8–9 March. Ottawa.

———. 1985. "Notes for Opening Remarks by the Honourable Grant Devine to the First Ministers Conference on Aboriginal Constitutional Matters." 2 April. Ottawa. CICS Document 800-20/030.

Dumont, Yvon. Métis National Council. 1990. "Minutes of Proceedings and Evidence of the Special Committee of the House of Commons to Study the Proposed Companion Resolution to the Meech Lake Accord." 12 April.

Erasmus, Chief Georges, Assembly of First Nations. 1987a. "Minutes of Proceedings and Evidence of the Special Joint Committee of the Senate and the House of Commons on the 1987 Constitutional Accord." 19 August.

———. 1987b. "Opening Remarks to the First Ministers Conference on Aboriginal Constitutional Matters." 26 March. Ottawa. CICS Document 800-23/007.

———. 1990. "Minutes of Proceedings and Evidence of the Special Committee of the House of Commons to Study the Proposed Companion Resolution to the Meech Lake Accord." 12 April.

Favel, Blair. Blackfoot Tribe and Siksika Nation. 1990. Testimony before the Royal Commission on Electoral Reform and Party Financing. 16 May. Blackfoot Indian Reserve, Gleichen.

Fleras, Augie. 1991. "Aboriginal Electoral Districts for Canada: Lessons from New Zealand." In *Aboriginal Peoples and Electoral Reform in Canada,* ed. Robert A. Milen. Vol. 9 of the research studies of the Royal Commission on Electoral Reform and Party Financing. Ottawa and Toronto: RCERPF/Dundurn.

Fontaine, Phil. Assembly of Manitoba Chiefs. 1990a. "Minutes of Proceedings and Evidence of the Special Committee of the House of Commons to Study the Proposed Companion Resolution to the Meech Lake Accord." 24 April.

———. 1990b. Testimony before the Royal Commission on Electoral Reform and Party Financing. 29 May. Winnipeg.

Fraser, Graham. 1987. "Bitterness, Relief Follow Native Meeting." *Globe and Mail,* 30 March.

Gazette (Montreal). 1991. "Legislature Seat for Inuit Gets Backing from Sirros." 1 May.

George, Ron. United Native Nations. 1990. "Minutes of Proceedings and Evidence of the Special Committee of the House of Commons to Study the Proposed Companion Resolution to the Meech Lake Accord." 4 May.

Gerber, Linda M. 1984. "Community Characteristics and Out-Migration from Canadian Indian Reserves: Path Analysis." *Canadian Review of Sociology and Anthropology* 21:145–65.

Getty, Don R. 1987. "Transcript of Proceedings of the First Ministers Conference on Aboriginal Constitutional Matters." 26–27 March. Ottawa.

Globe and Mail. 1981. "Native Leaders Shocked." 6 November.

———. 1991. "Indians Threaten Boycott of Talks." 19 August.

Gordon, Mark. Inuit Committee on National Issues. 1983. "Transcript of Proceedings of the First Ministers Conference on Aboriginal Constitutional Matters." 15–16 March. Ottawa.

———. Makivik Corporation. 1987. "Minutes of Proceedings and Evidence of the Special Joint Committee of the Senate and the House of Commons on the 1987 Constitutional Accord." 16 June.

Gougeon, Richard. 1991. "Native Task Force on Constitutional Issues Consented to." *Press Independent* (Yellowknife), 12 July.

Gould, Gary. New Brunswick Aboriginal Peoples Council. 1990a. "Minutes of Proceedings and Evidence of the Special Committee of the House of Commons to Study the Proposed Companion Resolution to the Meech Lake Accord." 4 May.

———. 1990b. Testimony before the Royal Commission on Electoral Reform and Party Financing. 5 June. Sydney.

Hall, Tony. 1986a. "Closing an Incomplete Circle of Confederation: A Brief to the Joint Parliamentary Committee of the Federal Government on the 1987 Constitutional Accord." *Canadian Journal of Native Studies* 6 (2): 197–222.

———. 1986b. "Self-Government or Self-Delusion? Brian Mulroney and Aboriginal Rights." *Canadian Journal of Native Studies* 6 (1): 77–89.

———. 1989. "What Are We? Chopped Liver? Aboriginal Affairs in the Constitutional Politics of Canada in the 1980's." In *The Meech Lake Primer: Conflicting Views of the 1987 Constitutional Accord*, ed. Michael D. Behiels. Ottawa: University of Ottawa Press.

———. 1991a. "Aboriginal Issues and the New Political Map of Canada." In *"English Canada" Speaks Out*, ed. J.L. Granatstein and Kenneth McNaught. Toronto: Doubleday Canada.

———. 1991b. "Minutes of Proceedings and Evidence of the Special Joint Committee of the Senate and the House of Commons on the Process for Amending the Constitution of Canada." 18 March.

Hawkes, David C. 1985a. *Aboriginal Government: What Does it Mean?* Kingston: Queen's University, Institute of Intergovernmental Relations.

———. 1985b. *Negotiating Aboriginal Self-Government: Developments Surrounding the 1985 First Ministers' Conference*. Kingston: Queen's University, Institute of Intergovernmental Relations.

Hawthorn, H.B., ed. 1966. *A Survey of the Contemporary Indians of Canada.* 2 Vols. Ottawa: Indian Affairs Branch.

Henton, Darcy. 1991. "New Native Chief Faces Big Challenge." *Toronto Star*, 10 May.

Hogg, Peter. 1985. *Constitutional Law in Canada*. Toronto: Carswell.

Inuit Committee on National Issues. 1983a. "Brief to the Special Joint Committee of the Senate and House of Commons on Senate Reform." Ottawa.

———. 1983b. "Opening Remarks to the First Ministers Conference on Aboriginal Constitutional Matters." 15 March. Ottawa. CICS Document 800-17/015.

———. 1983c. "Proceedings and Evidence of the Special Joint Committee of the Senate and House of Commons on Senate Reform." 25 October.

———. 1984. "Opening Remarks to the First Ministers Conference on Aboriginal Rights." 8 March. Ottawa. CICS Document 800-18/034.

———. 1985. "Opening Remarks by Zebedee Nungak and John Amagoalik." First Ministers Conference on Aboriginal Constitutional Matters. 2 April. Ottawa. CICS Document 800-20/026.

Langlois, Charles A. 1990. Letter to the Royal Commission on Electoral Reform and Party Financing. 24 July. Ottawa.

LeClair and Associates. 1991. "Report on Consultations with Aboriginal Peoples Concerning Guaranteed Aboriginal Representation in the House of Commons." 12 February. Ottawa.

Lougheed, Peter. 1983a. "Opening Remarks to the First Ministers Conference on Aboriginal Constitutional Matters." 15 March. Ottawa. CICS Document 800-017/011.

———. 1983b. "Transcript of Proceedings of the First Ministers Conference on Aboriginal Constitutional Matters." 15–16 March. Ottawa.

Louis Riel Métis Association of British Columbia. 1983. "Minutes of Proceedings and Evidence of the Special Joint Committee of the Senate and of the House of Commons on Senate Reform." 6 October.

Manitoba. 1983. Manitoba Métis Rights Position Paper. First Ministers Conference on Aboriginal Constitutional Matters. 15–16 March. Ottawa. CICS Document 800-17/017.

Manitoba (Attorney General) v. Canada (Attorney General), [1981] 1 S.C.R. 753.

Manitoba. Public Inquiry into the Administration of Justice and Aboriginal People. 1991. Report of the Aboriginal Justice Committee of Manitoba. 2 vols. Winnipeg.

Manitoba Keewatinowi Okimakanak Inc. 1990. Testimony before the Royal Commission on Electoral Reform and Party Financing. 20 April. Thompson.

Marchand, Len. 1990. Testimony before the Royal Commission on Electoral Reform and Party Financing. 13 March. Ottawa.

Marchant, C.K. 1982. Representation of Aboriginal People in Government Institutions. Ottawa: Capital Cities Consultants.

Matchewan, Jean-Maurice. Algonquins of Barrière Lake. 1990. "Minutes of Proceedings and Evidence of the Special Committee of the House of Commons to Study the Proposed Companion Resolution to the Meech Lake Accord." 20 April.

McCormick, Christopher. Native Council of Canada. 1990. "Minutes of Proceedings and Evidence of the Special Committee of the House of Commons to Study the Proposed Companion Resolution to the Meech Lake Accord." 12 April.

McKenna, Frank. 1990. "Minutes of Proceedings and Evidence of the Special Committee of the House of Commons to Study the Proposed Companion Resolution to the Meech Lake Accord." 9 April.

Mercredi, Ovide. 1988. "Aboriginal Peoples and the Constitution." In *After Meech Lake: Lessons for the Future,* ed. David E. Smith, Peter MacKinnon and John C. Courtney. Saskatoon: Fifth House.

———. Assembly of First Nations. 1990. Testimony before the Royal Commission on Electoral Reform and Party Financing. 19 April. Winnipeg.

Métis Association of Alberta. 1983. "Minutes of Proceedings and Evidence of the Special Joint Committee of the Senate and of the House of Commons on Senate Reform." 20 September.

Métis National Council. 1983a. *Compendium.* First Ministers Conference on Aboriginal Constitutional Matters. 15–16 March. Ottawa. CICS Document 800-17/007.

———. 1983b. "Minutes of Proceedings and Evidence of the Special Joint Committee of the Senate and of the House of Commons on Senate Reform." 19 September.

———. 1984. "Opening Remarks to the First Ministers Conference on Aboriginal Rights." 8 March. Ottawa. CICS Document 800-18/012.

———. 1987. "Minutes of Proceedings and Evidence of the Special Joint Committee of the Senate and the House of Commons on the 1987 Constitutional Accord." 19 August.

Morin, Gerald. Métis Society of Saskatchewan. 1990. Testimony before the Royal Commission on Electoral Reform and Party Financing. 17 April. Ottawa.

Morse, Bradford W., ed. 1985. *Aboriginal Peoples and the Law: Indian, Métis and Inuit Rights in Canada.* Ottawa: Carleton University Press.

———. 1989. "Obligations, Aboriginal Peoples." In *Aboriginal Peoples and Government Responsibility: Exploring Federal and Provincial Roles,* ed. David C. Hawkes. Ottawa: Carleton University Press.

Moss, Wendy. 1987. *Aboriginal People: History of Discriminatory Laws.* Ottawa: Library of Parliament.

———. 1989. *Indian Self-Government.* Ottawa: Library of Parliament.

Mulroney, Brian. 1985a. "Notes for an Opening Statement by the Rt. Hon. Brian Mulroney, Prime Minister of Canada, to the First Ministers Conference on Aboriginal Constitutional Matters." 2 April. Ottawa. CICS Document 800-20/017.

———. 1985b. "Proposed 1985 Accord Relating to the Aboriginal Peoples of Canada." First Ministers Conference on Aboriginal Constitutional Matters. 2–3 April. Ottawa. CICS Document 800-20/013.

———. 1987a. "Federal Draft: Schedule – Amendment to the Constitution of Canada." First Ministers Conference on Aboriginal Constitutional Matters. 26–27 March. Ottawa. CICS Document 800-23/028.

———. 1987b. "Notes for an Opening Statement by the Rt. Hon. Brian Mulroney, Prime Minister of Canada, to the First Ministers Conference on Aboriginal Constitutional Matters." 26 March. Ottawa. CICS Document 800-23/014.

———. 1987c. "Notes for Concluding Remarks – First Day Session." First Ministers Conference on Aboriginal Constitutional Matters. 26 March. Ottawa. CICS Document 800-23/026.

———. 1991. "Address to the First Nations Congress." 23 April. Victoria.

Nagle, Patrick. 1991. "PM Promises Natives a Seat at Future Constitution Talks." *Ottawa Citizen.* 30 August.

Native Council of Canada. 1981. *Native People and the Constitution of Canada: The Report of the Metis and Non-Status Indian Constitutional Review Commission.* Ottawa: Mutual.

———. 1982. "Recommendations on Provision to be Added to or for Amendment to the *Canada Act 1981.*" Federal-Provincial Meeting of Officials on Aboriginal Rights. 17 November. CICS Document 840-245/004.

———. 1983a. "Minutes of Proceedings and Evidence of the Special Joint Committee of the Senate and of the House of Commons on Senate Reform." 27 September.

———. 1983b. "Opening Statement to the First Ministers Conference on Aboriginal Constitutional Matters." 15 March. Ottawa. CICS Document 800-17/020.

———. 1983c. "Parliamentary Representation for the Native Peoples of Canada. Federal–Provincial Meeting of Officials on Aboriginal Rights." 15–16 February. CICS Document 840-256/004.

———. 1984. "Opening Statement to the First Ministers Conference on Aboriginal Rights." 8 March. Ottawa. CICS Document 800-18/025.

———. 1990a. Submission to the Royal Commission on Electoral Reform and Party Financing. Ottawa.

———. 1990b. Testimony before the Royal Commission on Electoral Reform and Party Financing. 12 June. Ottawa.

New Brunswick Association of Métis and Non-Status Indians. 1983. "Minutes of Proceedings and Evidence of the Special Joint Committee of the Senate and of the House of Commons on Senate Reform." 16 September.

Norton, Joe. Mohawk Council. 1990. "Minutes of Proceedings and Evidence of the Special Committee of the House of Commons to Study the Proposed Companion Resolution to the Meech Lake Accord." 4 May.

Nungak, Zebedee. Inuit Committee on National Issues. 1987a. "Minutes of Proceedings and Evidence of the Special Joint Committee of the Senate and the House of Commons on the 1987 Constitutional Accord." 5 August.

———. 1987b. "Opening Remarks to the First Ministers Conference on Aboriginal Constitutional Matters." 26 March. Ottawa. CICS Document 800-23/018.

———. Makavik Corporation. 1990. Testimony before the Royal Commission on Electoral Reform and Party Financing. 24 July. Kuujjuak.

Ottawa Citizen. 1991. "Micmacs Deserve Seat, Premier Says." 20 April.

Platiel, Rudy. 1983. "Natives See Long Road to Control." *Globe and Mail,* 21 March.

———. 1991. "A Place in the Mainstream." *Globe and Mail,* 29 May.

Platiel, Rudy, and Graham Fraser. 1987. "Native Self-government Talks Stall over Question of 'Inherent' Right." *Globe and Mail,* 27 March.

Platiel, Rudy, and Jeff Sallot. 1985. "Mulroney Fails to Get Deal." *Globe and Mail,* 4 April.

Reference re term "Indians", [1939] S.C.R. 104.

Richardson, Don. 1991. "Seats Won't Replace Autonomy: Erasmus." *Telegraph-Journal* (Saint John), 21 November.

Robinson, Ron. Nisga'a Tribal Council. 1990. "Minutes of Proceedings and Evidence of the Special Committee of the House of Commons to Study the Proposed Companion Resolution to the Meech Lake Accord." 20 April.

Robinson, Viola. Native Council of Nova Scotia. 1990a. "Minutes of Proceedings and Evidence of the Special Committee of the House of Commons to Study the Proposed Companion Resolution to the Meech Lake Accord." 4 May.

———. 1990b. Testimony before the Royal Commission on Electoral Reform and Party Financing. 5 June. Sydney.

Robinson, Eric, and Henry Bird Quinney. 1985. *The Infested Blanket: Canada's Constitution – Genocide of Indian Nations.* Winnipeg: Queenston House.

Romanow, Roy. 1985. "Aboriginal Rights in the Constitutional Process." In *The Quest for Justice: Aboriginal Peoples and Aboriginal Rights,* ed. Manno Boldt and J. Anthony Long. Toronto: University of Toronto Press.

St. Ann's Island Shooting & Fishing Club Ltd., [1950] 2 D.L.R. 225 (S.C.C.).

Sallot, Jeff. 1983. "Natives Will Get More Rights Talks but not a Veto." *Globe and Mail,* 16 March.

Sallot, Jeff, and Rudy Platiel. 1985. "Native Leaders Worried about Federal Rights Plan." *Globe and Mail,* 13 April.

Schwartz, Bryan. 1985. *First Principles: Constitutional Reform with Respect to the Aboriginal Peoples of Canada, 1982–1984.* Kingston: Queen's University, Institute of Intergovernmental Relations.

Sheppard, Robert. 1981a. "On Aboriginal Rights." *Globe and Mail,* 6 November.

———. 1981b. "PM Won't Open Pact to Reinstate Rights." *Globe and Mail,* 11 November.

Simpson, Scott. 1991. "Premiers Accept Self-government Concept after Presentation by Aboriginal Leaders." *Vancouver Sun.* 27 August.

Sinclair, Jim. Métis National Council. 1983a. "Transcript of Proceedings of the First Ministers Conference on Aboriginal Constitutional Matters." 15–16 March. Ottawa.

———. 1983b. "Minutes of Proceedings and Evidence of the Special Joint Committee of the Senate and of the House of Commons on Senate Reform." 29 September.

———. Métis National Council. 1987. "Minutes of Proceedings and Evidence of the Special Joint Committee of the Senate and the House of Commons on the 1987 Constitutional Accord." 19 August.

———. Assembly of Aboriginal Peoples of Saskatchewan. 1990. "Minutes of Proceedings and Evidence of the Special Committee of the House of Commons to Study the Proposed Companion Resolution to the Meech Lake Accord." 4 May.

Speirs, Rosemary. 1991. "Ottawa Launches Native Probe." *Toronto Star,* 28 August.

Tennant, Paul. 1985. "Aboriginal Rights in the Constitutional Process." In *The Quest for Justice: Aboriginal Peoples and Aboriginal Rights,* ed. Manno Boldt and J. Anthony Long. Toronto: University of Toronto Press.

Toronto Star. 1991. "Natives Lack One Voice in Unity." 20 August.

Trudeau, Pierre Elliott. 1983. "Opening Statement by the Rt. Hon. Pierre Elliott Trudeau, Prime Minister of Canada, to the Constitutional Conference of First Ministers on Aboriginal Constitutional Matters." 15 March. Ottawa. CICS Document 800-17/012.

———. 1984. "Opening Statement by the Prime Minister of Canada The Right Honourable Pierre Elliott Trudeau to the Conference of First Ministers on Aboriginal Rights." 8–9 March. Ottawa. CICS Document 800-18/023.

Turner, Randy. 1990. "Long-Shut Doors Open for Indians." *Winnipeg Free Press*, 22 November.

United Kingdom. *Constitution Act, 1867*, 30 & 31 Vict., c. 3, s. 91¶24.

———. *Constitution Act, 1871*, 34 & 35 Vict., c. 28.

———. *Constitution Act, 1930*, 20 & 21 Geo. V, c. 26.

United Kingdom. House of Commons. 1982. *Hansard*. 23 February.

Valpy, Michael. 1981. "The Sellout of Canadian Native Rights." *Globe and Mail*, 6 November.

Weaver, Sally M. 1984. "A Commentary on the Penner Report." *Canadian Public Policy* 10 (2): 215–21.

Weinstein, John. 1986. *Aboriginal Self-Determination off a Land Base*. Kingston: Queen's University, Institute of Intergovernmental Relations.

Wilson, Bill. First Nations Congress (BC). 1990. "Minutes of Proceedings and Evidence of the Special Committee of the House of Commons to Study the Proposed Companion Resolution to the Meech Lake Accord." 27 April.

Winnipeg Free Press. 1991. "Defining the Aboriginal Role." 21 August.

2

ABORIGINAL ELECTORAL DISTRICTS FOR CANADA
Lessons from New Zealand

~

Augie Fleras

C ENTRAL AUTHORITIES THROUGHOUT the liberal-democratic world have struggled to find an acceptable formula for integrating minorities into the political mainstream. The search for a suitable arrangement has been particularly urgent in countries where the indigenous minority population is alienated from political life and reluctant to get involved in the electoral process for various reasons. Such an interpretation may be applied to Canada, since meaningful involvement in the federal electoral process continues to elude most Aboriginal groups outside of the Northwest Territories. Different strategies have been explored to improve electoral participation and Aboriginal representation, but few have attracted as much attention as a proposed system of Aboriginal electoral districts (AEDs) integrated into the national framework and modelled after a comparable arrangement in New Zealand.

The system of separate electoral districts in New Zealand has contributed to, as well as detracted from, Maori aspirations for nearly 125 years. As a racially based option that overlays the existing pattern of territorial representation, Maori electoral districts have drawn both criticism and acclaim from observers at home and abroad. On the one hand, Maori seats have taken on a considerable aura over time and are widely regarded as integral to Maori status as the *tangata whenua o aotearoa* (indigenous occupants of New Zealand). On the other hand, the system of separate representation has been accused of sabotaging Maori aspirations for power sharing beyond the symbolic level. Maori concerns have been compromised, compartmentalized, diminished or derailed by what, arguably, serves as an instrument for containment and control. However, the recent restructuring of Maori Affairs by the Labour government has cast a new light on Maori seats, in the process suggesting a reassessment may be in store. Current shifts in the Maori agenda have focused attention on guaranteed Maori representation as part of a comprehensive struggle to restructure *tangata whenua* relations vis-à-vis the New Zealand state.

It is within this context of ambiguity and change that this study addresses the feasibility of applying a parallel system of separate Aboriginal representation to Canada. The goal is to assess and evaluate the principles that may shape the design of a proposed outline for a system of AEDs in Canada in light of New Zealand's experience with Maori representation. To properly discharge this obligation, a number of questions regarding Maori electorates (electoral districts) are posed with respect to structure, function and process as well as in terms of desirability, fairness or effectiveness. These questions include: What are Maori seats? What is the nature and basis of Maori representation? Why did Maori seats originate? Why do Maori seats continue to exist? How did they develop and evolve? Where are the anomalies within the system? What are the benefits and drawbacks? What is a fair and equitable basis for Maori representation? How can the effectiveness of Maori seats be maximized in Parliament? and What lessons can be derived from the New Zealand experience and applied to Canada?

Our conclusion is one of cautious optimism: the rationale underlying a system of AEDs is fundamentally sound and workable, provided it is considered in conjunction with a comprehensive range of mutually agreed-upon initiatives for political, social and economic self-determination. Even so, the implementation of any system of AEDs is likely to be fraught with difficulties in light of the highly politicized context underlying Aboriginal–government relations.

TANGATA WHENUA O AOTEAROA: THE MAORI OF NEW ZEALAND

New Zealand is a small, liberal democracy in the South Pacific with a largely urbanized population of just over three million, comprising both the majority *pakeha* (whites) and the indigenous Maori (at around 12.5 percent of the total population). The *pakeha* constitute the majority in both the numerical and political sense. They comprise a loose designation of non-Maori and non-Polynesians, many of whom trace their ancestry back to Britain or northern Europe. Lesser concentrations of other Polynesian groups from Samoa, Tonga and Niue are also located in New Zealand, particularly in the cities of Auckland and Wellington. Racial minorities such as the Chinese or East Indians are in evidence. Their numbers are relatively small, as might be expected in light of New Zealand's once restrictive immigration laws.

The various tribes collectively known as the Maori represent the indigenous inhabitants of New Zealand (*tangata whenua o aotearoa*) who occupied this country for nearly 1 000 years prior to European contact. Protracted intertribal hostilities precluded the creation of a common identity and name (Maori) until well after European contact and settlement (Sorrenson 1986).

Maori tribes shared much in common with their Polynesian ancestors, notwithstanding the cultural differences created by historical and environmental forces. They lived in relatively self-sufficient communities of *whanau* (related extended families), deriving subsistence from horticultural and foraging practices. The unit of political reality rarely extended beyond the *iwi* (tribal level), although on occasion a group of *waka* (related tribes) collaborated on a joint effort for military or economic purposes. Maori society could be described as communal and constructed around the principles of kinship and residence. Formal hierarchies of status and rank were important, reflecting and reinforcing the values associated with personal honour, revenge and competition (see Metge 1976 for thorough review).

This sociocultural design persisted relatively intact until the early part of the 19th century, at which time an inexorable demise began in the wake of wholesale European settlement. Competition over land and power eventually culminated in the Land Wars of the 1860s, which further dislodged the Maori as a significant presence in New Zealand. By the turn of the century, the Maori population had dropped to about 46 000 (from a high of about 250 000) because of disease and the government's assimilation policies, which left many Maori poorly equipped for modern society.

The 20th century has not substantially altered the peripheral status of the Maori. The population has risen to 404 775, according to 1986 census data (New Zealand 1990). Yet the Maori continue to be overrepresented in those areas that count least (unemployment and imprisonment) but underrepresented in those domains that count most (education and income). Compounding the material impoverishment is the shaky status of Maori language, culture and identity. A reversal in Maori fortunes is anticipated, however, as the national agenda embraces the recognition of the Maori as the *tangata whenua o aotearoa*, with a corresponding claim to power and resources (Fleras 1991).

WHAT ARE MAORI SEATS?

New Zealand stands as an independent member of those Commonwealth nations whose political systems are organized around a British

Westminster model of parliamentary democracy (see Fleras 1985a for earlier discussion). Yet parliamentary structure here is characterized by a number of anomalous features. Among these "quirks" are the absence of a formal written constitution and rejection of an upper chamber in favour of a unicameral structure.

Provision of separate Maori seats constitutes one of the more contentious aspects of New Zealand's pioneering efforts at managing race relations. Two distinct types of representation – the Maori and the general – are integrated into a single, comprehensive system. The distinction between Maori and general ridings does not reflect differences in content or style. Each of the 97 general and 4 Maori seats elects one candidate every three years in a first-past-the-post electoral (plurality) system. Maori representatives do not sit in a separate chamber but possess full voting rights on all issues dealt with by their parliamentary colleagues. All major political parties nominate Maori candidates for the Maori seats and contest them every three years as part of the general election. Maori voters are likewise indistinguishable from their counterparts in the general electorate. Those who choose to exercise the "Maori option" (see below) follow the same procedures and are subject to similar restrictions as voters on the general roll.

Differences exist, instead, over the question of candidacy and voting eligibility. First, general electorates are characterized by a territorial (where you live) system of representation coupled with the principle of universal suffrage (McRobie 1981). By contrast, Maori representation is based on a racial criterion (who you are) because only Maori can vote in these ridings.

Second, nominations for election to Maori seats are restricted generally (but not exclusively) to Maori candidates. At one time, only "full-blooded" or "half-blooded" Maori could stand as candidates in Maori electoral districts. This discriminatory distinction was abolished in 1967 when the government opened candidacy to both races in the Maori and general ridings. It is interesting to note that a non-Maori contested one of the Maori seats in the 1981 national elections – with predictably dismal results.

Third, differences also arise from qualifications of the voting public. Only a New Zealand Maori – a Maori being a person of the Maori race of New Zealand, including any descendant of such a person as set out in the *Electoral Amendment Act* of 1980 – has the option of voting for a candidate in one of the four reserved seats (Maori option). Once having exercised the option to register on the Maori roll, however, a transfer to the general roll is not allowed until the following quinquennial census.

As we shall see in ensuing sections, the system does not necessarily work according to plan. Rather, the concept is riddled with inconsistencies that leave it open to criticism and demands for its reform or abolition.

ORIGINS AND HISTORY

The *Maori Representation Act* of 1867 introduced a dual system of representation by superimposing four Maori seats upon the existing arrangement in the House of Representatives. The Act was intended to give the Maori representation until such time as they qualified for inclusion on the European roll. The Act was meant to last five years while Maori landholdings were being converted from communal land to individual freehold.

The Act divided New Zealand into four electoral districts and entitled Maori males to elect one representative from the Northern (North Island), Southern (South Island), Western or Eastern electoral districts. All adult Maori males not previously convicted of treason or of any "infamous offence" received the right to vote irrespective of any property means test – 12 years before universal male suffrage was extended to Europeans. "Half-castes" were permitted to cast a ballot on the Maori roll, the common – or both, if they met the appropriate property qualification (Love 1977). Passage of an act in 1893 abolished the double vote for qualified Maori and officially inaugurated a separated electoral process. From then until 1976, full- or half-blooded Maori voted on the Maori roll; others were assigned to the general roll. Only a full-blooded Maori could stand as a candidate for election to a Maori seat, but this provision was repealed in 1967.

The conferral of Maori seats was not entirely unprecedented in New Zealand history. Gold miners in South Island and pensioners in Auckland were also allotted temporary representation during the 1860s. But unlike these seats, Maori seats became firmly entrenched as part of New Zealand's political landscape (Jackson 1973). The terms of the *Maori Representation Act* were extended indefinitely in 1876, partly to offset the flood of Maori voters into marginal ridings in North Island (Sorrenson 1986).

The original intent to restrict Maori seats for five years undermined the credibility of the first Maori representatives. Maori MPs were regarded instead as observers with speaking rights over issues of relevance only to the Maori. As intermediaries poised between the government and the Maori, these MPs primarily articulated Maori concerns by coordinating a two-way flow of information. Acceptance of this interpretation helps to explain certain anomalies within this system. Maori electorates have long been exempted from provisions that updated the number, size and boundaries of the general electorates. Maori voters did not receive the right to secret ballot until 1937, some 67 years after its inception for the general electorate. In Maori ridings, compulsory registration was introduced in 1956, the first electoral rolls in 1949, and same-day voting in 1951 – long after comparable innovations had taken place in general ridings. Also, provisions routinely taken to facilitate general enrolment and voting practices have rarely been extended to the Maori electorate (Mahuta 1981). Such diffidence is seen as having undermined the credibility of Maori MPs as bona fide contenders in New Zealand's legislative process.

PROTECTION OR CONTAINMENT?

Much has been made of the motives behind the establishment of Maori seats. Why did the extension of voting privileges to the Maori precede universal male suffrage by 12 years and female suffrage by another 14 years? Did separate representation convey an enlightened response to protect Maori interests? Was it nothing more than a deceptively manipulative ruse of political expediency for social control (Walker 1989)? Ostensibly, Maori seats were established to organize Maori viewpoints into a coherent format; to express Maori aspirations at the national level; and to protect special Maori status and corresponding claims derived from this status (Tabacoff 1975). More realistically, the seats originated as part of a calculated scheme to meet the political needs of the expanding *pakeha* population while appeasing the indigenous people at a time when Maori–*pakeha* relations had been pushed to the brink by protracted hostilities. Also looming large were practical concerns pertaining to the "Maori problem," namely, the need to:

- pacify a defeated, yet formidable, adversary whose cooperation would facilitate in the orderly development of New Zealand society;
- assimilate the Maori as quickly as possible without imposing an undue burden on the colony or Colonial Office;
- safeguard settler interest for as long as it took to acquire Maori land and to secure the frontier against unfriendly Maori;
- preclude any attempt by the Maori to set up a separate power base with which to circumvent parliamentary authority;
- reward Maori loyalists, placate Maori rebels and assure the British Colonial Office of justice and fairness in dealing with the Maori;
- preserve the existing balance of parliamentary power between North Island and South Island (South Island received one Maori

seat and three gold miner seats, while North Island was entitled
to three Maori seats and one pensioner seat in Auckland); and
• defuse Maori resistance to settler authority and amalgamate them
  into the political fold (Sorrenson 1986).

The proposed arrangement undermined Maori interests by restrict-
ing them to four seats instead of the nearly 20 they would have been
entitled to had the principles of proportional representation been put
into effect. This gerrymandering of the Maori electorate saw the entire
Maori population of 60 000 assigned to four ridings, in contrast with
some 250 000 settlers who were distributed over 72 ridings (Mitchell
1969). The decision to extend this system beyond the initial five-year
period attested to its usefulness in shoring up *pakeha* interests. These seats
posed a minimal threat to settler ambitions, yet they conveyed an image
of New Zealand as a beacon in the management of harmonious race
relations. The Maori, in turn, found they had little choice except to cling
to this imperfect arrangement in the absence of any meaningful alternatives for power sharing (Sorrenson 1986). Once comfortably in place,
the system's continued existence was due as much to inertia and res-
ignation as to any proven ability to improve Maori interests.

DEVELOPMENT AND CONSOLIDATION

The first Maori members of Parliament as a whole did little to impress
their colleagues or constituents (Jackson and Wood 1964; Jackson 1973).
The effectiveness and impact of the Maori MPs were hampered by structural flaws that sabotaged any hope for success. Members of the House
tended to treat Maori representatives with barely concealed disdain,
refusing to acknowledge them as anything but a token contribution to
the political life of the nation. Many of the early parliamentarians lacked
the political acumen or basic English skills to influence the outcome of
legislation pertaining to the Maori race (Williams 1969). Shifting political coalitions exposed Maori representatives (not to mention European
members) to unscrupulous elements who took advantage of widespread
political naïvety for personal gain (Dalziel 1981).

The largely independent status of the early members may have
accounted for this loss of efficacy. The first unified Maori party did not
evolve until the 1930s, under the leadership of T.W. Ratana. With Ratana,
the party captured all four Maori seats, transformed them from trib-
ally based alliances to a network of class-based branches, and aligned
them with the rising fortunes of the Labour Party. Ratana support for
Labour was based on Maori access to the comprehensive social secu-
rity system erected by the Labour government rather than on any

ideological preference for party policy or politics (Walker 1989; Vasil 1990). While the Ratana grip on the Maori electoral process has loosened somewhat in recent years (Chapman 1986), Maori members of Parliament remain loyal to Labour nearly to a fault, with an unquestioning commitment – for good or bad – to toe the Labour line in all policy and party issues.

Only recently has a new Maori political party emerged to contest this complacency, reflecting in part Maori disenchantment with and alienation from Labour policies during the 1970s and 1980s (Vasil 1990). Known as *Mana Maori Motuhake* (Maori self-determination), the party comprises disaffected elements such as urban youth and academics who collectively seek an independent voice for Maoridom in Parliament. To date, *Motuhake* candidates have not been able to dislodge the Labour majority in the four Maori ridings. Nevertheless, there are signs of a *Motuhake* beachhead into Labour support. *Motuhake* candidates captured 9.1 percent of the valid vote (5 989 votes) in 1984; Labour captured 77.6 percent (Sorrenson 1986). In 1987, the Labour proportion of the popular vote dropped to 70.9 percent, reflecting an increase in the number of *Motuhake* voters to 9 789. The 1990 results saw *Motuhake* capture nearly 24 percent of the popular vote (10 864 votes), whereas Labour support declined to 65.6 percent and National support to 10.4 percent. As well, the *Motuhake* candidate in the North electorate came close (994 votes) to upsetting the Labour incumbent (*New Zealand Herald* 1990).

Still, the prospect for an independent Maori voice in Parliament remains bleak. That a party showcasing one of the foremost Maori leaders has not made much of an impact on the Maori except in the North electorate reflects to some extent the difficulties of organizing a pan-Maori political party in a society where loyalty to the *iwi* (tribe) is paramount (Vasil 1990). Ballot-box failure, however, has not blunted the emergence of a politically assertive Maori activism outside parliamentary circles. But the extent to which Maori MPs in the recent Labour cabinet were able to capitalize on this activism to push through extensive reforms is open to debate (Fleras 1991).

REACTION AND RESPONSE

The presence of Maori seats has elicited a broad spectrum of opinion within New Zealand, much of it "highly emotional, ethnocentred and contradictory" (Mahuta 1981). Proponents and opponents alike are locked in shifting rhetoric over its benefits or drawbacks, strengths and limitations, and successes and failures. Those at one end of the continuum fixate on various disadvantages of separate representation and demand its immediate repeal. Maori seats are denounced as a "symbol without substance" whose diversionary and divisive effect ensures the political containment of the *tangata whenua*. Others at the opposite end admire the positive properties of Maori representation and prefer to retain the system as is. Balanced somewhere in between the poles of rejection and retention is a pervasive ambivalence about a system that simultaneously enhances yet detracts from Maori aspirations as the *tangata whenua*. The principle of guaranteed representation is endorsed as part of Maori identity and a symbol of their *mana* (power, or status), albeit in a form refashioned to meet the challenges of modern Maori society.

Repeal

Many New Zealanders believe the system of Maori representation is wrong and should be abolished forthwith. Numerous public opinion polls and surveys reveal a widespread *pakeha* antipathy to Maori seats (Stokes 1981). Opponents of the system have long argued that Maori seats are racist in assigning electoral privileges on racial rather than territorial grounds. An electoral system based primarily on ethnic considerations (who you are) rather than on universal suffrage (where you live) is rebuked as inconsistent with New Zealand's political culture (McRobie 1981). Others disparage the perpetuation of separate Maori representation as nothing short of paternalistic and discriminatory in an egalitarian society (McLeay 1980). It denies a similar privilege to other minorities with an allegedly similar claim for political inclusion. Still others consider Maori seats obsolete as a forum for Maori aspirations but formidable as a force for interracial strife and societal disharmony.

High-profile Maori leaders have also taken the system to task. Foremost among Maori grievances is the lack of fair representation that derives from restriction of Maori seats to four (Vasil 1990). Equally upsetting is the "compartmentalization" of Maori issues into the political sidestream. Robert Mahuta, Director for the Centre of Maori Studies at Waikato University in Hamilton, is especially critical of an arrangement that discounts the relevance of Maori issues in general ridings, since representatives are not obligated to chase the Maori vote (Mahuta 1981). Another critic, Dr. Ranginui Walker of Auckland University, argues that Maori seats constitute a political cul-de-sac whose ineffectiveness is directly attributable to the parliamentary principle of majority rule. The inclusion of four Maori seats in a parliamentary system dominated by two major political parties ensures the Maori presence is permanently outvoted and excluded by the "tyranny of majority rule" (Walker 1979). Compounding this disadvantage is the relatively poor showing of Labour since the Second World War. The relegation of the Labour Party to long stretches as the opposition in Parliament has had the effect of confining Maori members to a role of institutionalized backbenchers. Small wonder then that Maori seats are criticized as an exercise in political futility and useful only for the control and containment of the Maori.

Reform

The commitment to reform Maori seats appears typical of Maori opinion in general (New Zealand, Treaty 1985). The historical antiquity of Maori representation has assured it of a relatively permanent stature among those who defend the system as indispensable to the long-term interests of the *tangata whenua*. Separate representation is at once valued for its role in organizing Maori viewpoints, articulating them nationally and protecting the Aboriginal interests of the *tangata whenua*. It continues to be endorsed as a deep-rooted symbol of Maori *mana* and identity, with the power to catapult Maori concerns into the nation's decision-making process. So too are Maori representatives held in esteem by the Maori electorate. While criticized at times for personal or political reasons, they are bestowed a degree of honour, deference and respect in accordance with their political *mana* (Searnacke 1979).

Strangely enough, Maori endorsement of separate representation is not reflected in practice. The percentage of Maori voters on the Maori roll has declined in recent years, while their numbers on the general roll have risen. By July 1984, only 77 564 of the estimated 209 600 eligible for the Maori vote had enrolled (Sorrenson 1986). The count declined further to 70 564 only two years later in 1986 (New Zealand, Royal Commission 1986). This "flight" from the Maori to the general roll may reflect either a disenchantment with Maori seats or the adaptation of a creative strategy to expand the Maori base in Parliament. No less worrisome are the large number of Maori who fail to vote in the Maori ridings. Only 49 494 of those enrolled cast a ballot in the 1990 general elections (compared with 54 352 in 1987 (Norton 1988)), although the drop may have been the result of a boycott called by the Maori Council of Churches to protest grievances against the *Treaty of Waitangi*. Yet the Maori defend the symbolic value of guaranteed representation as central to identity and survival. They bristle at any move to abolish Maori seats without prior consultation or alternative arrangement. Doing so, it is argued, would undermine Maori political interests, delegitimize their involvement in the political process and jeopardize their ability to focus pressure on central authorities.

Most proposals for reform are couched in terms of increasing the number of Maori seats in proportion to general ridings. Other recommendations focus on the unique status of the Maori as a justification for an increase (New Zealand, Treaty 1985). A conference sponsored by the New Zealand Maori Council in April 1985 proposed a resolution to increase the number of Maori seats to 25. It also recommended the election of representatives on a tribal rather than a geographical basis (*Dominion* (NZ), 30 April 1985). This increase in size and selection was endorsed as critical for accentuating Maori influence as a third-party political force in coalition arrangements. Other observers, including Professor Hirini Moko Mead, Chair of Maori Studies at Victoria University of Wellington, have gone one step further. They have mooted the creation of a semi-independent Maori Parliament, one in which the Maori would enjoy a more realistic type of representation without fear of political reprisals (Mead 1979). The anticipated number of seats – between 12 and 25 – would not only encompass current increases in Maori population but also respect Maori tribal divisions and urban concentrations. A consensual consultative style of political debate would prevail, in accordance with traditional styles of leadership and decision making among the Maori. To date, a separate Maori presence in Parliament has not materialized.

Retention

The major political parties are at the forefront of those who wish to retain the political status quo. In theory, the Labour Party is strongly committed to the perpetuation of Maori seats; the National Party is opposed (Daniell 1983). Labour, by all accounts, has a vested interest in the present arrangement. Labour candidates consistently capture all four Maori seats – frequently by astonishing margins. Maori seats provide the party with a coordinated and reliable mechanism of communication in planning public policy. Maori members identify relevant issues for the party, as well as alert party officials to trends in Maoridom that would otherwise escape the attention or interests of party strategists (see Weaver 1983). This legitimized access to broadly based advice confers an advantage on Labour; the National Party, on the other hand, has limited consultative privileges at the parliamentary level.

To the surprise of no one, Labour strategists have tried to increase the number of Maori seats according to a formula based on Maori voter registration. A measure to increase Maori seats by one was passed in 1975, only to be rescinded the following year by the incoming National government. Recently, Labour strategists have begun to revise their thinking about the value of Maori seats. On statistical evidence alone, the number of votes cast for Labour candidates in Maori seats is grossly in excess of what is required for victory. With Maori seats siphoning off far more votes than necessary, potentially useful votes are diverted from marginal general ridings where they could play an important role in tipping the balance toward Labour's advantage. Not unexpectedly, there is talk among Labour strategists of transferring Maori voters onto the general roll on the unfounded assumption that the subsequent influx will consolidate overall party strength (see Simpson 1981).

The National Party is similarly unclear over the status of Maori representation. Party leaders have traditionally ignored involvement in Maori seats, partly out of principle and partly from Maori antipathy to National policies. National has preferred instead to search for electoral support outside of these narrow limits. Maori have been encouraged to vote on the general roll, and qualified Maori personnel have been put forward as candidates in general ridings. The tactic has attained moderate success: since 1975, several National Maori candidates have served as ministers for the Department of Maori Affairs, including Ben Couch (1977–84) and, most recently, Winston Peters (since October 1990). But National policy is remarkably low key over the issue of Maori seats. Maori voters have been encouraged to forsake the Maori roll, yet nothing has been done to hasten the process. If anything, party leaders have endorsed retention of the status quo on the strength of its ability to dissipate Labour strength harmlessly throughout the electorate.

In conclusion, neither the Maori nor the major political parties have initiated fundamental reforms to correct inherent flaws within the system of separate representation. Politicians of different stripes have agreed on the eventual demise of separate Maori representation but remain coy about proceedings that may upset the prevailing balance of political power. Reluctance to take a stand over Maori seats is not indicative of increased sensitivity to Maori aspirations. Nor does this equivocation embody a commitment to respect Maori wishes for political self-determination. Such indecision represents an act of calculated expediency over fears of unleashing a swarm of unpredictable Maori votes onto the general roll. It also reinforces the perception that the future of the Maori electoral process is beyond the control of those who are directly affected by any changes.

THE PROS AND CONS OF MAORI REPRESENTATION

The notion of separate Aboriginal electoral districts (AEDs) has attracted considerable debate as a strategy for Maori political inclusion. But it is one thing to seek out criticism of Maori seats. It may be quite another to assess the strengths and weaknesses of these arguments in light of current realities. What precisely are the strengths and drawbacks of Maori seats? A look at the pros and cons of guaranteed representation will leave us in a better position to delineate the key features of the New Zealand experience for application to Canada.

Drawbacks and Limitations

Conferral of the franchise on racial instead of universal grounds has fomented its share of negative reaction. Separate representation has been indicted as a kind of "political limbo" (Mahuta 1981) or "electoral ghetto" (Simpson 1981), both irrelevant and reactionary to the point of apartheid. The conferral of separate voting privileges represents an act of "arrested development" (Jackson 1973), designed to unobtrusively appease the Maori yet foster the outward appearance of democratic power sharing. Detractors have argued that, far from drawing minorities into the policy-making channels of society, AEDs may undercut any contribution to the political arena (Canada, House of Commons 1983). There is little doubt New Zealand's system of separate representation is riddled with inconsistencies to the detriment of the Maori electoral process. Limitations abound, but the more serious are as follows:

- The number of general ridings has risen from 72 in 1867 to the current 97 in response to population growth. But Maori seats remain fixed at four for reasons of political expediency rather than of appeals for fairness or equity. Restriction of Maori representation to four ridings puts a strain on representational principles, since Maori members are cut off from anything more than nominal contact with their constituents (Metge 1976). Refusal to increase the number of Maori seats also consigns Maori representation to the peripheries of a system designed to suit majority interests (Walker 1979).
- The boundaries of general ridings are reassessed every five years by the Electoral Representation Commission according to a set formula. The new boundaries come into effect at the expiry of that particular parliamentary term (New Zealand 1990). Maori electoral boundaries, by contrast, have remained virtually intact since their inception despite the displacement of Maori from rural regions to urban centres. The major exception occurred in 1954, when the Southern riding was extended into the Western riding. It thus became not only one of the geographically largest ridings by area within the British Commonwealth but also one that encompassed 45 general ridings in the process (Sorrenson 1986). The recent "retribalization" of Maori society has reinforced

the artificiality of these boundaries, making them seem even more remote and irrelevant to Maori social reality.

- Discrepancies in voter distribution are sufficiently pronounced to discredit the representational basis of Maori seats. First, the number of ballots cast in Maori ridings may vary considerably. During the 1978 election, for example, nearly 33 000 ballots were cast in the Northern riding, but only about 14 000 in the Western district. Second, the Maori ridings' population are grossly under-represented by comparison with the general electorates' population (*Christchurch Press*, 26 February 1985). In 1986, the four Maori seats represented a total Maori population of 404 775, while the 97 general ridings were answerable to approximately 3 million non-Maori. However, the average Maori electoral population (adults enrolled in the Maori roll, plus children) was 35 515 per seat, only about 2 500 more than in the general riding (Sorrenson 1986). Third, the number of ballots cast in Maori ridings is consistently less than in general ridings, leading some to argue that Maori are overrepresented. In 1984, the average valid vote per seat in the Maori electorate was 14 783, in contrast with an average of 20 550 in the general ridings (ibid.). This total had declined to 13 589 in 1987, then to 12 374 in the 1990 election.
- Difficulties also arise in the confusion over the Maori option as it pertains to the Maori roll. To exercise the Maori option, a person who is 18 or older and of Maori ancestry must complete a special form that accompanies the quinquennial census. Failure to do so, or to do so incorrectly, invalidates access to the Maori option until the following census period. Technicalities disqualify a disproportionately large number of Maori voters. For example, all but 456 of the 2 885 special ballots cast during the Northern Maori by-election in 1980 were disqualified for one reason or another. Special votes arise because certain polling booths do not carry Maori rolls, thus requiring a Maori voter to fill out a complicated form in the presence of witnesses (Mahuta 1981). Disqualified Maori votes in the 1975 elections totalled 21.4 percent of the ballots cast, compared with only 3.9 percent of the general votes (*Northern Age*, 26 February 1985).
- It is well known that Maori members are confronted by enormous problems when trying to reconcile the opposing demands of party loyalty and electoral integrity (Metge 1976). No less an authority than Matiu Rata, a veteran of the parliamentary trenches since 1963, confirmed this when he described his colleagues as victims of constant compromise, torn between the needs of their

constituents and the imperatives of party politics (Daniell 1983). As captives of the Labour machine, Maori representatives are expected to defer to Labour on all controversial issues. Failing that, they are required to remain silent whenever politically expedient to do so (Cleveland 1979). The tyranny of majority rule is reinforced by forcing Maori members to ingratiate themselves to an established political party in hopes of securing a reliable base of power. As proof of this containment by party affiliation, Labour carried the elections of 1946 and 1957 on the strength of its Maori mandate in Parliament. Yet few substantial concessions were made to Maori in return, nor did the Maori MPs capitalize on their advantage (Love 1977).

• The calibre of Maori representatives is regarded as erratic at best. Candidates for the Maori ridings are nominated and voted into office not necessarily because of their political skills, but because of personality characteristics or tribal affiliations. Not unexpectedly, their influence rarely extends beyond the community level, never mind over broad territorial constituencies composed of numerous tribes and artificial boundaries. Once elected, moreover, most Maori MPs remain in office until retirement or death, thereby eliminating competition and the infusion of fresh talent. The background of Maori MPs has also changed in recent years. Candidates with a strong labour union background have now given way to those from professional middle classes. A corresponding shift in style has followed, with greater emphasis on pragmatism and compromise than on ideological purity (Chapman 1986).

The concept of guaranteed Maori representation is susceptible to scrutiny and debate. The system lends itself to criticism by virtue of its perception as counterproductive, divisive, undemocratic and irrelevant. In defence of Maori representation, similar accusations have been levelled against a wide array of general parliamentary practices. Nor should we automatically assume that weaknesses associated with Maori ridings apply automatically to AEDs in principle. Limitations in Maori representation may reflect features inherent in the design and execution of Maori ridings rather than anything intrinsic to the concept itself. Keeping this distinction in mind allows us to separate the idiosyncrasies of Maori representation from the concept of AEDs in general.

Benefits and Potential
Maori seats are widely upheld as a symbol of Maori *mana* and identity. Few would bother to dispute the symbolic salience of Maori

representation to New Zealand's political landscape. What many have failed to realize is the benefits of Maori representation above and beyond the symbolic. Significant shifts in restructuring Maori–government relations have come about when Maori members were charged with ministerial responsibility for Maori Affairs. The *Treaty of Waitangi* of 1975 and the *Maori Official Language Act* of 1987 are but two examples. Of even greater importance are the recent revisions to the Maori agenda since 1984.

Maori–government relations have undergone a period of unprecedented change and sweeping reform under the Labour government, in many ways commensurate with the upheavals of state restructuring in the public and private sectors (Walsh and Wetzel 1990; Kelsey 1990). The magnitude of these changes for restructuring the Maori agenda is profound, especially at policy and administrative levels. Foremost in this collective redefinition is tacit acceptance of biculturalism as a policy construct, followed by the transformation of formerly monocultural institutions to reflect New Zealand's dual heritage (Walker 1987). Key innovations in this restructuring process include:

- recognizing Maori structures – namely, *whanau* (extended family) and *iwi* (tribes) – as vehicles for development following passage of the *Runanga a Iwi Act* in September 1990;
- dismantling the Department of Maori Affairs and replacing it with the Iwi Transition Agency as the agency of empowerment for Maori *iwi*;
- creating *Manatu Maori* (a Ministry of Maori Affairs) to serve as an advisory-monitoring agency;
- enshrining Maori as an official New Zealand language in courts and Parliament;
- mainstreaming federal agencies to ensure *te taha Maori* (a Maori dimension) to the public service;
- strengthening the powers of the Waitangi Tribunal over grievances retroactive to 1840; and
- accepting of the *Treaty of Waitangi* as a solemn contract between the founding partners of *Aotearoa*.

Of special note has been government commitment to the *Treaty of Waitangi* as the central motif in redefining the status of the *tangata whenua*. Under Labour, the *Treaty of Waitangi* had evolved from a position of "legal nullity" to the status of a social contract between two equal partners. Under the terms of the Treaty, northern Maori tribes ceded *kawanatanga* (legal authority) to the Crown for establishment of law and order, yet political sovereignty and control over resources were retained in the hands of the *tangata whenua* (McHugh 1989). The Treaty did not extinguish Maori sovereignty but reaffirmed it by guaranteeing the rights of *rangatiratanga* (absolute Maori chieftainship) to the *tangata whenua*. From this reading a set of bicultural principles may be discerned as a guide for devolving *iwi*–government relations. They include:

- The Treaty establishes the principle of two nations with two distinct cultures within a single overarching political framework known as the state or the Crown.
- The Treaty is interpreted as a declaration of *iwi* independence from and Maori sovereignty over *Aotearoa*, promotion of inalienable Maori rights over land and culture, protection of indigenous human rights, and unrestricted access over natural resources (Armstrong 1987; Williams 1989). The Treaty has inaugurated new levels of national discourse for redefining the mutual rights and reciprocal obligations between partners in a bicultural arrangement. It has also empowered the courts to make judgements that strengthen the legitimacy of *Aotearoa* as a bicultural state.
- The Treaty extends the rights and privileges of British citizenship to the *tangata whenua*, including the rights to Maori language, identity and culture. Recognition of the bicultural focus of the Treaty has conferred two sets of entitlements to the *tangata whenua*, namely, equality rights as partners and citizens of *Aotearoa*; and special rights vested by virtue of the *rangatiratanga* reference in Article 2 of the Treaty (see Temm 1990).
- The Treaty guarantees Maori rights and interests as well as authority to protect and promote those *taonga* (treasures) of concern to the *tangata whenua*. The role of the state is not merely to recognize these rights and interests but to become actively and positively involved in the protection and promotion of relevant cultural values (New Zealand, Ministerial Committee 1987).

In sum, the *Treaty of Waitangi* has contributed to the restructuring of Maori–government relations along bicultural lines. From 1986 until defeat in 1990, the Labour government had taken an active stand in relation to the Treaty. Central to the government's Treaty policy was limited recognition of the principle of redress (through the Waitangi Tribunal); the principle of cooperation, consultation and communication (partnership perspectives); the principle of equality (special measures and affirmative action) and the principle of *rangatiratanga* as intrinsic to Maori renewal and self-determination. This combination of developments has elevated the Treaty to the status of a constitutional instrument that obligates the government to negotiate with the Maori as partners in a bicultural arrangement (Walker 1989).

The Labour government was clearly committed to a bicultural interpretation of New Zealand society. As the Minister responsible for Maori Affairs, Mr. Koro Wetere had presided over this largely unprecedented revamping of Maori Affairs in a manner that advanced both Maori interests and party policy. Nevertheless, it is difficult to determine the role of other Maori members in this restructuring process. Some, such as Ranginui Walker (1989), maintain that transformations in Maori–government relations have stemmed largely from relentless Maori activism outside parliamentary corridors for the past 150 years. Other evidence suggests a pivotal role for Maori MPs in transforming Maori activism into politically acceptable programs (Fleras 1985b, 1991). Indications are Maori MPs have guided the Labour government through a difficult period, and their contribution to a redefining of Maori–government relations requires further exploration.

SEPARATE REPRESENTATION IN A COMPARATIVE CONTEXT

The system of separate representation is not unique to New Zealand. Other countries have likewise tried to address the issue of integrating the minority population into the political process. In the United States, for example, the dependencies of Guam and Puerto Rico are guaranteed a representative to Congress. The state of Maine provides legislative representation by way of two representatives from the largest tribes, but the representatives have no voting rights (Cox 1991). In Zimbabwe, the constitution of 1980 established a system whereby 20 reserved seats were set aside for the whites – whose 33 000 voters constituted 0.5 percent of the voting public – and 80 seats were set aside for 2.9 million Blacks. Reserved seats in India cater only to candidates from scheduled castes or tribes (New Zealand, Royal Commission 1986). South Africa also possesses a system of separate representation. Three separate parliaments co-exist, with representatives from the Asians, coloureds and whites – but not Blacks – combining to form an electoral college.

These global initiatives pale by comparison with the international profile of separate Maori electoral districts. From their inception to the present, Maori seats have been widely perceived as contributing to New Zealand's lofty image as a land of racial harmony. Yet the principles and practices of Maori representation continue to elicit negative response (Davies 1981–82; Mahuta 1981). Ambiguities within this strategy of conflict management are shown not only to have detracted from its lustre as an instrument for political advancement, but also to have postponed its acceptance elsewhere by indigenous minorities likewise intent on redefining their status in society. Admittedly, political institutions and practices of relevance to one political context may be irrelevant in another in view of history, geography and social dynamics. Professor Sally Weaver of the University of Waterloo writes: "In the international context of indigenous affairs there is a tendency to believe 'the grass is greener on the other side of the fence' in regard to national political organizations, and to the relationship between indigenous minorities and the nation-state, and this uncritical emulation of models and practices in other countries should be tempered by a careful examination of these models to ensure that inappropriate or ineffectual ones are not advocated or adopted" (Weaver 1983, 109).

The system of guaranteed representation along ethnic lines is one such political arrangement with perhaps restricted utility outside of New Zealand. Take the case for Aboriginal electoral districts (AEDs) in Canada. Maori tribes constitute just under 13 percent of New Zealand's population, with the majority concentrated in urban centres across North Island. Contrast this with the Aboriginal population in Canada, who constitute about 3.5 percent of the population (756 430, according to the 1986 census), concentrated primarily in non-urban settings. Differences in history and geography, in addition to demographic features, complicate the issue.

Debating AEDs in Canada

Aboriginal demands for political self-determination have taken on a sharper focus since the 1960s. Canada's Aboriginal leaders concur about the need for self-governing powers but remain divided over strategies to maximize their access to political power. Of the many avenues for self-government explored by the Aboriginal sector, few are as provocative – or as enticing – as the system of guaranteed representation. The concept of constitutionally guaranteed Aboriginal seats in Parliament has been raised in the past and continues to receive moderate degrees of support as one means of influencing the policy process. The impetus behind this support rests on the observation that Aboriginal voters are excluded from the electoral process south of the 60th parallel (Marchand 1990). Even when Aboriginal people constitute a sizable proportion of the population, according to Senator Len Marchand (the first status Indian person elected to Parliament in 1968), their presence is diluted because of higher concentrations of non-Aboriginals (Paltiel 1991).

Various recommendations have been put forward to compensate for Aboriginal disadvantages in the federal system. Proposals for an

Aboriginal-based self-government in the Northwest Territories have included discussions about guaranteed Aboriginal representation in the legislative assembly (with jurisdiction over matters of Aboriginal importance such as land and culture) in tandem with a majority-rule principle for decision making (Watt 1990). Another development has seen a proposal to set aside at least one non-voting seat in the New Brunswick legislative assembly, despite a lack of consultation with key Aboriginal leaders in the province (Cox 1991).

Yet numerous obstacles stand in the path of implementing a system of AEDs. Nor is there any guarantee that increased presence in the federal electoral process will translate into enhanced influence over the political outcome. A key government report on Aboriginal self-government (Canada, House of Commons 1983) concluded as much when it claimed that any advantages from bolstering Aboriginal participation in the electoral process were offset by the potential to distract central authorities from more fundamental social, economic, political or cultural concerns. Others also have spurned the concept of AEDs as irrelevant in advancing Aboriginal interests; logistically nightmarish, given the diversity and breadth of an Aboriginal constituency; and inconsistent with the values and principles of Canada's political culture.

What, then, should be done to modify the electoral process in Canada? How do we establish an electoral system that addresses Aboriginal claims for a self-governing status yet ensures Aboriginal involvement in the political mainstream? Are the demands for Aboriginal political self-determination and those of Aboriginal representation mutually exclusive? Do we proceed by more fine-tuning of the present system? Or is it time to introduce bold initiatives that reflect, reinforce and advance the unique status of Aboriginal people? What lessons can we learn from the New Zealand experience that will serve as a guideline for implementing a comparable system of AEDs in Canada?

LESSONS FROM THE NEW ZEALAND EXPERIENCE

The system of Maori representation has been around since 1867, garnering both praise and criticism at home and abroad. Even with historical antiquity on its side, the concept of Maori electoral districts continues to perplex, provoke and pose certain questions. Questions are varied but often address the nature and basis of Maori electoral districts in terms of principle, practice or process (New Zealand, Royal Commission 1986):

- Who should be entitled to vote or to stand as a candidate in a system of guaranteed Aboriginal representation?

- What is the appropriate number of Maori seats that can adequately represent Maori interests in Parliament?
- Should Maori electoral districts reflect the tribe as a fundamental unit of social reality? Is an alternative set of criteria preferred?
- How do we determine the boundaries of the Maori electorates? How often should they be readjusted?
- How can a system of separate representation be reconciled with Maori cultural values and the political aspirations of the *tangata whenua*?
- Is there a formula that can more accurately convert the number of votes cast in special electoral districts into actual representation at the parliamentary level? Is the current system – plurality with a separate roll – inferior to a proportional system with a common roll?
- How do we define a fair, equitable and effective level of representation that reflects the Maori's history, their socio-economic standing, and their special status as *tangata whenua*? Is it possible to devise a system of representation that embraces some degree of equity, access, responsiveness, accountability and representativeness?
- What can we reasonably expect in terms of impact and effectiveness from a system of Aboriginal electoral districts?

Responses to these questions provide a framework for organizing our assessment of Maori seats. Yet caution must be exercised. The fact that the following answers are vigorously contested and elude even nominal levels of consensus should alert us to stay clear of glib generalizations. Still, these responses furnish us with a frame of reference for assessing the relevance of New Zealand's system for Canada. Such a point of departure is consistent with the mandate to delineate the principles by which to guide the design of a system of AEDs for Canada in the wake of lessons derived from the New Zealand experience. Convenience dictates that we organize the lessons from the New Zealand context into three major categories, namely, the nature and basis (rationale) of separate representation; the electoral process itself with respect to the mechanics of the system; and the effectiveness, fairness and equality of Maori representation.

The Nature and Basis of AEDs
Understanding the nature and basis of Maori representation is a necessary first step in articulating the principles that may serve as a guideline for a comparable system of AEDs in Canada.

LESSON ONE: The political context underlying a system of AEDs will influence its public acceptance and political effectiveness. Even a flawed system of representation cannot be discounted if the rationale for its existence is consistent with the empowerment of Aboriginal people.

Even the most ardent admirer of Maori representation will admit to improprieties within the system of Maori seats. Flaws in the design and execution of Maori electoral districts have undermined support for Maori seats, as reflected by declining enrolments and sporadic voting patterns. Such a cool response is not surprising in light of the political context that surrounded the genesis, development and persistence of Maori seats. The introduction of Maori seats sought to encourage Maori cooperation with *pakeha* laws and participation in institutions. This arrangement was less enthusiastic about enhancing Maori interests through effective political representation (New Zealand, Royal Commission 1986). This suggests many of the inadequacies associated with Maori seats are not intrinsic to the concept of guaranteed representation per se. Rather, the problem lies in the uneven application of that principle throughout all facets of the Maori electoral process. To put it bluntly, Maori seats were established and perpetuated for the wrong reasons, and growing Maori indifference toward involvement in the system is the price that is now being paid.

Exposing the logic behind separate representation (its origins, growth and present status) draws our attention to the political context that defines, justifies and legitimizes the existence of AEDs. The rationale for separate representation is not fixed and immutable. Its relevance fluctuates with the prevailing social and political forces that shape the dynamics of government–Aboriginal relations. Consider the current situation. As the *tangata whenua*, the Maori constitute a domestic, yet sovereign, nation with corresponding rights to self-determination. They prefer to be cast as a relatively autonomous "nation within," with the power and authority that emanate from such sovereign jurisdiction. What is widely rejected is a view of themselves as another racial or ethnic minority in need of integration through special programs.

The impact of this collective redefinition is crucial in terms of the logic underlying the system of Maori representation. The significance of Maori seats is diminished when political discourse is focused around their role as agents of assimilation or of party politics. It is equally diminished if promoted as a political gesture to placate the Maori while absolving other MPs of their responsibility for Maori issues. The potential of Maori representation is enhanced, however, when authorities are willing to accept Maori representation as a minimal precondition for meeting Aboriginal political, social, economic and cultural aspirations. From this we can infer that any system of AEDs is likely to be more effective and acceptable if established in consultation with Aboriginal leaders and people from the grass roots. Conversely, no one should be surprised if electoral support and legitimacy are withdrawn when a system is imposed unilaterally for the express purpose of cooling out an increasingly troublesome constituency.

> LESSON TWO: Even as a symbol, the principle of AEDs may have a powerful impact in sending out positive messages about the status of Aboriginal–government relations and the restructuring of Aboriginal relations with the state.

Public debate about guaranteed representation is frequently couched in terms of its symbolic value. Maori seats are referred to as a symbol embodying the special status of the *tangata whenua*. Symbolically, Maori electoral districts guarantee a Maori presence in Parliament: the system has been put there by Maori voters, is answerable to the Maori electorate, and collectively strives to promote Maori interests over land, culture and identity. Attaching a symbolic label to Maori seats is not without its perils, however. Such labelling may imply their impact is more nominal than real – a poor substitute as it were for a fair and productive system that ensures power sharing.

Even if primarily symbolic, Maori seats are a symbol with formidable substance. A complex symbol such as Maori seats elicits varying messages and multiple meanings in response to evolving contexts. It provides a guideline (blueprint) in legitimizing a certain course of government action vis-à-vis the Maori (and vice versa); a rationale to justify a specific set of government actions and Maori responses; and a yardstick by which to evaluate government policies and programs for the Maori. For these reasons alone, the symbolic value of separate electoral districts should not be taken lightly. Maori seats may symbolize a *pakeha* perception of the Maori as the *tangata whenua o aotearoa*. Conversely, the very presence of Maori seats symbolizes a Maori commitment to the legitimacy of the parliamentary process. They also serve as a symbol of Maori identity and distinctiveness as set out in the *Treaty of Waitangi*. Taken together, the existence of Maori seats provides a highly charged symbol that touches on the nature and status of Maori–government relations at a point in time. This in turn suggests Maori seats may be interpreted as a "contested terrain" involving the forces of Maori resistance and empowerment on the one hand, and *pakeha* hegemony and co-optation on the other.

A similar line of argument can be applied to Canada, where Aboriginal people have had difficulties in expressing themselves in Parliament (Marchand 1990). Even symbolic representation may provide a starting point for presenting an Aboriginal viewpoint to decision makers in Canada. Yet why should Aboriginal people be singled out for special electoral treatment when other minorities such as persons with disabilities, women or visible minorities are equally underrepresented? The answer lies in the fact that Aboriginal people are Canada's first citizens and as such represent a special case in need of preferential action programs. With few exceptions, as noted by Jeffrey Simpson (1991), Aboriginal people have found it difficult to become involved in the electoral process. The result is nothing short of worrisome, since the Aboriginal concerns are inadequately articulated in a forum where grievances could otherwise be given the national exposure they so desperately require.

The Electoral Process

New Zealand's electoral process in general is fraught with difficulties and inconsistencies that make it a highly alienating experience for Maori voters. This is particularly true with respect to the system of Maori representation. Here the debate over the mechanics pertaining to the Maori electoral process provides insights into the administration of AEDs that may serve as a guideline in other contexts.

> LESSON THREE: The technicalities associated with the Maori option are so complex that a certain paralysis has set in. Simplification is critical, especially if much of the voting population as a group does not possess the educational credentials of the general population.

Maori seats are plagued by two inconsistencies that threaten to foreclose the system by default if not by design. Such discontinuities are not altogether absent from general ridings, but their impact is less noticeable there. First, a large number of Maori refuse to register on the Maori roll (only 70 564 of the 1 920 256 eligible voters in all New Zealand were registered on the Maori roll in 1986). Compare this with the 145 087 that were duly registered on the Maori rolls only 10 years earlier (McRobie 1981). In fact, it is estimated that about one-third of all Maori do not bother to register on either the Maori or general roll (New Zealand, Royal Commission 1986). Second, there is an alarming number of invalid ballots cast, the net impact of which dampens the perception of Maori seats as fair and representative. What is the problem, and what can be done?

In the first case, Maori refusal to get involved in the electoral process may reflect a belief that Maori seats are irrelevant, counterproductive and meaningless. Modifications are necessary to revive the relevance of Maori seats as a genuine alternative to the general system. The Maori seats must be seen as created by the Maori, for the Maori and in pursuit of Maori interests. Elected Maori MPs must possess both the *mana* and resources to take advantage of their presence as power brokers in Parliament. They must be free of party containment, at least to the point where they independently decide to act as a separate Maori party or to pursue a coalition agreement with a major political party.

The second problem can be resolved by simplifying the enrolment procedures, especially as they pertain to the special vote. As it stands now, the large number of spoiled ballots reflects a procedure for enrolment so technical and complicated as to dissuade all but the most dedicated follower (McRobie 1981). Problems in defining who is a Maori make it difficult to determine the eligibility of voters in separate electorates. This may lead to problems in registration associated with the periodic Maori option. A system that is simple, safe and familiar is required if guaranteed representation is to make a meaningful impact on its constituents.

LESSON FOUR: Electoral boundaries must reflect the realities of Aboriginal tribal organization, not merely the prerequisites of administrative convenience or electoral expediency.

Maori electoral boundaries have remained virtually intact with only minor modifications since their inception in 1867. Many observers have criticized this feature of the system, arguing that the boundaries do not correspond in any meaningful way to the realities of Maori tribal society (see Stokes 1981). Such arbitrariness makes it difficult for the Maori electorate to express a positive or meaningful identification. The boundaries are not only artificial but also rarely adjusted, thus precluding the flexibility to accommodate demographic trends. Ideally, it would appear that Maori seats should be organized along tribal lines as one measure of electoral relevance. This is problematic enough in New Zealand, where tribal reality is paramount. The existence of numerous tribes and subtribes with disputed boundaries may pose an additional challenge to central authorities and Aboriginal leaders in countries such as Canada.

LESSON FIVE: The number of AEDs must remain flexible if they are to reflect changing realities and new directions. Decisions to increase the number of AEDs must rest to some extent with those who are affected by the adjustment.

Few aspects of the electoral process rankle the Maori as the reluctance of central authorities to increase the number of Maori seats. Numbers in the general ridings are carefully adjusted prior to each election to ensure representational fairness. But Maori seats have remained fixed at four since their inception, in seeming disregard to the number of general seats, the size of the Maori population and the number of Maori on the Maori roll (New Zealand, Royal Commission 1986). Fairness alone dictates the number of Maori seats must reflect some element of responsiveness to changing political and demographic trends. Otherwise, the system loses its relevance and acceptability to Maori voters.

What, then, is a fair basis for Maori representation? There is no consensus regarding whether the electoral quota should be calculated on the basis of total population or of adults qualified to vote. The major political parties have tended to dominate the debate in this assessment. The Labour Party argues the Maori are underrepresented on the strength of total population. Whereas MPs in general ridings represent approximately 32 000 constituents, Maori members represent approximately 100 000 constituents. The National Party, however, suggests the Maori are overrepresented because of low voter turnout and declining enrolment figures (McRobie 1981). The partisan politics involved in these decisions reveals clearly how the debate is peppered with party self-interest. Who can be surprised, then, by the growing chorus of Maori voters who are abandoning the scheme for alternative political strategies?

LESSON SIX: The size of Maori electoral districts is a chief cause of problems pertaining to representativeness and involvement. Perhaps the size of the electorate is less critical than the creation of a riding that bears some meaningful reality to the Maori population.

Maori ridings are uniformly large, thus exacerbating an already difficult situation of representation and fairness. In 1983, for example, the Northern Maori riding covered 18 general ridings; the Eastern, 8; the Western, 17; and the Southern, 45, including all of South Island as well as the area around Wellington. The average electoral population in the Maori electoral districts in 1983 was 7.8 percent higher than the average for the general electoral districts. Some allowances have been made to compensate for the Southern Maori riding, but the difficulties continue to undermine the development of an effective grassroots party organization, leading to lower enrolments and voter turnout (New Zealand, Royal Commission 1986).

The Effectiveness of AEDs

The New Zealand case provides a number of lessons from which we can draw inferences with regard to the effectiveness and impact of Maori electoral districts. The notion of effectiveness is somewhat elusive, of course. What precisely do we mean by effective: effective for whom, who decides, by what criteria? More importantly, what strategies should Maori members employ to maximize their presence in Parliament? A major test of New Zealand's electoral system rests with its capacity to provide for effective political representation of Maori interests on the basis of certain principles (New Zealand, Royal Commission 1986). Principles for effective Maori representation can be enumerated as follows:

1. In a parliamentary democracy based on majority rule, minority interests must be adequately and effectively represented if they are to compete for influence on public policy. Exclusion of any minority from having a stake in the political process is likely to lead to indifference, alienation and rejection of the political system. Innovative steps must be taken to ensure a lively Maori presence throughout the entire electoral process.
2. Maori members must represent Maori interests in Parliament. Voices of the *tangata whenua* cannot be appropriated by representatives of the general electorates.
3. Maori representatives are a necessary but insufficient means to protect Maori interests. All political parties must be expected to take an interest and compete for the Maori vote.
4. Both Maori and general members should be held accountable to the Maori electorate.
5. The system of separate electoral districts must be reorganized to allow all Maori a meaningful voice in the electoral process.
6. The system of Maori electoral districts cannot be justified apart from Maori demands for recognition of their *tangata whenua* status in New Zealand.

It is our belief that the effectiveness of AEDs, at least in terms of fair representation, will rest on the adequacy of political responses to these principles.

LESSON SEVEN: A system of AEDs is but one component in a comprehensive overhaul of Aboriginal–government relations.

Introducing AEDs without comparable initiatives along a wide political, economic or social front may be interpreted as little more than
a public relations exercise devoid of relevance to the *tangata whenua*.

We contend that a system of AEDs can serve in a positive way to
enhance Aboriginal goals. Yet such a system cannot be expected to
independently carry the entire load of Aboriginal aspirations. Recent
events in New Zealand reveal how a restructuring of Maori–government
relations has come about from the combined impact of diverse sources
and agencies in collective pursuit of *tangata whenua* status. In addition,
powerful formal channels such as the New Zealand Maori Council
serve in an advisory-monitoring capacity (Fleras 1985b). A highly vocal
network of activist organizations also plays a significant role in keeping the government aware of Maori concerns (Walker 1984). Collectively,
these organizations provide a broad spectrum of Maori opinion, so that
each in its own way contributes to the political process. Independently,
in other words, the impact of Maori seats on the political agenda is rendered less effective. In conjunction with broader initiatives, however,
the same system can serve as a useful organizing principle for mobilizing
Maori resources to improve the social, economic and cultural lot of the
tangata whenua.

> LESSON EIGHT: Meaningful dialogue and consultation are critical
> before decisions can be made about the structure, function or pro-
> cess of AEDs.

Maori ambivalence toward Maori seats may reflect a lack of meaningful involvement and consultation in the design and implementation of separate representation. It goes without saying that Aboriginal
input is crucial at all phases of the electoral reform process if there is
to be any hope of success. Consultations need to be conducted in the
spirit of power sharing, which ideally involves a broad cross-section
from the grass roots to national leaders.

> LESSON NINE (A): Maori representation may be effective when aligned
> with a major political party.

> LESSON NINE (B): The presence of an independent Maori party may
> also be effective, although there is no way of determining its impact.

Maori members have three options open to them for maximizing
their presence within the existing parliamentary set-up. In theory, they
can stand as independents, as members of a major party or as members

of a separate Maori party. In the past and until the 1930s, Maori MPs stood as independents and only rarely entered into coalitions with any staying power. A notable exception was the Young Maori Party of the early 20th century. Sir Apirana Ngata of the Young Maori Party initiated a number of concessions of community renewal and land development. But much of the land reform was conducted when Ngata occupied a ministerial position under the Reform Party during the 1920s.

The second alternative is for Maori members to align themselves with a major party in hopes of capitalizing on increased resources and exposure. Since the late 1930s, Maori members have clung tenaciously to the Labour Party banner. Recent polls suggest this affiliation has not wavered significantly, despite growing support for *Mana Maori Motuhake* as a viable alternative. Although many dispute the effectiveness of such an arrangement (see section on pros and cons), the Labour–Maori alliance has been productive when one or more Maori members are accorded an influential ministerial position. The productivity is further enhanced when the party in power is predisposed toward support of Maori demands. This most certainly has been the case in recent years where a Maori minister for Maori Affairs has presided over a span of unparalleled reform in redefining Maori–government relations. But Labour's loss in the general election of 1990 may again diminish the profile of Maori members and restrict their impact to the status of onlookers and backbenchers.

The third option is for Maori members to act *en bloc* as a separate Maori voice in Parliament. Such an arrangement would appear to have considerable merit for exerting a concerted and unified pressure on the party in power. Ideally, a separate Maori party would transcend party constraints for service on behalf of Maori constituents. At present, all evidence points to widespread Maori indifference to this alternative, as evidenced by the relatively poor showing of *Motuhake*. The tribal basis of Maori society may further militate against establishment of a pan-Maori political organization.

LESSON TEN: The effectiveness of Maori representation is improved through implementation of a system of proportional representation with a common roll.

We concur with critics who argue that New Zealand's system of separate Maori representation is intrinsically flawed and subject to unwarranted constraints that restrict its potential. Structural limitations suggest the present system, even with adjustments, is incapable of addressing Maori needs. The major weakness stems from the fact that both Maori and non-Maori representatives are accountable only to the particular community that elected them. An arrangement such as this, the Royal Commission on the Electoral System argues, isolates the Maori agenda by encouraging non-Maori MPs to pigeon-hole Maori concerns away from the political centre (New Zealand, Royal Commission 1986). Such a diversionary tactic has pre-empted Maori electors from using their formidable voting power to negotiate concessions from political parties.

The Royal Commission has roundly criticized the concept of a separate roll within New Zealand's plurality system of representation. A first-past-the-post system is unfair to small parties and minority groups (New Zealand, Royal Commission 1986). This is true even in Maori seats where the Labour hold is sufficiently secure that there is no party incentive to contest for the Maori vote or to commit resources to the riding. Mindful of these anomalies, the Royal Commission has advocated scrapping the plurality system with separate seats and replacing it with a proportional system with a common roll (no Maori option, no Maori rolls, etc.) as the most effective form of representation. Under a common roll, each person is entitled to one vote, and this vote is the same for everyone within that particular geographic setting.

The operation is straightforward on the surface. For example, the number of seats in Parliament allocated to the Maori would depend on the percentage of votes cast for a Maori party. A Maori party would be allocated one seat for 25 000 votes, two seats for 37 500, and so on. Such an arrangement would provide an incentive for other parties to take Maori concerns into account by running Maori candidates in winnable ridings. As well, it would ensure competition between the major political parties for Maori votes on a nationwide basis. Competition for Maori votes would result in a more effective and independent role for Maori members within the party. No longer split between two rolls, Maori would exert a substantial minority status (12.5 percent of the electorate in 1986) within the electoral system. Maori participation in the electoral process would increase in response to a more meaningful, representative, flexible and opportunistic arrangement in Parliament.

> LESSON ELEVEN: The fairness and effectiveness of AEDs can be further improved by introducing a system of double voting for Aboriginal people.

Problems exist with the New Zealand system in meeting acceptable standards of Maori representation. But the Royal Commission's conclusions did not go far enough in restructuring Maori representation at a time when fundamental change was in progress. The essential fault of the Royal Commission lay in its failure to read the highly politicized nature of Aboriginal demands. While the idea of integrating Maori and *pakeha* into a common roll has a certain intrinsic appeal, such a proposition appears diametrically opposed to Maori aspirations for consolidating what is distinctive about them at symbolic levels. It is difficult to imagine Maori consent for a scheme that would sacrifice a cherished and distinctive symbol at a time when Maori aspirations as a sovereign nation are currently contested and politicized. How, then, do we create a system of AEDs that combines Maori insistence on separate and guaranteed representation with a meaningful Maori input in the corridors of parliamentary power?

The solution perhaps lies in a compromise between the current system of plurality with separate seats, on the one hand, and the proportional system with a common roll as espoused by the New Zealand Royal Commission on the other. The compromise arrangement confers on all persons of Maori ancestry the right to cast two votes. Under a system of double voting, one ballot is reserved for the Maori seats, and the other, for a candidate to the general pool.

This set-up would leave the present system of Maori representation intact (although the number of Maori seats might be subject to readjustment) while ensuring Maori input into the general system of representation. The concept of dual voting is not as unprecedented or preposterous as it may seem on the surface. Male Maori property owners at one time possessed the right to vote on both the Maori and the general roll between 1867 and 1893. Similarly, a proposed system of double voting need not be condemned as discriminatory or unfair. Entitlement to a double vote may be justified as consistent with Maori Aboriginal claims to special status (citizen-plus) derived from first principles and enshrined in the *Treaty of Waitangi*. Nor should double voting be regarded as inimical to the principle of equality. In situations characterized by inequality, there is nothing intrinsically fair about recourse to mathematical equality and colour-blind universality. Attainment of true equality may entail special considerations that redefine the grounds for entitlement. A double vote constitutes one such concession with which to overcome the additional disadvantages confronted by Aboriginal people.

The benefits of a dual franchise are self-evident in other ways. Symbolically, it acknowledges the Maori as an integral component of New Zealand society without diminishing their unique status as the original occupants of the land and their inalienable rights. Conferral of a double vote overcomes the electoral paradox that compartmentalizes Maori concerns in the present system yet risks swallowing up these issues in the clutter of a proposed common system. The concept also possesses the virtue of simplicity. Eliminating the Maori option and separate rolls does away with many of the logistic entanglements that have induced voter apathy. To be sure, the bestowal of a dual vote as an Aboriginal right is not without its problems.

First, it does not address issues pertaining to the size, number and boundaries of electoral districts. Second, it is likely to meet with resistance and resentment. Many will be outraged by a scheme at odds with the values of New Zealand's political culture. But such an arrangement is an enlightened and imaginative proposal to incorporate the principle of indigenous rights in the electoral process. It provides the Maori with the political clout they need to overcome their peripheral position in society and to assume their rightful status as Treaty partners and *tangata whenua*. It also enhances the possibility of greater Maori involvement in the electoral process, coupled with a livelier commitment to work with the *pakeha* to forge a world-class bicultural society.

CONCLUSION: PUTTING AEDs INTO PRACTICE

Evidence appears to support the principle and practice of AEDs, although the soundness of this arrangement has been tarnished by charges of political indifference, electoral neglect and party considerations in New Zealand. There is no difficulty in defending a system of guaranteed AEDs but only as part of a wider restructuring in Aboriginal–government relations. Such an arrangement could conceivably assist Aboriginal people in formulating input at the highest level of decision making. It could also enhance Aboriginal participation in the electoral system at a time when the very legitimacy of Canada as a unified society is tottering on the brink of collapse.

The concept of separate Maori representation provides a useful departure point for designing a viable system of AEDs in Canada. Focusing on the logic, structure and implementation of Maori representation has alerted us to the danger of conflating the peculiarities of Maori electoral districts with the principles of AEDs in general. Foremost in terms of lessons from New Zealand is the acknowledgement that AEDs constitute but one component in the overall drive to entrench Aboriginal rights through Aboriginal self-determination along political, social, economic and cultural fronts. An equally important lesson is the necessity to have Aboriginal input in the design and implementation of a new electoral process. Anything less than this can only squander the potential of AEDs amidst charges of appropriating Aboriginal rights to self-determination. Finally, AEDs must be established in the spirit of power sharing, not as a conflict-management device with public relations overtones. Otherwise, what we have is a system that nominally reintegrates an Aboriginal voice into the electoral process but whose underlying logic detracts from any standard of what is fair, just and equitable.

What constitutes a fair and equitable system of AEDs? Four possibilities prevail on the basis of lessons derived from the New Zealand experience.

- Maintain the present system (that is, plurality with separate roll), albeit with modifications, to sharpen representivity and responsiveness to Maori electors and members.
- Abolish Maori seats; merge the Maori roll with the general one to create a common roll, but make no changes to the first-past-the-post system of representation.
- Repeal the existing system in favour of one based on the principles of proportional representation and common roll, as recommended by the Royal Commission.
- Introduce a system of proportional representation with separate electoral districts and a separate Maori roll that entitles all persons of Maori ancestry to two votes. Conferral of a double vote to all eligible voters has two major benefits: it simplifies the enrolment and voting procedures that have crippled the Maori electoral process; and it secures a guaranteed Maori voice in Parliament by reinforcing the *tangata whenua* status of the Maori. At the same time, the major parties are forced to compete for the other Maori vote as part of the national agenda. The end result is an electoral process not only more accountable to Maori voters, but also one consistent with New Zealand's multicultural ideals.

We anticipate a proposal for double voting would be greeted with disbelief and dismay – even derision – by many Canadians. After all, introducing a racially based system of representation in Canada is contentious enough. Even more disruptive is a double-vote system that clashes with many of our most cherished political values, that is, "one person, one vote." Yet if the events at Oka and Akwesasne have taught us anything, it is an awareness that Aboriginal commitment to Canadian society is brittle and amenable to rupture. Fine-tuning the existing system through electoral add-ons may not be enough in the post-Oka era. Imaginative and bold proposals must be articulated and debated if we are to ensure an Aboriginal involvement in Canada's electoral system that is fair, equitable and productive. The introduction of AEDs is but one measure of that commitment.

REFERENCES

This study was completed in June 1991.

Armstrong, M. Jocelyn. 1987. "Interethnic Conflict in New Zealand." In *Ethnic Conflict*, ed. J. Boucher, D. Landis and K.A. Clark. Beverly Hills: Sage.

Canada. House of Commons. Special Committee on Indian Self-Government. 1983. *Indian Self-Government in Canada*. Ottawa: Queen's Printer.

Chapman, Robert. 1986. "Voting in the Maori Political Sub-System, 1935–1984." In New Zealand, Royal Commission on the Electoral System, *Report: Towards a Better Democracy*. Wellington: Government Printer.

Cleveland, Les. 1979. *The Politics of Utopia: New Zealand and Its Government*. Wellington: Methuen.

Cox, Kevin. 1991. "N.B. Seat Proposed for Natives." *Globe and Mail*, 19 March.

Dalziel, R.D. 1981. "The Politics of Settlement." In *The Oxford History of New Zealand*, ed. W.H. Oliver and B.R. Williams. Wellington: Oxford University Press.

Daniell, S. 1983. "Reform of the New Zealand Political System: How Likely Is It? A Survey of the Attitudes of the Members of the New Zealand Parliament to Reform Proposals." *Political Science* 35:151–89.

Davies, Iona. 1981–82. "Rights and Wrong. New Zealand: Land of Discrimination." *Canadian Forum* 61:42–43.

Fleras, Augie. 1985a. "From Social Control to Political Self-Determination? Maori Seats and the Politics of Separate Maori Representation in New Zealand." *Canadian Journal of Political Science* 18 (3): 551–76.

——. 1985b. "The Politics of Maori Lobbying: The Case of the New Zealand Maori Council." *Political Science* 38:39–52.

——. 1989. "Inverting the Bureaucratic Pyramid. Reconciling Aboriginality and Bureaucracy in New Zealand." *Human Organization* 48 (3): 214–25.

——. 1991. "Te Tira Ahu Iwi: Devolving Maori–Government Relations in Aotearoa." In *Nga Take Ethnicity and Race Relations in Aotearoa New Zealand*, ed. Paul Spoonley, David Pearson and Cluny McPherson. Palmerston North, NZ: Dunmore Press.

Halligan, J. 1980. "Continuity and Change in the New Zealand Parliament." Ph.D. diss., Victoria University, Wellington.

Jackson, W.J. 1973. *New Zealand: Politics of Change*. Wellington: A.W. and A.H. Reed.

Jackson, W.K., and G.A. Wood. 1964. "The New Zealand Parliament and Maori Representation." *Historical Studies: Australia and New Zealand* 11:383–96.

Kelsey, Jane. 1990. *A Question of Honour? Labour and the Treaty 1984–1989*. Wellington: Allen and Unwin.

Levine, S., and A. Robinson. 1976. *The New Zealand Voter – A Survey of Public Opinion and Electoral Behaviour*. Wellington: Price Milburn.

Love, Ralph Ngatata. 1977. "Policies of Frustration: The Growth of Maori Politics. The Ratana/Labour Era." Ph.D. diss., Victoria University, Wellington.

Mahuta, Robert. 1981. "Maori Political Representation: A Case For Change." In *Maori Representation in Parliament*, ed. Evelyn Stokes. Hamilton, NZ: Waikato University.

Marchand, Len. 1990. "Aboriginal Electoral Reform." A discussion paper. Ottawa.

McHugh, P.G. 1989. "Constitutional Theory and Maori Claims." In *Waitangi. Maori and Pakeha Perspectives of the Treaty of Waitangi*, ed. Hugh Kawharu. Auckland: Oxford University Press.

McLeay, E.M. 1980."Political Arguments About Representation: The Case of the Maori Seats." *Political Studies* 28:43–62.

McRobie, Alan. 1981. "Ethnic Representation: The New Zealand Experience." In *Maori Representation in Parliament*, ed. Evelyn Stokes. Hamilton, NZ: Waikato University.

Mead, Hirini Moko. 1979. "A Pathway to the Future: He Ara Kite Aomarama." Paper presented to the New Zealand Planning Council, Wellington.

Metge, A. Joan. 1976. *The Maoris of New Zealand*. Rev. ed. London: Routledge and Kegan Paul.

Mitchell, Austin V. 1969. *Politics and People in New Zealand*. Christchurch: Whitcombe and Toombs.

New Zealand. *Electoral Amendment Act, 1980*, No. 29.

———. *Maori Official Language Act, 1987*, No. 176.

———. *Maori Representation Act, 1867*, No. 47.

———. *Runanga a Iwi Act, 1990*, No. 125.

———. *Treaty of Waitangi Act, 1975*, No. 114.

———. *Westland Representation Act, 1867*, No. 48.

New Zealand. 1990. *Official Yearbook of New Zealand*. Wellington: Dept. of Statistics.

New Zealand. Ministerial Committee of Inquiry into Violence. 1987. *Report*. Wellington.

New Zealand. Royal Commission on the Electoral System. 1986. *Report: Towards a Better Democracy*. Wellington: Government Printer.

New Zealand. Treaty of Waitangi Hui. 1985. "Report of the Proceedings." Waitangi, NZ, 4–6 February.

New Zealand Herald. 1990. "Electorates Return to Their Old Ways." 29 October.

Norton, C. 1988. *New Zealand Parliamentary Election Results 1946–1987*. Wellington: Victoria University.

Paltiel, Rudy. 1991. "Natives Polled on Constitutional Idea." *Globe and Mail*, 18 January.

Searnacke, Monty. 1979. Vice-president's address to the National Party (Maori section). Quoted in Robert Mahuta, "Maori Political Representation," in *Maori Representation in Parliament*, ed. E. Stokes. Hamilton, NZ: Waikato University, 1981.

Simpson, Alan. 1981. "Redistributing the Maori Vote." In *Maori Representation in Parliament*, ed. Evelyn Stokes. Hamilton, NZ: Waikato University.

Simpson, Jeffrey. 1991. "The Primary Idea of Creating Specific Parliamentary Seats for Natives." *Globe and Mail*, 26 March.

Sorrenson, M.P.K. 1986. "A History of Maori Representation in Parliament." In New Zealand, Royal Commission on the Electoral System, *Report: Towards a Better Democracy*. Wellington: Government Printer.

Stokes, Evelyn. 1981. *Maori Representation in Parliament*. Hamilton, NZ: Waikato University.

Tabacoff, D. 1975. "The Role of the Maori MP in Contemporary New Zealand Politics." In *New Zealand Politics: A Reader*, ed. S. Levine. Melbourne: Cheshire.

Temm, Paul. 1990. *The Waitangi Tribunal: The Conscience of a Nation*. Auckland: Random Century.

Vasil, R. 1990. *What Do the Maori Want?* Auckland: Random Century.

Walker, Ranginui. 1979. "The Maori Minority and the Democratic Process." Paper presented to the New Zealand Maori Council, Wellington.

———. 1984. "The Genesis of Maori Activism." *Journal of Polynesian Society* 93:267–82.

———. 1987. "Maori Aspirations and Social Policy." A preliminary review of submissions to the Royal Commission on Social Policy. Wellington.

———. 1989. "The Maori People: Their Political Development." In *New Zealand Politics in Perspective*, ed. H. Gold. Auckland: Longman Paul.

Walsh, Pat, and Kurt Wetzel. 1990. "State Restructuring, Corporate Strategy and Industrial Relations: State-Owned Enterprise Management in New Zealand." Paper presented to the 5th Biennial Conference of the Association of Industrial Relations Academics of Australia and New Zealand, 4–7 July, University of Melbourne, Melbourne.

Watt, Keith. 1990. "N.W.T. a Model for the World?" *Globe and Mail*, 31 December.

Weaver, Sally. 1983. "Towards a Comparison of National Political Organizations of Indigenous Peoples: Australia, Canada and Norway." Paper delivered to the Institute of Social Sciences, University of Tromso, Norway.

Williams, J.A. 1969. *Politics of the New Zealand Maori: Protest and Cooperation, 1891–1909*. London: Oxford University Press.

Williams, Joe. 1989. "Indigenous Human Rights in New Zealand from an International Perspective." In Proceedings of the Aotearoa/New Zealand and Human Rights in the Pacific and Asia Region, 26–28 May, Wellington.

3

ABORIGINAL PEOPLES AND CAMPAIGN COVERAGE IN THE NORTH

~

Valerie Alia

The phone lines are down to the Yukon's most remote community. The people of Old Crow won't have any way of letting the Chief Returning Officer know who won in their riding, short of renting a plane and flying the results in. Those results could be crucial. – CBC Radio, Whitehorse.

(Ford 1985)

NORTHERN CANADIAN POLITICAL life is a complex mix of innovation and tradition. Cultures, weather, topography, transportation and communications connect in special ways. Northern interdependency among people in communities of 50 to 3 000, linked to cities tiny by southern standards, makes politics personal, informal and small-scale. Yet the nature of the circumpolar North also makes its politics uniquely global.

The following questions guide this work: How did Aboriginal people participate in the 1988 federal election and in recent territorial and provincial elections? How did they view their participation? What is the nature and extent of access to news media? What other avenues of communication are available? Do media encourage or discourage electoral participation of Aboriginal and northern people? Does the nature and size of the constituencies of northern and Aboriginal candidates mean that these candidates require greater media access? What is the general nature of the relationship among Aboriginal people, federal elections and media in the northern territories and provinces?

The study of Yukon Territory, the Northwest Territories (NWT) and the northern regions of the provinces was conducted between September 1990 and January 1991, months that figure importantly in the campaign/elections process. The researchers experienced many of the conditions described by those interviewed. The principal researcher worked from a northern home base, aware of the value of experiencing conditions first hand and also of the fact that people who study the North from the "Outside" are treated with (justifiable) suspicion.

The research had a Yukon home base because the researcher was least familiar with this region and because the Yukon has received little attention in other studies and has played important roles in national, regional and Aboriginal politics. It is home to the nation's first female national party leader, Audrey McLaughlin of the New Democratic Party (NDP). She and Premier[1] Tony Penikett, leader of the Government of the Yukon, have attracted national media attention and have used that forum to bring northern and Aboriginal concerns to a wider public.

The research followed several paths. A qualitative literature review included media coverage of the 1988 federal election and northern and Aboriginal campaigns/elections since 1987; transcripts of the 1990 public hearings of the Royal Commission on Electoral Reform and Party Financing; relevant elections literature and other materials; political history of northern Canada and Aboriginal governance; Aboriginal communications societies; and print and broadcast media. Time, personnel and funding did not permit quantitative analysis.

Interviews were conducted by the principal researcher and assistants based in Yukon Territory, the Northwest Territories and London, Ontario, with Aboriginal and non-Aboriginal politicians in all northern provinces and territories; print and broadcast journalists, including leaders of several Aboriginal communication societies; First Nations community and organization leaders.[2] Those interviewed were guaranteed anonymity; therefore, except where given publicly, their comments are protected from attribution in this text. In addition to conducting interviews, the principal researcher participated in three very useful conferences.[3]

With federal campaigns and elections at the centre, the interviews also covered territorial and provincial campaigns because a fuller picture was desired and because northern electoral districts have too few federal candidates for a significant study of politicians (e.g., one Member of Parliament in the Yukon and two in the Northwest Territories). The final component of this study includes consultation with leaders and community members from northern provinces and territories, and the principal researcher's four-month participant-observation-based case-study of Yukon communities.

In this study, North means those regions designated Middle, Far and Extreme North on the map that follows, based on Hamelin's mapping of Canadian nordicity (Hamelin 1978, 25–40).

Figure 3.1
Nordicity zones
(Arrows indicate the region called "North" in this study)

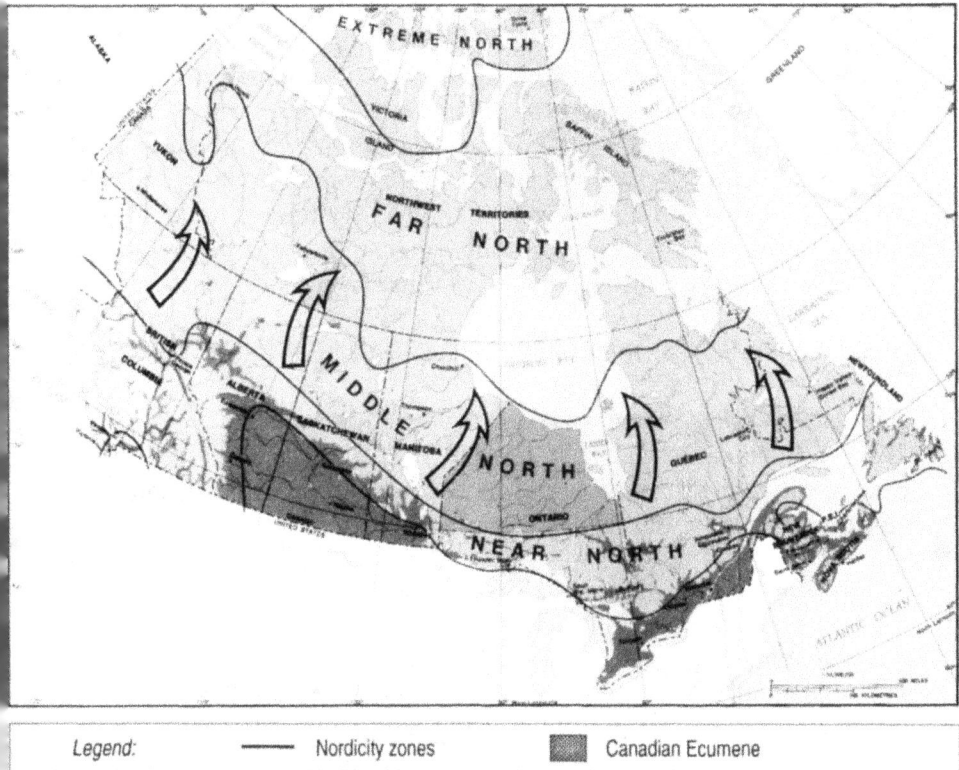

| Legend: | ——— Nordicity zones | ▨ Canadian Ecumene |

Source: Ontario Royal Commission on the Northern Environment.

INTRODUCTION

The special character of northern political life colours all media/elections relationships. The Northwest Territories (NWT) is Canada's only region without political parties and with an Aboriginal-majority government. Here and in the rest of the North, where parties do exist, voter decisions are based more on issues and personalities than on party loyalty.

Information about how long First Nations peoples have lived in the North varies; figures range from 7 000 to over 35 000 years.[4] Many Aboriginal people say they have always lived here. More to the point, First Nations emphasize that their governments long preceded any idea of Canada.

According to historical texts and many Aboriginal leaders, earlier Aboriginal governments were not elected. Community members were related by language, clan and family; there were no elected chiefs, councils or administrative centres. Decision making was consensus-based – a political foundation still important to northern governments today.

Full Aboriginal participation in electoral politics is recent: the Inuit were first allowed to vote in 1950. Indian people on reserves waited over a decade more before all vestiges of denied voting rights were removed, the last Canadians to be granted full electoral participation.[5] This newness and the ongoing process of exploring how Aboriginal people fit into the electoral system provide the context for the study at hand. The issues that follow were identified most often in the testimony to the Royal Commission hearings and in our interviews concerning the relationship between communications and elections.

ABORIGINAL PEOPLE, COMMUNICATIONS AND ELECTIONS: KEY ISSUES

First Nations Voting Patterns and Perceptions of Representation

Voter turnout varies widely among provinces and territories, regions and communities. In general, Aboriginal voter turnout is low; among the causes cited by Aboriginal people are the following:

- inadequate media coverage;
- insufficient availability of media;
- failure to provide voter and candidate information in Aboriginal languages; and
- perceptions of alienation from the electoral process.

The major exceptions occur in the Yukon and Northwest Territories. In the 1988 federal election, the Yukon vote was 12 849 out of 16 396 eligible voters. The western NWT vote was 12 847 out of 18 721, while the eastern Arctic – Nunatsiaq riding – was 8 469 out of 11 392 (Canada, Elections Canada 1990).

Only three of the 295 sitting members in the House of Commons are of Aboriginal descent, and two are from the two Aboriginal-majority ridings in the NWT (Marchand and Leclair 1990).

Many of the problems in the North are also found in remote Aboriginal communities elsewhere in Canada. Saskatchewan has two extremes – one reserve district with 100 percent voter registration but only a 30 percent vote, and another with an 80 percent vote. The officer for the latter district says people travelled 300 miles to voter education classes in Saskatoon "and brought their ballot boxes back for us ... this was the type of cooperation we received ... a great experience" (Werezak et al. 1990).

Gould (1990) and Robinson (1990) attribute low New Brunswick turnouts to alienation, candidate disinterest in Aboriginal issues and failure to present campaign materials and issues in Aboriginal languages. Craven (1990) reports very low turnout in British Columbia's Saanich–Gulf Islands. In Alberta, Crowfoot and Young Man (Crowfoot 1990) report that despite a move to make polling stations more accessible to citizens of the Blackfoot Tribe and Siksika Nation, voting in the last election remained weak, because of "... lack of representation ... some of them didn't even know who was running ... there were posters all over the reserve but we never see these people around here" (ibid.).

Chief Strater Crowfoot (1990) of the Siksika Nation in Alberta mentions reserve size, vehicle scarcity and history: "[Our] older people aren't used to voting and ... don't feel that our concerns are being addressed by the people that are on the ballot, so why bother."

This view, repeated in many interviews in the North, suggests that communications media cannot replace the importance of personal voter–candidate contact. Many of those interviewed stressed the importance of Aboriginal-majority electoral districts as a means of encouraging Aboriginal participation. For example, several people attributed the near-100 percent turnout in Old Crow, Yukon, to redistricting that gives the Vuntut Gwich'in First Nation a crucial voice in election outcomes.

To improve the relationship between Aboriginal campaigns and media coverage, we must understand the relationship between politics and communications in Aboriginal societies. Bobbi Smith, director of Yukon Women's Directorate, described political participation in her northern British Columbia coastal village: "When we were kids, we were *expected* to be in the Longhouse. Around 6:00 [PM], someone would come around to all the houses and tell everyone to be in the longhouse for council meeting. Children were expected to be there, and you were expected to be quiet. You might not understand everything that was going on, but you would understand some of it, and you'd be part of it" (Smith in Alia et al. 1990–91a).

In many Aboriginal cultures, political information is not relayed through media to a remote public but is part of a forum in which politicians and leaders engage in intimate dialogue with the whole community. Elders don't retire, they are the political centre, and children are participants, not bystanders.

With this in mind, the NWT funded an education program, organized by the Yellowknife B Band, to help elders regain their place in Native politics. Program recruiter Roy Erasmus says "we would like to see some of the leaders currently being left out – because of their language and educational difficulties – from their normal leadership roles" (Native Press 1990).

Elijah Smith (Liberal, Tatchun) ran for a seat in the Legislative Assembly in the Yukon at age 75. Non-Aboriginal leaders often retire in late middle age. Programs designed without First Nations participation or direction tend to miss important cultural differences. Bruce Cottingham reports: "I asked a woman I was working with [on an Aboriginal language project] what the word for 'government' was in her language. She told me. I asked what the word means, and she said 'grandmother' " (Alia et al. 1990–91a).

Effective reform of the communications-elections relationship requires that kind of Aboriginal–non-Aboriginal dialogue. Understanding why government and grandmother are the same word is crucial to the comprehension of deep and long-standing differences between Aboriginal and European traditions of government.

Language, Literacy and Education

Concerns about language, literacy and education permeate the hearings and interviews in the North. Saskatchewan Aboriginal people say they need greater access to post-secondary education, "not recognized as a treaty right"; ceilings limit the number of Aboriginal people entitled to post-secondary education, and funds to primary education have been cut (Alia et al. 1990-91b).

A northern Manitoba Aboriginal leader proposed developing a variety of voter/candidate education strategies that use the familiarity and friendliness of informal gatherings and traditional community-inclusive government. Northern Manitoba returning officer Walsh sees a particular need to teach people about enumeration but is uncertain how to reach people: "you just, physically, cannot go and put on a school in every community when you have 72 communities" (Walsh 1990). Across Canada, Aboriginal-run schools are increasing, as First Nations take control of their own education. The electoral reform process can use these schools and other programs to develop electoral education strategies directed by and relevant to Aboriginal people. The schools are grounded in Aboriginal cultures (for example, the Chehalis Public School was built to longhouse design and is run by the Sumas Band, one of 12 Aboriginal-run schools in BC) (Shiell 1990). Many combine old and new, Aboriginal and non-Aboriginal programming and teaching methods. One example is the Kipohtakaw Education Centre in Alexander, Alberta (Schiller 1987).

Big imaginations and small funds can have innovative results. In Pelly Crossing, Yukon (Selkirk First Nation), adult educator Richard

Lawrence (Alia et al. 1990–91a) put up a year-round literacy tent, and school principal Jim Tredger started a new tradition – twice-monthly community lunches he and the students prepare together to bring more people into the school. The lunch I attended was an overwhelming success; people stayed to read posted information and visit classrooms and each other.

By applying techniques such as these and building on existing institutions, electoral education programs can link voter education with more general – but related – goals of improving literacy. Assembly of First Nations figures for 1990 show a functional illiteracy rate (less than a grade nine education) for Aboriginal people of 45 percent, or two-and-a-half times the non-Aboriginal Canadian rate of 17 percent. The research reveals widespread concern about illiteracy/functional illiteracy in the North. Fifty-two percent of NWT people are functionally illiterate (Cotterill and Sorensen 1990). We must be careful not to assume causality. While illiteracy is unquestionably a problem in the NWT it has not always meant either lack of *electoral literacy* (see the following section) or low voter turnout. Hamilton attributes similar turnout figures for federal and territorial elections in part to an educated electorate (Hamilton 1990). Presumably, he does not mean a "literate" electorate, because he and several others propose putting candidates' photographs on ballots (see Cotterill and Sorensen 1990; Barkley 1990).

Whitehorse attorney Shayne Fairman proposes that Elections Canada develop a comprehensive education program – what Commissioner Don Oliver calls "a road show across Canada" (Fairman 1990). The road-show principle is especially well adapted to northern conditions. Northern rail lines and bus routes, where available, would be ideal conduits for contemporary circuit riders to bring elections education to remote communities. A proposal for developing this idea appears in the concluding suggestions in the final section of this study.

Electoral Literacy

To clarify the elections picture, I have introduced the term *electoral literacy* to our vocabulary. It is clear that functional illiteracy can coexist with electoral literacy. One of the preconditions for functional electoral literacy is the ability to understand the language of elections and elections coverage. In 1990, the NWT enacted historic legislation, amending the NWT *Official Languages Act*, "the first time a Canadian jurisdiction has recognized Aboriginal languages as equal to English or French. Under the new law, Chipewyan, Cree, Dogrib, Slavey, Gwich'in and Inuktitut (which includes the Inuvialuktun dialects and Inuinnaqtun) will share the same status as French and English ... which have always represented the minority of northerners" (Smellie 1990b).

Elsewhere in the North, there is demand for increased availability of elections materials, broadcast and other news media, speeches, public meetings and workshops in Aboriginal languages. At the same time, federal funding cuts have cancelled or limited many Aboriginal language programs. One Aboriginal Yukon politician (Alia et al. 1990–91b) says it is elders who have lost the most, since budget cuts forced CHON-FM (the radio station of Northern Native Broadcasting, Yukon) to curtail translation for political campaigns. This politician has also observed a decline in Aboriginal language use over the past 30 years and says that leaving elders out of the information system undercuts their traditional importance as political leaders.

Just before cuts to Labrador Inuit media, a journalist praised the region's bilingual (English-Inuktitut) news media for meeting the needs of a largely Inuktitut-speaking population (Alia et al. 1990–91b). It is important to review language policy and funding priorities in the light of electoral literacy. Informants have said that media often make a difference. This will be explored further throughout the study.

The following discussion demonstrates that the literacy climate isn't the only climate that affects northern elections and addresses the inseparability of northern weather and communications.

TRANSPORTATION, WEATHER, GEOGRAPHY, TOPOGRAPHY: WHAT IT'S REALLY LIKE TO VOTE, CAMPAIGN, SURVIVE AND SERVE IN THE NORTH

Foul weather isolates Yukon.
Snow storms ... and ice fog have disrupted ... flights for nearly two weeks.
(Buckley 1991, 3)

In many places, weather is a subject for small talk. In the North, it's the stuff of hard news and serious concern. Virtually everyone interviewed said northern weather and travel conditions are inadequately addressed in electoral policy. The concerns cut across party lines. These concerns affect all voters and candidates, with the important difference that Aboriginal communities, voters and candidates have fewer resources with which to do their work under these conditions.

Communication and transportation are inseparable in the North. Federal funding provisions are inadequate – drop-in-the-bucket remedies for ocean-sized problems. It is hard for southern urbanites to picture vast regions in which many people never see candidates' faces or names or hear their voices. It is equally difficult to imagine having to charter a helicopter or airplane merely to exercise the right to vote or run for office.

In the Yukon, January 1991 began with record-breaking cold – Whitehorse was blanketed in ice fog so thick it was hard to see across a well-lit street. Taxis and trucks gave out, planes were grounded for days, people were stuck in town or out, and mail went nowhere. In an unguarded moment, I slipped into the "Outside" mentality and dashed across town (48 below, no visibility) to the post office to use Priority Post. Only after queuing up with others did I realize how silly we looked clutching our precious packages. It was several days before the mail went out. In the communities, there are a couple of dogsled mail runs, but none from Whitehorse to Ottawa.

David Hamilton, Clerk of the NWT Legislative Assembly, recalled: "We've had to drop ballot boxes into ridings by helicopter. We have had situations where we couldn't open the poll because of a whiteout ... the vast distance between communities in some districts can deter a potential candidate from travelling to file nomination papers" (Hamilton 1990).

Ken Collin, of the Thompson, Manitoba, Progressive Conservative (party) Association, said that "lack of funding and the tremendous expense of a northern campaign ... has always been a deterrent to potential candidates." Elected members get extra budgets; candidates are drastically underfunded (Collin 1990b).

For NWT Amittuq MLA Titus Allooloo, campaign communications are tied to boundary concerns. He tried (unsuccessfully) to have his riding divided into two, because he can't spend enough time with constituents in Hall Beach, Igloolik and Pond Inlet – communities far from each other and from airline schedules. It costs about $10 000 to charter an aircraft between any two of the communities; adequate representation of his constituency would require a $100 000 annual travel budget (Smellie 1990a, 1,2).

As in the NWT, "weather plays a large role in northern Manitoba" (Zebrinski 1990). A Thompson returning officer concurs with Allooloo, calling it ludicrous that voting in his region can mean having to charter aircraft (Walsh 1990). Federal Progressive Conservative Association President Richard Whidden (1990) agrees: "You're really asking potential candidates ... to either take a leave of absence [or] terminate employment ... a serious constraint upon anyone who may wish to engage in active political life."

Familiarity with the eastern Arctic's fly-in-only conditions led to the researcher's wrong assumption that roads meant greater campaign access in Yukon. As a Yukon journalist said, "If it's minus 45 or 50 you don't drive at all; if you get stuck somewhere, you die" (Alia et al. 1990–91a).

In this climate, in which transportation is often frustrating, communication links are crucial. If they, too, were not underfunded, media could help bridge the gap between politicians and constituents. As it is, northern Aboriginal and non-Aboriginal journalists told us that even before federal cutbacks, they could not afford to travel enough to provide adequate coverage. Their budgets for future elections look even slimmer. The single bright spot is Television Northern Canada (TVNC), which now provides a circumpolar satellite link for television across the North. Administered by an all-Aboriginal board of directors who represent Inuit and Indian people across the Canadian Arctic, TVNC is the only program that has maintained its (start-up) funding level.

The following sections address northern communications media, communication styles and strategies for improvement.

Communications I: News Media

Canada is a world leader in Aboriginal broadcasting. In 1987, there were 30 First Nations radio stations in Canada, only 20 in the United States, a few Aboriginal-run stations in Latin America, a few stations in northern Scandinavia run by Sami (northern European indigenous people) and "brief Maori broadcast services ... carried over Radio New Zealand" with a radio network run by Maori (New Zealand's indigenous people) scheduled for 1990. Not until late 1985 did the first exclusively Aboriginal station in Australia begin broadcasting at Alice Springs (Browne 1990, 111–12). Australia's Northern Territory is akin to Canada's North – vast spaces, small communities, several languages. Despite its lead, Canada might benefit from studying the experiences of other countries.

Of all northern media, newspapers and magazines – particularly Aboriginal media – suffered most from 1990 federal budget cuts. Publications have always been scarcer than radio and television programming. Print media are often the only way voters see candidates' faces. They publish First Nations meeting notices, clan announcements, campaign advertisements and political dialogue encompassing columns, events coverage, candidate forums, opinion pieces and letters to editors on a scale unknown in the urban South. They are a readily available resource for Elections Canada information programs.

There are numerous efforts to strengthen and maintain these media. Most are likely to continue in scaled-down formats, which will mean even less coverage in future elections. The price paid by publications and staff is high. Overwork and burnout are reported almost universally. The commitment to keep Aboriginal publications alive is strong; some editors research, write, edit and sell ads – and take salary cuts or volunteer when funds run out.

While it cannot address the needs of Aboriginal and northern print media and does not remedy those cutback casualties, Television Northern Canada (TVNC) will help sustain scaled-down broadcast operations. It is likely to have a major impact on future elections coverage, because of its own programming capacity and its ability to bolster existing programming in every northern region.

Figure 3.2
Native communication societies of Canada

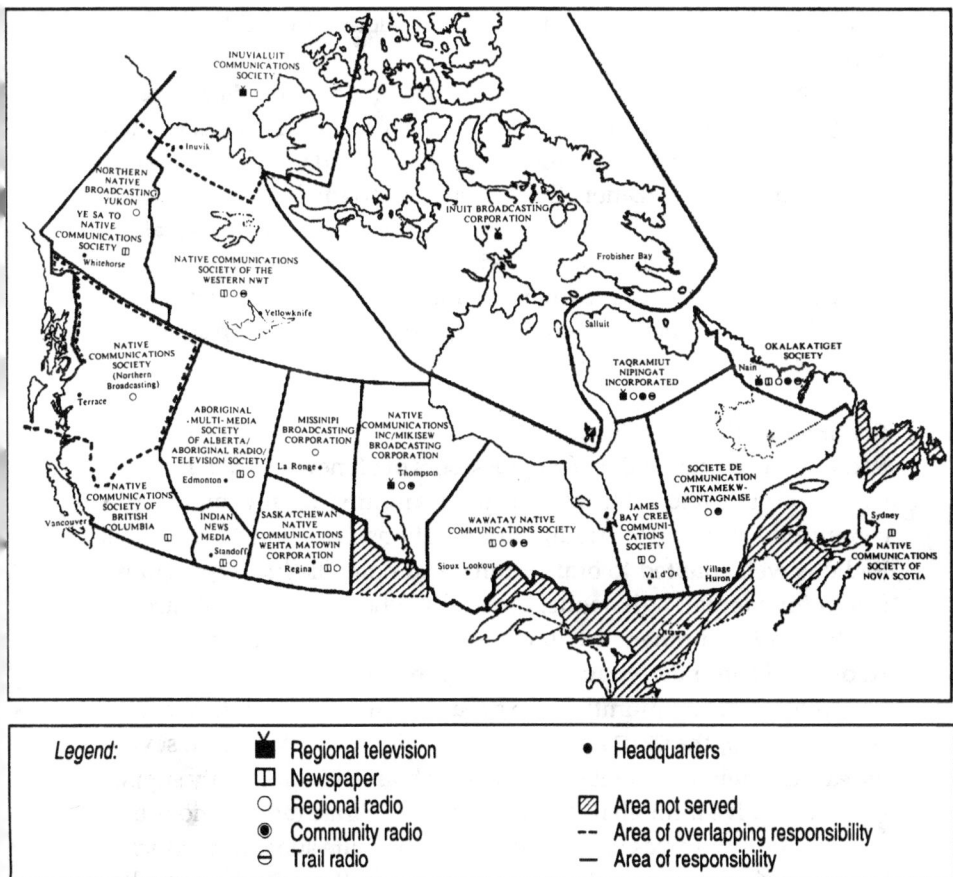

Legend:

Symbol	Description	Symbol	Description
Regional television		•	Headquarters
Newspaper			
○	Regional radio		
⊙	Community radio	▨	Area not served
⊖	Trail radio	--	Area of overlapping responsibility
		—	Area of responsibility

Source: Lougheed and Associates 8/86.

In 1989, Roth and Valaskakis celebrated the then-evolving TVNC as one of many initiatives in an improving communications picture. The $10 million satellite transponder is "dedicated exclusively to the distribution of Aboriginal television programming throughout Canada's North." TVNC President Ken Kane, head of Northern Native Broadcasting Yukon, said the system, which began operating in January 1992, will link all Aboriginal peoples in northern Canada. His vision for the system does not stop at the Canadian border; he said TVNC may eventually encompass the non-Canadian circumpolar North, to include Greenland, Alaska and Siberia (Kane, in Alia et al. 1990–91a).

On 8 July 1991, the Canadian Radio-television and Telecommunications Corporation (CRTC) held a public hearing to consider TVNC's application "for a Native television network in Northern Canada consisting of cultural, social, political and educational programming" (CRTC 1991). Throughout its development, TVNC has been praised by citizens, politicians and journalists. Several politicians said they look forward to this as an important resource in future elections.

TVNC will enhance, not replace, the native communication societies. The societies will continue to play a crucial role in northern election coverage. These regional societies cover all of Canada and are connected to an umbrella organization, the National Aboriginal Communications Society (NACS). Several of the societies cut or suspended publications and broadcast programming following federal budget cuts in 1990 and 1991, and in 1991, NACS moved its national headquarters from Ottawa to Lac La Biche, Alberta, to save money. The preceding map shows the societies as they stood before budget cuts.

Community Radio in the North
Radio has been called the most grassroots of all news media. It ranges from sophisticated international programming to informal single-community stations, including pirate stations, ham and CB networks. Radio is well adapted to oral cultures and nomadic life. It provides a forum for campaign dialogue, especially where some people are out on the land and others are in communities. In 1989 there were 139 Aboriginal community radio stations (Fox 1989).

Aboriginal community radio began in Inuit communities in 1961. A decade later, the CRTC licensed community radio stations in several Indian and Inuit communities. Volunteer labour and community support keep radio alive through fluctuating budgets. Pirate radio stations exist in some northern areas and are reputed to be quite successful. Much of the pioneering work was done by the Inukshuk Project, which resulted in the formation of the Inuit Broadcasting Corporation (IBC). IBC has

Table 3.1
Community radio in the North

Provinces	Number of stations	Territories	Number of stations
Quebec	42	Northwest Territories	45
Ontario	27	Yukon Territory	6
Saskatchewan	10		
Newfoundland	7		
Manitoba	2		

flourished and has been an important and highly creative part of northern communications. The following review derives from a qualitative analysis of the past three years of northern election coverage and a review of national coverage of Aboriginal issues and elections.

Northern Election Coverage: 1987–90
The survey of media elections coverage nationally reveals news headlines that underscore the growing importance of Aboriginal electoral participation:

- "NDP (Kenora–Rainy River) Winner Credits Heavy Native Support," (*Winnipeg Free Press*, 5 September 1984, 8);
- "Prince Rupert: Native Voters Hold the Key – If They Use It," (*Vancouver Sun*, 18 August 1984, E3);
- "Native Vote Could Influence (24) Ridings," (Halifax *Chronicle-Herald*, 18 August 1984, 12);
- "Micmacs Seek Political Clout: NS Aboriginal Peoples' Liberal Assn. to Hold First Meeting Today," (Halifax *Chronicle-Herald*, 16 February 1990, B1).

Moving from the national headlines to the text of news media coverage of Aboriginal and northern issues, we find that certain patterns emerge.

(1) Only nationally prominent leaders (e.g., Audrey McLaughlin, Ethel Blondin and Elijah Harper) merit coverage in national, regional or urban medias.

(2) Alberta Attorney General Dick Fowler offered an example of a missed opportunity to cover a significant *positive* issue: In November

1990, a land agreement granted Indian people over 100 000 acres. Despite the presence of several mainstream journalists at the signing in the Legislature, "the event and underlying issues got just a 'blurb' on CTV. On the same day, three cows escaped from the Premier's farm, and that non-event received significantly more coverage than the [land agreement]" (Hardie 1990, 4).

In another instance, a newspaper wire feature on Quaqtaq, Quebec, Mayor Eva Deer is so full of stereotypes one loses count. The politician portrait focuses on Deer as a female, an Inuk, and as a challenger of drugs, alcohol and men, in that order. The packaging of the story distorts it even further:

"Drug problem 'epidemic,' female Inuit mayor says" (Abramovitch 1990). In one line, the newspaper gratuitously identified the (Aboriginal) politician (Mayor Eva Deer) by gender, culture and negative subject (drugs). No one would suggest that people's problems, or politician's agendas, should be censored; but Aboriginal politicians and communities receive disproportionately negative coverage. Euro-Canadian communities and politicians are seldom covered in comparable ways.

(3) Northern and Aboriginal elections merit coverage when they directly affect concerns of southern Canadians.

(4) Northern topics are covered when southern economic development (oil or gas exploration, for example) or tourism is involved, that is, when southern Canadian, national or international interests are at stake.

(5) The standards expected of southern and international news coverage are not imposed on coverage of the North. I have lost count of the number of misspelled references to "Iqualuit" (Iqaluit) or some other variation. Countless news stories confuse and misuse Inuit (plural), Inuk (singular) and Inuktitut (the language). Yet reporters and editors are expected to learn preferred/accepted spellings of peoples everywhere outside the North.

(6) Northern electoral issues are covered in the South only when they fit into the boundaries outlined above.

The survey of press coverage of the most recent territorial and federal elections includes some exceptions to the above rules. The *Winnipeg Free Press* and *Calgary Herald* provided the broadest coverage of the urban dailies. Over the past four years, they covered First Nations campaign and election activities in detail. They interviewed Aboriginal leaders relatively often and showed Aboriginal participation in federal and Aboriginal governments. Both newspapers devoted most space to regional issues, but included national issues as well.[6]

The Montreal *Gazette* tended to concentrate on "fear and trouble" – crises before (and during) Oka and Kanesatake. Elections appear only where regionally based, with the exception of a couple of pieces on the NWT territorial election.[7]

The *Globe and Mail* preferred economic issues but moved steadily toward increased coverage of northern elections.[8] The *Toronto Star* rarely covered northern or Native issues unless they affected Ontario or Toronto. A notable exception was the Labrador Innu challenge of low-level flights and proposed NATO base, an issue followed by all major papers.[9]

All of the dailies covered the 1989 election in Yukon, especially Audrey McLaughlin's NDP leadership win. Other coverage was slim. The *Vancouver Sun* ran an occasional story on land claims, regional elections, etc. (e.g., Glavin 1990).

In general, the politicians and political workers interviewed were least critical of radio and most critical of television. They had harsh words about the quality of print coverage: many Aboriginal leaders remarked on ethnocentrism; fear of remote communities and Aboriginal people; ignorance of Aboriginal political priorities, traditions and values; and a tendency to assign low priority to Aboriginal issues.

Television was criticized for being largely absent. The lack of on-the-spot coverage and, in some cases, the unavailability of any television or print media are often connected to budget cuts or restrictions. Some Aboriginal newspapers and magazines on which candidates relied in previous elections are not expected to survive into the next election.

The widespread call for increased attention to literacy is undermined by the loss of print media in regions most affected by illiteracy. The chief electoral officer for Canada has stated that illiteracy "raises serious questions about the complexity of our voting procedures" (Canada, Chief Electoral Officer 1989, 47).

Communications II: Alternative Community Resources

Alternative communications are more highly developed in remote communities than in urban areas. People tend to drop by the store or band office daily, making bulletin boards a central rather than a marginal medium. In fact, in some ways, we might reverse the terms mainstream and marginal with respect to remote communities – when a daily or weekly newspaper arrives days or weeks late, bulletins faxed, phoned or radioed in are far more reliable news sources.

Bobbi Smith's earlier account of child-to-elder participation in Aboriginal politics identifies a tradition which continues in today's public meetings and informal gatherings. Meetings, feasts, potlatches and public events of all kinds are important – often central – communications media in northern Aboriginal communities.

Some mainstream media start as alternatives. The northern Ontario Wawatay Communications Society's broadcast programming began as a trail radio rental service to trappers out on the land; the small high-frequency transmitters formed an emergency communications system based in the communities.

In most communities in the northern provinces and territories, both old-fashioned and computer bulletin boards serve as primary, not supplementary, information sources. MacGregor (1989, 61) describes the transmission of crucial political information in northern Quebec during the James Bay Treaty negotiations: "[Inuk Senator] Charlie Watt was walking into the post office at George River when he noticed other Inuit gathered about a bulletin board, talking excitedly." News is posted at band offices, post offices, general stores, schools and other public places.

The Aboriginal cultural institutes are communication centres that could assist in elections education and translation. The Dene Cultural Institute (founded in 1985), affiliated with the Native Communications Society of the NWT and the Dene Nation, produces literature, educational and cultural programming.

The Avataq Cultural Institute has served northern Quebec Inuit from its Inukjuak headquarters since 1981. It sponsors conferences, educational programs, literature, archaeology and a place-names program; works with youth and elders; and is a potential base for electoral education forums. The Inuit Cultural Institute, in Arviat, provides similar programming, with an emphasis on language. It has produced dictionaries, oral histories and an annual elders conference.

As this discussion has suggested, the term alternative must be used with care. Especially where northern and Aboriginal communications are concerned, alternative does not mean marginal, unprofessional or inferior. Time after time, we see examples of innovative survival strategies that evolve into so-called mainstream communications – pirate stations that go "legit," bulletin boards that become newsletters, newsletters that become newspapers or magazines, and local newspapers or magazines that become regional, national or even international. Alternative media merit full attention and credibility. (European Canadians may recall their own oral town-crier–troubadour traditions.)

Communications III: Advertising

New CRTC policy set in September 1990 may offset some losses from the above-mentioned 1990 federal cutbacks to northern and Aboriginal news media and communication societies. At the same time, it may contribute to the development of greater independence, because Aboriginal radio stations are now permitted to earn advertising revenues; those without competitors are allowed almost unrestricted advertising – up to 250 minutes of sales spots per day (Langford 1990). The new policy permits extensive, sometimes virtually unlimited advertising on previously non-commercial radio stations (e.g., Native communications society stations). CHON-FM began broadcasting commercials soon after my arrival in the Yukon in September 1991. Not everyone was pleased about the program interruptions, but most people said the inconvenience was justified if it meant the station's survival.

Communications IV: Phone, Fax, Frustration: Special Needs of Northern Constituencies

Northerners are often more familiar with high-tech communications than southerners. Sophisticated computers have been commonplace in eastern Arctic adult education and other centres for years. Satellite dishes sit on ancient rocks in tiny settlements whose inhabitants still spend much of their lives on the land. At the 1989 Inuit Circumpolar Conference (ICC) General Assembly, in Greenland, Inuit Cultural Institute representatives demonstrated the direct translation program that changes English into Inuktitut syllabics.

Fax machines have caught on all across the North. "I think there is a fax machine in all but two communities in the western Arctic. These machines are ... sometimes the only way to get a voters list out of a community ... I hope that new legislation would allow faxed documents to be accepted as if they were originals. This would also make it easier for people to send proxy forms ... and other important election documents to the Returning Officer" (Cairns 1990). Cairns and several others also recommend using telephone answering machines for easier after-hours access.

Facsimile mail (fax) has become a fact of northern life. Phone lines are the most reliable and least fallible means of reaching other communities and the "Outside":

> The consensus is that electoral machinery has not kept pace with modern elections innovations such as facsimile mail (fax), and that its allowed use in the voting infrastructure would be helpful to Aboriginal, remote and underserved communities. (Alia et al. 1990–91b)

> It's amazing ... it has just sort of mushroomed and the smallest community has a fax machine to the point where some people seldom use

the mails ... any more. You sort of wonder how you existed without it. (Mayer 1990)

Fax machines in municipal offices, post offices and other public places could help candidates distribute political information. Legalizing faxed documents would save time and expense and eliminate missed deadlines and the frustration of potential candidates and voters, unnecessary travel and air fares. Although technically illegal, fax is already in use for northern electoral emergencies. A recent episode clarifies the urgent need for reform. In October 1991, "Wicked winter storms forced some snowbound travellers to send in their ballots by facsimile machine Tuesday in the Northwest Territories' election." Most voting districts experienced blizzard conditions that "stranded planes and voters in an otherwise uneventful political race." Rankin Inlet voters stranded in Whale Cove voted by proxy from fax machines; other voters in the Western Arctic did the same (Canadian Press 1991b, 1,2).

Northerners use fax as an alternative to costly air freight and slow postal service.[10]

Yet the fax is not problem-free. Some northern communities have only a single telephone, which means adding fax to already overused facilities. And fax machines can be used only where there is phone service. All northern communities have some phone service, but phones are often scarce (Germain 1991). To use facsimile mail regularly, Elections Canada would need to study each community's resources. However, Hamilton (1990) and others say fax machines won't work for sending secret ballots.

These reservations notwithstanding, the creative possibilities are enormous, and the ways of using facsimile in campaigns and elections barely explored. The technology can provide ways to economize on funds, personnel and time – all crucial to northern electoral politics.

The following sketches are intended to provide an overview of Aboriginal campaigns and communications in the provincial and territorial North.

NORTHERN PROVINCES AND TERRITORIES

I. The Provincial North

A particular climate permeates campaigns and media coverage of the provincial North: "The ... Canadian provincial north, is a truly forgotten area. It has little or no place in the public consciousness ... There has never been any general agreement on the territorial extent of the provincial north" (Weller 1983, 480).

The northern regions have more in common with the Yukon and the NWT than with the southern regions of their own provinces. Their citizens perceive themselves to be Northerners. As in the territories, campaigns are often based more on individual candidates and issues than on parties. Media coverage varies widely, depending on geographic, cultural and economic conditions.

Northern Ontario

Those interviewed in Northern Ontario cited the need for improved coverage of northern issues and Aboriginal concerns and political campaigns. As in many other regions, television coverage gets the lowest marks. Politicians, citizens and political workers cite "very poor service," especially in smaller communities. One region has no regional TV at all.

Radio got the highest rating. Candidates said print media were responsive and fair, except for one community paper with a favoured candidate. In general, election coverage was seen as fair and adequate, with the following criticisms and suggestions for improvement.

Politicians and political workers said journalists should be more aware of northern issues, particularly those affecting Aboriginal peoples. Media coverage is "never specific enough." Campaign and other news coverage needs more depth, more analysis and less sensationalism. As one person put it, northern and Aboriginal news should be "treated as part of the national political agenda."

One suggestion is a daily or weekly election section in newspapers, focused on Northern Ontario issues, with a reporter assigned to cover Aboriginal issues for each campaign. More reporters are needed, especially at election time.

National broadcast media should send people to remote areas "to learn what politicians must deal with" – travel by snowmobile or air, cold, fog, delays and breakdowns.

The quality of coverage is not the only issue. Access is sometimes a greater concern. With most reserves accessible only by air, informants said "news often doesn't get out."

They cited the "moccasin telegraph" as the most prominent of alternative communications. People expect candidates to come in person, but riding size makes it impossible. With no contact between elections, it is hard to learn who candidates are. There were no community meetings or all-candidate meetings. Useful alternatives include bulletin boards in stores and band offices.

An Aboriginal community leader said reporters don't come often enough or quickly enough (Thorbes 1990).

Northern Alberta, Manitoba and Saskatchewan

None of those interviewed recalled specific problems arising out of the 1988 federal election, but there was general dissatisfaction with the level of coverage. Aboriginal politicians at the federal and provincial levels agreed that the region has enough Aboriginal publications. Aboriginal newspapers do "a good job of raising awareness and covering issues given the constraints they are under."

The radio program "Native Perspectives" originates from Lac La Biche, Alberta, and is broadcast via satellite, broadcast again on FM transmitters and re-broadcast yet again over CBC television in the morning for two hours before television programming begins (Germain 1991). The program was praised, but "one program two hours per day is not enough to cover Native issues."

As one interviewee commented, "There are problems getting the mainstream media to cover Native issues adequately. During elections, provincial and federal issues of concern to Indians are put on the table, but these are never the leading issues" (Hardie 1990, 5). Several people mentioned the need to educate journalists to challenge stereotypes and "apprehension about visiting the communities ... unfounded fears for their safety" (ibid.).

Saskatchewan Indians say mainstream media "tend to stress the tragedies and ignore the triumphs." Erratic communications networks are a continuing problem for campaigns. Non-Aboriginal journalists should use Aboriginal sources in their stories more often. Development of Aboriginal newspapers and news networks should be a priority. More news should be provided in Aboriginal languages.

Underfunding is the primary obstacle confronting Aboriginal broadcasters. Media need enough funding to "hire reporters to track candidates and issues" and provide an adequate broadcast distribution system. The *Saskatchewan Indian*, a major Indian newspaper with nationwide influence, folded after 1989–90 government funding cuts. Until it restarted in the summer of 1991, there was "no single organ that reaches and unifies the Indian community." *Native Network News* (a monthly Alberta newspaper published in Edmonton) is owned by the Métis Nation and has been published independently since 1988. It circulates 15 000 copies to 60 000 readers in Alberta, Saskatchewan, BC, Yukon and the NWT and is entirely self-supporting.

Especially outside major cities, publications have a hard time surviving. They now depend on advertisers, and some find that Aboriginal publications are not considered viable places to advertise.

Saskatchewan's 60 000 Métis, represented by the Métis Society of Saskatchewan, kept the newspaper *New Breed* alive after federal funding cuts by going monthly. The circulation is approximately 10 000.

Informants in this region said there are too few Métis politicians (among them Saskatchewan MLA Keith Goulet). A First Nations politician predicted an increase in mainstream media coverage as the number of Aboriginal politicians increases. He predicts that Aboriginal politics will move from basic administrative issues to larger concerns, such as the maintenance of Aboriginal languages and cultures.

Some reserves in this region cannot get broadcast news because they don't have cable service; few stations are available. Most Aboriginal communities are accessible by road (four in Saskatchewan are not).

Informants said the new TVNC network linking CKNM–Yellowknife, CKNR–Terrace, British Columbia, CHON-FM–Whitehorse and CFWE–Lac La Biche would probably improve the picture. They emphasized the importance of encouraging Aboriginal people to use the service fully.

Northern Quebec

Most people found 1988 campaign and election coverage inadequate – "not much more than publication of the results." The 1988 election was covered primarily from CBC Montreal, one Aboriginal leader said, adding that there was "very little [election] coverage on CBC North [focused on] northern issues." Another watched "Newswatch" or "The National" and avoids CBC North's Cree programming "because of the inaccuracy ... and the biased approach of reporting the issues."

An Aboriginal politician expressed more general detachment from the electoral system and said "there isn't a wide interest among northern Native people in federal or provincial politics ... many don't care about who is in power because their concerns are never met anyway." This politician said that Quebec has never had an Aboriginal member of the Quebec National Assembly. Arsenault observed that the politician "spoke of the Canadian political process ... as if he were describing the government of a foreign land. In many respects, this is the overwhelming response I received during the study: 'Their politics is not our politics' " (Arsenault 1990, 2).

CBC North's Cree programming is "not sufficient" and "often bears little resemblance to the realities of the communities." Politicians and other leaders want more "analytical programming ... we only have information services; we [need] tools to criticize [people] or issues." They repeated the complaint heard in every northern region – that coverage of northern and Aboriginal news is crisis oriented.

Most Aboriginal politicians, political workers and journalists interviewed were fluent in several languages (Arsenault 1990, 8). A problem raised in the western provinces and the Yukon, as well as in Quebec, is that satellite television has brought in predominantly U.S. programming.

Not all Canadian programming is relevant. The only Canadian coverage northern Quebec residents receive is British Columbia Television (BCTV) and CBC. A politician complained that "there is little or hardly any coverage related to issues in northern Canada or ... northern Quebec," because most comes up from CBC Montreal rather than down from CBC North.

People did not feel that media access or quality of coverage have improved over the past few years. One leader was concerned that "the people do not know the different political parties in the North ... [or] understand the political issues the parties are talking about [or] ... the platform of the various parties. There's a very serious language barrier in Northern Quebec between the organizations and Native people."

Language and culture barriers were a recurring theme. "In my own riding, my choice is always between candidates who do not even speak my own language ... do not know our people, our culture, our communities, our needs or our problems" (Coon Come 1990).

As in other regions, television came in for the most criticism. But one politician wanted to turn it around. He said most northern Quebec people "love to watch television and they can sit for hours in front a television set ... if we can get access to that television set I believe that most people will be up to date on what is happening" in elections and political events.

Chief Billy Diamond called for a specifically northern, comprehensive media literacy program, "a thorough Northern Education Program in the North concerning ... how issues can be solved by using the media, and how you can tell your story by telling the media" (Diamond in Alia et al. 1990–91a).

The territory's vastness makes it impossible for politicians to visit communities or for either mainstream or alternative media to cover the issues adequately.

Labrador

Labrador seems to have a "tightly knit Aboriginal community" that encompasses several smaller communities. It was easy to locate political candidates and Aboriginal journalists, because communities seemed in touch with one another. Although communities and communications are often separate, there has been cooperation between Innu and Inuit around social and political issues of mutual concern. There were complaints about the continuing misidentification of Innu (Indian) and Inuit people.

There are 20 hours a week of Aboriginal radio programming in Inuktitut and English, distributed via a community FM radio network, and five hours a week carried on CBC Labrador.

An extensive "Trail Radio" network of HF and VHF radios, located in each north coast community, provides the only two-way emergency communication service available to hunters and fishers in remote locations. This kind of service is seen elsewhere in remote regions and often evolves into more conventional broadcast service. (See the section on community radio in the Yukon.)

The television magazine *Labradorimiut* (People of Labrador) is broadcast two-and-a-half hours a month by IBC and CBC North to over 40 communities in the NWT, northern Quebec and Labrador and via the Atlantic Satellite Network to Atlantic Canada. Its distribution will expand across the North, over TVNC.

Print media are limited. The Nain area receives the *Globe and Mail* "a week late, if at all." The local newspaper was cut by half after February 1990 budget cuts. "Labrador Native people feel left out of mainstream communications" (Arsenault 1990). They want more media, better educated journalists and candidates, and a better educated and a more involved electorate.

Communities have either road or air access and good inter-community (including alternative) communications networks. There is poor access to media and information from outside Labrador.

Northern British Columbia

Northern British Columbia was the most difficult region for researchers to access. Korbin found "many northern Aboriginal communities, with few effective links, [and no apparent] comprehensive communications structures. I found it very difficult to get names of local, provincial or federal politicians" (Korbin 1990, 1).

Media access is adequate, but there is a lack of connection with other Aboriginal communities in northern British Columbia. Most Aboriginal communities have broad access to radio stations, CBC, the *Vancouver Sun* and the *Province*, and local weekly or daily newspapers. Mainstream media cover Aboriginal issues, but scarce funds inhibit development of Aboriginal media. The absence of an Aboriginal communication network has many causes, including diversity of communities, interests, problems and geography.

A candidate in the 1988 federal election felt that running as an independent led to less media coverage than the campaigns of party-affiliated candidates.

We interviewed representatives of several Aboriginal friendship centres and obtained a picture of great diversity and inconsistency. People in Fort Nelson, BC, have broad access to mainstream broadcast media – CBC North, BCTV, CITV Edmonton, and an array of print media, including The *Fort Nelson News, Vancouver Sun* and Vancouver *Province.* People were satisfied with Aboriginal media coverage, particularly *Native Network News.*

Larry Guno, an Aboriginal MLA, is from the Terrace, BC area. Terrace is a production centre for Northern Native Broadcasting. Of the two local newspapers, *Prince Rupert This Week* provides "much better coverage of Native issues." Mainstream television and radio is abundant, along with radio and television programming from Northern Native Broadcasting.

Although Chetwynd's population is 50 percent Aboriginal, Aboriginal people have no control over or input into local media and "generally feel very left out." They have "very limited knowledge about other northern Native communities, or politicians, in BC" (Korbin 1990, 3).

The Provincial North: Conclusions

In general, the quality and quantity of news coverage is inadequate throughout the provincial North. Non-Aboriginal media must be willing and able to provide adequate campaign and election coverage of remote and Aboriginal communities. More education is needed to inform non-Aboriginal and non-northern journalists about the politicians, constituents, issues and communities. Access to particular media varies greatly, but there is near-universal protest against inadequate television access and coverage. The narrow picture is better than the broad one. Several communities have extensive media access, but media are often based outside the North, for example, the widely available programming from Detroit and Chicago through cable networks (Canadian Press 1991a).

Elections Canada can make more creative and extensive use of alternative communications media and linkages, including conventional and computer bulletin boards, fax machines, trail and community radio, public meetings, and local and regional newsletters.

II. The Territorial North

The Northwest Territories
The NWT's Aboriginal-majority legislature of 24 Independents, who make decisions by consensus, is unique among Canada's governments. The eastern NWT has a substantial Inuit majority. The western NWT has a sizable population of Dene, Métis and Inuvialuit (western Inuit). Yellowknife is nearly 90 percent non-Aboriginal.[11]

The Assembly meets in nine official languages – Chipewyan, Cree, Dogrib, English, French, Gwich'in (Loucheux), Inuktitut, North Slavey and South Slavey. In setting no time limit, the question period that follows legislative debate differs from those in the provinces and Yukon. The House has a full committee system but is not divided along party lines. Despite pressures to assimilate into the party system, NWT politicians continue to support the current structure. In a 1990 survey of NWT MLAs, 19 of 24 opposed "having political parties involved in NWT politics" (Native Press, 1990, 3).

Liberal MP Jack Anawak (who as a federal politician does have a party affiliation) said that the "Inuit vote is based on personality – individuals, not parties" and that campaigning must be "personalized" (Roth 1991b). Even where parties do enter the picture, they are not treated with the reverence or attention to boundaries that characterizes southern politics.

Northern people "need more information, a lot quicker." Aboriginal politicians say *Nunatsiaq News* (published in Iqaluit and based in the eastern Arctic) has done the most consistent job of covering campaigns and elections but that coverage remains "limited." Television again gets low ratings, as TV is not at all effective in campaigns. There should be more TV coverage for individual candidates, plus purchased air time (Roth 1991a).

One candidate said the (central) Keewatin region needs a newspaper of its own because it is caught between the eastern (Iqaluit-based) *Nunatsiaq News* and the Fort Smith *Journal*.

Radio is the universal news medium, especially where Inuktitut programming is available. Radio was widely used in the 1988 federal election, when each candidate received about five minutes of air time in each language (English and Inuktitut).

Conflicts among radio stations can undermine Aboriginal coverage. Yellowknife radio station CJCD "fought tooth and nail" against the licensing of Aboriginal radio station CKNM (Thorbes 1990).

The Inuit Broadcasting Corporation (IBC) provided candidate access and other programming. As of May 1991, IBC was broadcasting four to four-and-a-half hours a week over CBC, cut back two hours from 1990. Two hours a week of programming from Taqramiut Nipingat Inc. (TNI, northern Quebec) is carried by IBC over CBC, and there is a half-hour every other week of programming from Labrador (Roth 1991a).

Language access is an important concern. Eastern Arctic candidates say many of their constituents speak only Inuktitut and rely on translation (Smythe 1990). In May 1991, Canadian Airlines acknowledged the importance of information access by introducing in-flight safety and other messages in seven Aboriginal languages. The system of providing tapes on request could be a useful model for Elections Canada.

Candidates in the eastern Arctic say "visiting communities is very important." During the 1988 election, two of them visited 20 to 30 communities each. Many Aboriginal candidates say they are more comfortable talking to people "face to face" than on radio or television. One said poor media coverage was the reason he had to visit each community. More effective use of media would probably result in lower travel costs.

Lack of travel funds was the principal issue cited by NWT journalists and political leaders. They said mainstream media coverage would improve if journalists travelled more (Thorbes 1990). *Press Independent* editor Lee Selleck agreed that travel is important, especially during elections, but said his newspaper's near-70 percent budget cut makes travel impossible.

Selleck would like media organizations to sponsor cross-cultural workshops for Aboriginal and non-Aboriginal journalists. Elections Canada might consider becoming involved in this kind of project.

Among the criticisms levelled at television were "too little background to stories" and "oversimplification," leading journalists to fall into "stereotypical traps." NWT-based media are preferred to most national coverage of northern and Aboriginal issues.

Inter-cultural cooperation and more frequent publication are two positive outcomes of post-cutback northern journalism. Pressured by funding shortages, the *Press Independent*, originally a Dene paper, is working more closely with the Inuvialuit newspaper *Tusaayaksat* to share coverage in communities shared by Dene and Inuvialuit. This development could contribute to better relations among peoples who might become co-citizens of a new western NWT, with the advent of the NWT division and the creation of the Inuit homeland, Nunavut.

The Yukon Territory

The following discussion offers a more in-depth profile, based on my four-month residence in the Yukon.

The Yukon is home to 30 000 people, 21 000 of them in Whitehorse. The small territory has had a large impact on Canadian politics. It has produced a national party leader, a landmark coalition of Aboriginal people (the Council for Yukon Indians (CYI)), a prominent premier and numbers of political breakthroughs. Among Canada's northern citizens, Yukoners are perhaps the least alienated from federal politics.

I mistakenly assumed that access to Yukon communities would be much greater and travel much less costly than in other northern regions, because all but Old Crow are accessible by road. I learned that costs are often as high and scheduling as complex as for fly-in regions. Roads are dangerous or impossible to negotiate, especially for the uninitiated and especially in winter. And winter in the Yukon corresponds roughly to mid-fall through spring in the south, encompassing most campaign/elections periods.

In three-and-a-half months, I was able to visit most, but not all, Yukon communities. Complicating factors included politicians' schedules; weather; road access; vehicle availability; limited bus, van and airline schedules; and accommodation – not all communities have overnight facilities. (Billeting and room sharing remain common across the North.)

Before trade and commerce entered the Yukon, around 1840, it was populated by Indians and Inuvialuit. Today, Inuvialuit live only in the western NWT, some just over the Yukon border. The 1896 Klondike Gold Rush led to the creation of the Yukon Territory; parliamentary government got its start in 1909, with the first all-elected council.

The Yukon Indian Advancement Association, founded in the late 1960s, included non-Indian supporters. It was replaced in 1970 by the Yukon Native Brotherhood. The Yukon Association of Non-Status Indians went its own way. The Brotherhood focused on comprehensive claims and then (15 November 1973) brought non-status Indians in and took the name Council for Yukon Indians, Canada's first coordinated movement of status and non-status Indians (Alia et al. 1990–91a).

Political parties entered the Legislative Assembly in 1978, marking a turning-point from federal to strong territorial government. Chief Electoral Officer and Assembly Clerk Patrick Michael reports that since 1978, there have been two general elections and four by-elections, with only one win by an independent (Michael 1987, 7).

Although few candidates run as Independents, the Yukon tolerates diversity and party crossovers. Tatchun MLA Danny Joe, former Selkirk First Nation Chief, has been a candidate for the Progressive Conservative party, for the Liberal party, and, most recently, for the New Democratic Party.

Yukon elections "tend to be marked by close results," one explanation for high voter participation. Electoral district boundaries were redistributed in 1978, creating at least three Aboriginal-majority districts. One reason was the sudden influx of non-Aboriginal workers on the Beaufort Sea and Dempster Highway projects (Michael 1987, 15).

According to Michael, Yukon Indian people were "largely forgotten" in early territorial politics. The first Aboriginal candidates ran in the 1974 general election; the first Aboriginal candidates to win joined the Assembly in 1978. Since then, the numbers have increased to the present total of five Aboriginal MLAs, including Assembly Speaker Sam Johnston.

Johnston, a member of the Teslin First Nation, brings his Tlingit heritage into the parliamentary system. He wears a Tlingit ceremonial robe at the start of each week's session and uses decision-making principles honed in 14 years as Teslin Chief in his role as speaker.

Communications in the Yukon   Radio dominates the picture. Its long history began with the Yukon Telegraph, whose Dawson City–Whitehorse line (with Atlin, BC, a central point) was "the last wilderness undertaking of its kind in North America, costing [in 1900] several millions of dollars, but serving the nation for almost half a century" (Lawrence 1990, 40). The primary stations are CHON-FM (the radio service of Northern Native Broadcasting Yukon, – NNBY), which reaches virtually all communities, and CBC, which combines southern and northern programming. CHON-FM provides weekly reports from most communities and occasional remote broadcasting.

Most media-related complaints from politicians and community leaders were about scarce or poor television election coverage. Audrey McLaughlin and Tony Penikett both mentioned inadequate television resources (Alia et al. 1990–91a; 1990–91b). There is a closed parliamentary channel, with daily broadcasts from the Yukon Territorial Assembly (while the Assembly is in session). CBC-TV's broadcast day is southern based, with short bursts of CBC's "Focus North" (news and features) and Northern Native Broadcasting, Yukon's NEDAA-TV (public affairs, features). Television programs come via satellite from British Columbia, Chicago and Detroit – cities whose news and time zones are out of sync with the Yukon day.

Whitehorse has two newspapers, the *Whitehorse Star* and the *Yukon News*. The latter does more territory-wide coverage and is distributed more widely in the communities.

The 1991 suspension of *Dannzha'* magazine (which evolved from *Yukon Indian News*) and its summer edition *Shakat* left a huge gap, with no Aboriginal print media in the Yukon except for community newsletters, which surface and disappear according to time, energy and funds. Former editor Doris Bill says Ye Sa To (which sponsored the magazine) was the least-funded of all Native communication societies. "All I want to be is a journalist, and I keep having to be a lobbyist," she said just after the magazine folded. A few months later, *Dannzha'* was reborn on a more modest scale, as a twice-monthly newspaper, still sponsored by the Ye Sa To communication society.

Community newsletters such as the *Pelly Button* remain the dominant print media in Yukon First Nations communities. Some are excellent; but the nature of their production lives makes them unreliable.

They are usually produced by volunteers who work full-time at other jobs. One editor has the equivalent workload of two full-time jobs in addition to the work of hunting and trapping (Alia et al. 1990–91a). Election coverage is likely to be a major casualty of the Aboriginal print deficit.

My four-month Yukon stay revealed a surprising feeling of community among diverse and remote groups of people. Figure 3.3

Figure 3.3
Map of Yukon Territory with communities visited

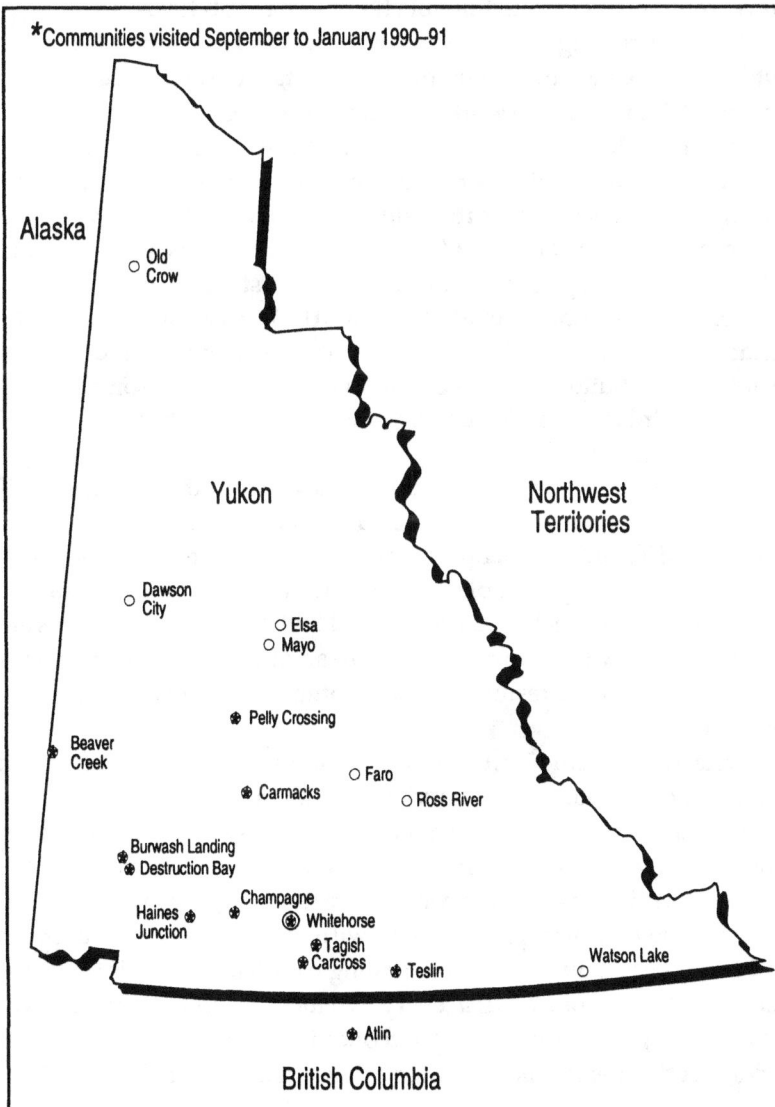

and notes on the communities visited are intended to flesh out the campaign/communication picture.

Yukon Community Sketches   Burwash Landing, with a population of 83 (most of them members of the Kluane Tribal Council), has its own newsletter. Council Director Florence Sparvier revived the newsletter because "people are too far out and can't get information." She says many people don't trust Indian Affairs and want their own information source.

Besides the newsletter, "Burwash people rely on CHON-FM." They read *Alberta Indian News* and other publications available in the council office, but radio is the medium of choice (Alia et al. 1990–91a).

In Pelly Crossing, 250 members of the Selkirk First Nation (Northern Tutchone) have their own bi-monthly newsletter, the *Pelly Button*, edited by Jerry Alfred, who also works full-time in land claims. The newsletter is delivered each month to every mailbox in the community. Pelly Crossing has a highly developed information network. People read the *Yukon News*, occasionally the *Whitehorse Star*, and the newsletter. "Everyone listens to CHON-FM," to which Ella Harper, who is also band office receptionist, phones in a weekly newscast.

Television stations include CBC, CBS (U.S.), BCTV and ITV. The MLA sends information to each home and also posts it in the band office, a beautiful new building with a couple of attractive hotel rooms for visitors. Other information is posted at the school, store, band office and Yukon College branch.

Apart from the weekly radio feed, news from the community is scarce – newspapers don't take regular news from Pelly.

Most of Teslin's 430 people are members of the Teslin First Nation, descendants of Tlingit people who moved from the Alaska and British Columbia coast. Chief David Keenan said that "a lot of First Nations are switching to new [government] structures," and that, following a decision three years ago, Teslin is the only community with a traditionally appointed chief.

Keenan said radio is the dominant medium, and "NEDAA (TV) and CHON-FM do a good job – interviews with chiefs, discussions of the issues. CBC Northern Service makes local news available – morning, evening. Land claims is the main thing and it's getting covered."

What's missing is regular community news: "Community newsletters are time-consuming; they go off with great zeal and fizzle. Teslin had a newsletter, but it's not functioning now. There's a print gap. We used to get *Shakat* or *Dannzha'* every two months but their budget was slashed. We get the *Yukon News* and once in a while, the *Alberta Indian News*, but the media's not versatile" (Keenan in Alia et al. 1990–91a).

The only road to Atlin, British Columbia, is through the Yukon. Just over the border, Atlin is included with the Yukon because of its unique status. Its 400 people are Taku River Tlingit First Nation and non-Aboriginal. A small community on a huge lake, it is the most north-westerly town in British Columbia. Among the residents are many artists. Mail comes three times a week on a van that takes passengers (such as me) if there's room. As is the case with ground traffic, flights go through Whitehorse. There are helicopter and fixed-wing charters, also through the Yukon. Going anywhere is costly. "It costs more to travel in our own province than to go to Ottawa and back, or Hawaii" (Alia et al. 1990–91a).

Atlin's identity is split between British Columbia and Yukon. People say they feel part of the Yukon, but "BC won't let us join the Yukon. We tried. BC won't let us go. But we get all our services from the Yukon" (Alia 1990). Some say Aboriginal people have little interest in politics outside their own community.

The telephone system exemplifies the complicated double status. "We pay both BC and Yukon phone companies – it comes in on one bill, but there are two sets of wires! All our doctors and lawyers are in Whitehorse. And most people move when their kids get high school age. Most of them go to Whitehorse" (Alia et al. 1990–91a). The BC government gives families subsidies to send high-school-age students to public or private schools in southern BC or Whitehorse. The public high school in Whitehorse maintains a dormitory for students from Atlin and remote Yukon communities.

Political campaigns are difficult. One person said, "The BC government sends flyers, but there's little campaigning." Another person said, "They don't listen to us; most band members could basically care less," referring to the Taku River First Nation, which has its own newsletter.

Federal funding arrives through Yukon, not British Columbia. Government Agent Fred Jenkins says, "the Whitehorse papers don't cover Atlin except if there's controversy." People tend to share news-papers – the *Vancouver Sun* when available or the *Edmonton Journal*.

Elections information is "never on the media. It comes through this office," says Jenkins. There are news releases on the counter, but people must go into the office to read them.

People say better media coverage would not do much to change voting patterns. After recent boundary changes, the MLA is even farther away than before – a reason many give for not voting. Two customs posts have absentee voters. "Getting them on the voters' list means a 500 mile trip. People don't see the point in voting in BC elections or federal. They don't feel their interests are represented" (Alia et al. 1990–91a).

Old Crow is the northernmost Yukon community, reachable only by air and vulnerable to ice, fire and flood. In the summer of 1990, the entire community was airlifted to Inuvik when forest fires came too close to homes; in spring 1991, floods threatened another evacuation. Most of the 270 people are members of the Vuntut Gwich'in First Nation.

Everyone says Old Crow is the key community at election time. Former commissioner and *Yukon News* editor Doug Bell recalled that in the last territorial election, Old Crow was "the giant-killer. We had all the votes in. It was tied 7–7 between the PC and NDP. We couldn't get Old Crow on the phone. I was still (Yukon) Commissioner. We got the Old Crow vote from a ham radio operator in Alaska" (Bell in Alia et al. 1990–91a). The ham operator was said to have picked up the results from a plane flying over and radioed them to the Whitehorse airport. Not without reason does Bell call ham operators "the real innovators." As noted above, the Old Crow vote is close to 100 percent in federal and territorial elections. "There's a mystique about Old Crow; it's famous. People Outside know about it" (Alia et al. 1990–91a).

All roads lead to Whitehorse; flights and buses connect with Alaskan cities and Vancouver; in summer, the White Pass and Yukon Railway is an alternate route to Skagway, Alaska (travellers must go a short way by bus to complete the connection). The population of 19 000 is both non-Aboriginal and Aboriginal (Kwanlin Dun First Nation).

Whitehorse is home to the Aboriginal and territorial governments – the Council for Yukon Indians and the Legislative Assembly. There are two newspapers and three radio stations (public – CBC, private – CKRW, and Native – CHON-FM); except for scant CBC North and NEDAA/TVNC (Native) programming, television is imported.

Whitehorse Star editor Jim Butler would like to cover elections more thoroughly. "We're a Whitehorse paper and only cover the bigger ridings outside Whitehorse. We do phone interviews with 99 percent of the candidates." Candidates are asked for photos, the only way many voters can see them.

Thinking ahead to the next federal election, he says: "I wish I could put somebody on the road. The only thing stopping me is money – hotels at $90 a night, food and gas – the worst – and salary. I can't free anyone from my present staff. To hire someone just to cover the campaign/election period – $600 a week plus around 600 miles a week plus food and lodging... we're a newspaper, but we're also a small business" (Butler in Alia et al. 1990–91a).

Coverage is not just thin, it is sometimes inaccurate. Premier Tony Penikett recalled that his landmark win was erroneously reported as a loss on CBC television.

The Territorial North: Conclusions

The northern territories and provinces experience most of the same problems of time, travel, climate, topography, language, culture and budget. However, there are significant differences in the ways various regions address those problems. It is easier for Yukon candidates to support one another; despite difficulty and inconsistent access, there is road access among all communities except Old Crow.

An eastern NWT candidate said community radio is more effective than CBC because candidates were able to get unlimited phone-in time – programs stayed on the air as long as callers kept phoning. This practice is seen in Aboriginal radio and television and connects with an oral tradition unlimited by non-Aboriginal broadcast principles of equal segments of limited programming. I observed the production of a Yukon television round-table in which participants (mostly politicians) were asked to return after lunch to continue a morning show because people were still phoning in and the discussion had not finished.[12]

There are other important lessons to learn from northern communications. The communications network (roads, telephone, fax, television, radio) is "better here in the Yukon than anywhere North of 50, except northern Alberta. Burwash Landing is better equipped than Port Severn, Ontario" (Alia et al. 1990–91a).

One reason for the advanced state of northern communications is that the North's extreme need makes it an ideal place to experiment (e.g., the Inukshuk Project and Television Northern Canada, TVNC). When needs aren't met in other ways, government goes in. When CBC lost funding and said it could no longer serve communities of less than 500, the Yukon government stepped in. "It's YTG [Yukon Territorial Government], not CBC, that gets CBC into the communities – funding, technology – 16 TV stations, 3 FM radio stations at Pelly Crossing, Stewart Crossing, Old Crow." The Government of the Northwest Territories supports 24 television rebroadcasts. "In 1976, they put a [satellite] dish at Teslin [Yukon]. It was not legal at the time, but YTG did it" (Alia et al. 1990–91a). The unofficial involvement of government, private citizens and communities in "illegal" communications activities (satellite dishes, pirate radio stations, etc.) belongs to the frontier mentality – the image of a North where benevolent "outlaws" hold sway. There is often a significant time lag between a project's outlaw origins and its legitimation in a system always struggling to catch up.

The inseparability of communications and transportation is underscored by new forms of communication that have transportation origins. The Yukon's UHF mobile radio communications network (600 mobile units, 26 repeaters) started for highway maintenance and the RCMP, and supported by Renewable Resources Yukon, is now in its second year.

CRTS community radio and television, also in the Yukon, was once the lifesaving "Timberline TV," set up to serve people out on the land. Today, it is one more resource for candidates and voters.

While Aboriginal politicians and community leaders say more materials and programs are needed, in all living languages, the specifics vary. Many do not want NWT language policy in Yukon: "I think the direction we'll go in, in Yukon, is more like the Chinese Canadian community. We will keep our languages for community support and our families. But seven different languages in this tiny territory – we can't afford to keep them official" (Alia et al. 1990–91a). The crucial concern is to avoid assimilation. Thus, party efforts to involve Aboriginal people have a down side: "We ... see a danger ... We don't want to be assimilated. We do want to work at a degree of integration which is suitable to us and to Canadian society" (Morin et al. 1990).

The following table represents an attempt to map some of the differences and similarities in the isolation experienced in the territories. It is intended as a sketch, to be developed further in future research. The general point is that Aboriginal people in the eastern NWT enjoy linguistic unity and access to print (although not to exclusively Aboriginal-run print media). They have greater difficulty accessing candidates than in Yukon, where roads facilitate access but Aboriginal print media are gone.

The western NWT – caught in the middle – is distinct but plays some mediative roles between Yukon and eastern NWT and shares assets and liabilities with both regions. The western NWT has linguistic diversity; yet most print media are in English. Its communities are divided between air and road access.

Isolation in the Territorial North

Yukon	Western NWT	Eastern NWT
7 Aboriginal languages	7 Aboriginal languages	1 Aboriginal language (Inuktitut)
sense of isolation is more mental than physical: roads and communications are in place, but language distances are bridged by English, and residents experience both northern and western remoteness from rest of Canada.	caught in the middle ...	sense of isolation is more physical than mental: there is linguistic unity, but remoteness is imposed by dependence on air travel, satellite communications.

It would be useful to develop more ways for the various northern regions to learn more from one another. Despite increased circumpolar cooperation among northern nations, there is a surprising amount of alienation among Canada's northern provinces and territories.

CONCLUDING SUGGESTIONS: STRATEGIES FOR IMPROVING CAMPAIGN COVERAGE AND SERVICE TO ABORIGINAL VOTERS, CANDIDATES AND JOURNALISTS

People from all regions and backgrounds addressed the difficulty of reaching northern and Aboriginal communities. Representatives of all political parties, in all regions, called for increased access and participation.

It is hard to avoid the conclusion that Aboriginal and other northern media should be strengthened and their services expanded. Despite considerable ingenuity applied to keeping media afloat and inventive alternative communication strategies, services have been lost to people who felt they were already receiving inadequate services.

The research indicates that remoteness is not in itself a cause of voter alienation and that not all Aboriginal people feel alienated from the electoral process. Alienation is a response to powerlessness and frustration – the feeling that one does not count and one's concerns are not addressed. Communications media figure importantly in this picture.

Atlin could be seen as a metaphor for Canada's north: isolated; caught among the several worlds of province (BC), territory (Yukon), federal government (Canada) and neighbouring government (Alaska/U.S.); and holding fiercely to its independence from all of them.

There is much to learn from the Yukon's high voter participation record – 77.97 percent in the 1989 general election. In Old Crow, it is far above the national average – 98.10 percent in the 1989 general election (Yukon, Chief Electoral Officer 1989, 3, 5). Here, all votes have mattered in election after election.

Improving media coverage is not likely to have a great impact on communities where voting is not highly valued and voter power is not a goal. Some First Nations leaders consider voting irrelevant; others, like Elijah Harper, see electoral participation and news media as means to address First Nations priorities.

Let us return briefly to the questions that guided this study.

How did Aboriginal people participate in the 1988 federal election and in other recent provincial and territorial elections? Participation varied considerably, according to region, culture, perception of voting power, geography, transportation, literacy and communication. Meetings, feasts and public events of many kinds attest to the importance of so-called alternative media, which help to connect traditional and federal governments. Participation and perception of involvement were affected by media that tend to cover nationally prominent leaders (Aboriginal and non-Aboriginal) and negative Aboriginal issues.

How do Aboriginal people view their participation in elections? The views range from suspicion to enthusiasm, depending on the perception of the usefulness of elections to Aboriginal communities. The cutbacks to media, particularly Aboriginal media, have been very demoralizing. Even where media survive, the human cost is great (understaffing, poverty, burnout). More media are needed – more relevant television access for candidates from a community or region (not just TV from Chicago, Detroit or Vancouver), and much more stable Aboriginal and non-Aboriginal northern print media, with journalists educated to understand the issues and candidates, and budgets allocated to provide adequate coverage.

The other major funding issue is the high cost of campaigning in the North. Representatives from all major parties supported the position that cost is a serious obstacle for potential candidates. Whether Aboriginal people see themselves as participants in the electoral system or as members of Aboriginal governments, the mood is cautious, impatient, suspicious.

High Aboriginal voter turnout is almost always linked to adequate media access and measurable influence, such as that seen in Old Crow, Yukon or the Eastern NWT. Such influence is sometimes measured in the number (and location) of Aboriginal politicians.

What is the nature and extent of news media access? Do media encourage or discourage participation of Aboriginal people? Not everyone thought these relevant questions. Those who say their votes don't count are unconcerned about campaign coverage. What everyone does care about is overall media treatment of Aboriginal people. Although there are exceptions, the general feeling is that media access for Aboriginal candidates is too limited.

Radio gets the best reviews. It is widely available and portable – important for people who live on the land. It provides a forum for campaign dialogue in which people in small, distant communities can participate. It is unintimidating, cost-effective, and – like northern and Aboriginal political styles – personal.

Television is weakest. Televised election coverage varies; in regions where the only TV available comes from distant communities such as Detroit and Vancouver, TV is irrelevant to the elections process.

Print coverage, when available, is better, but some regions are saturated, while others have no print at all. Journalists are criticized for "not doing their homework," for fearing Aboriginal people and remote communities, and for applying double standards to covering northern and southern, Aboriginal and non-Aboriginal issues. Most coverage of the North is a reflection of that in the South – issues are treated as if they matter only in relation to southern concerns. People say journalists must pay attention to the different perspectives of Aboriginal people, use Aboriginal sources in their stories and hire Aboriginal journalists. People want more analysis of campaign issues, more "tools to criticize." This is important for electoral literacy.

They want both better mainstream coverage and more news media of their own – Aboriginal news networks and continuity for Aboriginal newspapers, magazines and broadcast facilities. They want more coverage in Aboriginal languages.

Does the size and nature of northern constituencies mean that Aboriginal people in the North require greater media access? Unquestionably. People from every political party, every culture and every region said the same thing: It costs too much to campaign in the North.

The picture isn't all grim. Although everyone wants bigger travel and communication budgets and bigger budgets for media that cover the campaigns, there are ways to trim costs in other areas. Facsimile mail has the greatest potential for improving communication and lowering campaign costs. A fax is the ideal link between alternative media traditions and the future of northern campaigns. While no long-distance medium can replace the importance of face-to-face campaigning and on-the-spot campaign coverage, a fax can cut down on superfluous travel.

The other major medium of the future is satellite technology, which made a quantum leap with the coming of TVNC. To transmit a fax is possible almost everywhere; except for the occasional phone outage, it works (far more reliably than any other medium in bad weather).

It is no news that Canada's North is a vast region, sparsely populated. The next step is to use this knowledge to inform policy development. The North has a scattered electorate, who experience difficulties unique to the North as well as those found in low-income regions elsewhere (low employment, scarce housing, poor services). The difficulties inherent in remote, northern regions are compounded by problems specific to Aboriginal communities and compounded further by a funding climate that indicates less, rather than more, media access in future. Among the concerns that should be addressed are programs that undermine each other, such as the increased commitment to literacy promotion that coexists with a decreased commitment to print media. Better coordination could cut costs and improve service.

The research points to a number of issues that, it is suggested, should be considered by the Royal Commission on Electoral Reform and Party Financing. The following are suggestions for improving service to Aboriginal voters, candidates, political leaders and journalists in the northern territories and provinces.

Suggestions for Reform

1. Recognition by Elections Canada of the special needs of Aboriginal, northern and remote communities, including the following:
   a. Amending elections regulations to permit faxed documents. Fax machines are the least costly, fastest-moving, most widespread communication medium in the North.
   b. Recognizing alternative communications resources (community newsletters, conventional and computer bulletin boards, trail radio, fax and other "small" media) as valid media within the federal elections process.
   c. Making northern campaign budgets one-half greater than normal budgets to accommodate special conditions such as communication and transportation costs.
   d. Developing a policy that ensures full representation of Canadians, including Aboriginal people, in elections promotional materials.
   e. Developing an employment equity policy that ensures full representation of Canadians, including Aboriginal people, in the structure of Elections Canada.

2. Recognition of special educational needs, including the following:
   a. Production by Elections Canada of education packages for three target audiences – journalists, voters and politicians.
   b. Conferences for Aboriginal and non-Aboriginal journalists and politicians. Aboriginal leaders across Canada said politicians and journalists know little about Aboriginal concerns and fear visiting remote communities. One example of a low-cost conference that addressed these issues was developed in 1991 by the researcher and journalist Bud White Eye for students in the University of Western Ontario's Graduate School of Journalism. The now annual First Nations Intensive brought student journalists, First Nations leaders and journalists together for a day-long dialogue. The response was overwhelmingly positive, and results are being monitored.
   c. Innovative use of media for voter/candidate education, including television and radio short courses with Aboriginal teachers; education/information packages using low-cost audio and videotapes; elections learning modules using self-learning formats and existing

facilities (e.g., Yukon College, Arctic college and their distance education programs); and a travelling road show education package.

To capture the imagination and increase access to northern communities, this return to the days of circuit riding would use existing rail lines (Ontario's Polar Bear Express; the Churchill, Manitoba, run; the White Pass and Yukon route and others) and, where there are highways, buses. I suggest that Elections Canada run or rent rail cars and buses, much like the railroad school cars that once took education to northern Ontario communities over the Polar Bear route (Stamp 1974). The buses and rail cars can also serve as public meeting places and perhaps as mobile polls. Political parties might also consider this as a communications strategy.

3. Recognition of special needs in the areas of language and literacy, including
   a. translation of election materials into all languages in current use;
   b. expansion of Aboriginal language broadcasts;
   c. inclusion of in-use languages on ballots; and
   d. use of photo ballots.

General Principles   The following principles inform the measures suggested above: All materials should be prepared with Aboriginal people and cross-cultural principles in mind. They should be available in all northern languages, including the nine official NWT languages, Yukon Athabaskan and Tlingit languages, and all Aboriginal languages in current use in the northern provinces. I suggest reviewing the various instant-translation computer programs, some of which have been adapted to Aboriginal languages. The programs can accommodate different writing systems as well as direct translation. For example, an English/Inuktitut syllabics program is in use in the NWT.

When funding priorities are an issue, audiovisual materials should come first, printed materials second, the least costly to serve the broadest possible audience. Audiovisual media are accessible to those with limited reading skills (whether due to low literacy or language skills, visual impairment, etc.). We are told that in general, Canadians pay less attention to leaflets and brochures than to other media.

It is impossible to create an Old Crow out of every northern community. What is possible is to encourage and facilitate participation – through education, better media coverage, better multilingual/multicultural access, better transportation, and timing and funding that address the realities of northern campaigns and elections.

It is equally important to begin from the premise that learning and governing are two-way and that all programs should be developed with a spirit of cooperation and mutual concern. Aboriginal people should be involved in every step of the process.

ABBREVIATIONS

c.   chapter

R.S.C.   Revised Statutes of Canada

S.N.W.T.   Statutes of Northwest Territories

NOTES

This study was completed in June 1991.

The research team worked under challenging conditions; northern assistants were restricted by winter, transportation and weather. The Baffin interpreter had to work by phone; London researchers relied on phone, fax and courier lifelines. Fred Fletcher's guidance and encouragement were invaluable throughout the research process; Robert A. Milen provided crucial insight during the final stages. Bud White Eye coordinated the landmark First Nations Intensive, with Miles Morrisseau, Dan Smoke and Mary White Eye.

Warm thanks to Patricia Charlie (Old Crow/Whitehorse); Brian Eaton (Whitehorse); Clare Thorbes (London/Whitehorse); SharonAnne LaDue (Ross River/Whitehorse); Chitee Kilabuk (Pangnirtung, NWT); Adrienne Arsenault, Anthony Germain, Garth Hardie, Kelley Korbin, Dan Smythe, Karla Brun, Alan Chrisjohn, Judy LaForme, Lynn Larmour and Heather York-Marshall (London); the library staff of the Poynter Institute for Media Studies (St. Petersburg, Florida); Kathleen McBride; Carol Geddes (for friendship, insight and caribou stew at the eleventh hour); Jonleah Hopkins, Judith Merril, Dan Restivo, David Restivo, Lorna Roth, Shula Steinberg, and Gail Valaskakis, all of whom made it possible to live and work in two places at once.

Preliminary consultation with journalists covering the North took place in spring and summer 1990 under grants from the Social Sciences and Humanities Research Council and the University of Western Ontario.

1. The Yukon government leader adopted the title premier to emphasize the quest for status equal to that of the provincial leaders and the rejection of differential treatment for Canada's territories.

2. Note on language: Preferred usage varies among organizations and regions. Council for Yukon Indians prefers First Nations or Aboriginal. Indian is used widely in Yukon but is considered objectionable elsewhere. Although less favoured, Native is used widely. Indigenous appears internationally. In Canada, Inuit (singular Inuk, language Inuktitut) is preferred, except for

Inuvialuit. Inuit is used generically by Inuit Circumpolar Conference members, but Alaskans prefer Eskimo or the culturally specific labels, Yup'ik and Inupiat (Alia 1991).

The Athabaskan language Gwich'in (Gwitchin, Kuchin) is called Loucheux in some parts of the Yukon and NWT. Gwich'in, preferred by the Yukon Native Language Centre, is used, except in official titles (e.g., Vuntut Gwich'in First Nation).

3. The three were as follows: (1) Seventh Annual Inuit Studies Conference (including the researcher's participation on a panel on northern communications), in Fairbanks, Alaska, in August 1990; (2) Canadian Museums Association's "Literacy and the Museum: Making the Connections," in Ottawa, in November 1990; (3) "Ten Years After 'Jimmy's World': The Search for a Green Light Ethic," at the Poynter Institute for Media Studies, in St. Petersburg, Florida, 2–5 October 1990.

4. Although most sources no longer accept it, the 7 000 figure still appears in non-Aboriginal sources, such as the *NWT Data Book*.

5. To be precise, under the *Indian Act*, the enfranchisement process permitted Indian people to vote provided they ceased to be registered status Indians. Thus, they were allowed to vote if they declared themselves "full Canadians" and therefore non-Indians.

6. See, for example, *Winnipeg Free Press* 12 February 1987; 20 October 1989, 12; 15 October 1989, 1,4. See also *Calgary Herald* 16 January 1987, A1–2; 2 May 1989, B2; 10 December 1988, B6. The coverage ranges from specific issues (Lubicon claims) to band elections (Stoney band) to national concerns (NWT division/Inuit homeland).

7. See, for example, 31 August 1990, A4–7; 18 August 1990, A1; 15 May 1989, A4.

8. For example, 30 August 1990, A6; 26 October 1988, A8.

9. See, for example, *Toronto Star* 21 August 1989, A14.

10. Pro-fax proposals include those of the Iqaluit Chamber of Commerce (Kinnear 1990); and NDP representative Stephen Whipp, NWT (1990). Whipp recalls that a Tuktoyaktuk candidate "had to file his papers in Iqaluit ... thousands of dollars of air fare ... finally Elections Canada allowed him to fax it, but it took a lot of screaming ... and pushing to make that happen" (ibid.). Similarly: "I am not a salesman for a fax machine, but you ... look at the way you run elections and it is sort of 1932 technology" (Walsh 1990).

11. While it is not the task of this study to deal with broader issues, the long-discussed division of the NWT into two separate territories would have an enormous impact on campaigns, elections and media. In the east, a strong pro-division Inuit majority favours the creation of Nunavut ("our land" in

Inuktitut). The Western NWT is more complicated, because division would leave a territory-wide Aboriginal minority (Dene, Métis and Inuvialuit). Some have proposed calling the region Denendeh.

12. For a full discussion of the relationship between northern campaigns and the CBC, see Roth (1991a).

BIBLIOGRAPHY

Abramovitch, Ingrid. 1990. "Arctic Quebec: Drug Problem 'Epidemic', Female Inuit Mayor Says." *London Free Press.*

Adamson, Shirley. 1990. Interviewed by Ken Kane. Whitehorse: CHON-FM.

Alia, Valerie. 1990. "Northern News: Canada's Communication Cutbacks." Paper delivered to Seventh Inuit Studies Conference, Fairbanks, Alaska.

———. 1991. *Communicating Equality.* Whitehorse: Government of the Yukon.

Alia, Valerie, et al. 1990–91a. *Interviews and Participant Observation: Case Study of the Yukon.* Whitehorse.

———. 1990–91b. *Interviews: Politicians, Community and Organization Leaders, Journalists in Northern Provinces and Territories.* London.

Arsenault, Adrienne. 1990. "Summary of Research Findings." In Valerie Alia et al., *Interviews.* London.

Barkley, Dorothy. 1990. Testimony before the Royal Commission on Electoral Reform and Party Financing, 24 May, Yellowknife.

Bear, Leroy Little, Menno Boldt and J. Anthony Long, eds. 1984. *Pathways to Self-Determination: Canadian Indians and the Canadian State.* Toronto: University of Toronto.

Billingsley v. Northwest Territories (Attorney General), Northwest Territories Supreme Court, 17 October 1990.

Black, Martha. 1986. *Martha Black (My Seventy Years; My Ninety Years).* Edmonds: Alaska Northwest.

British Columbia. Elections BC. 1988. *Voter Registration and You.* Victoria: Queen's Printer for British Columbia.

———. 1990. *Election Reform in British Columbia: Making Voting More Convenient.* Victoria: Minister of Government Services.

Browne, Donald R. 1990. "Aboriginal Radio in Australia: From Dreamtime to Prime Time?" *Journal of Communication* 40 (Winter): 111–20.

Buckley, Andrea. 1991. "Grounded Planes Put Profits in Tailspin." *Yukon News,* 11 January.

Cairns, Rosemary. 1990. Testimony before the Royal Commission on Electoral Reform and Party Financing, 24 May, Yellowknife.

Calgary Herald. 1988a. "Candidate (Walking Wolf) Could Make History." 20 June.

———. 1988b. "Stoneys on Their Own (in Tribal Election)." 10 December.

Canada. *Broadcasting Act*, R.S.C. 1985, c. B-9.

———. *Cable Television Regulations*, SOR/86-831.

Canada. Chief Electoral Officer. 1987. *Report of the Chief Electoral Officer to the Speaker of the Legislative Assembly of the Northwest Territories.* Ottawa: Chief Electoral Officer of Canada.

———. 1989. *Report of the Chief Electoral Officer of Canada.* Ottawa: Minister of Supply and Services Canada.

Canada. Elections Canada. 1988. "Federal Election Information. If You're not on the Voters' List, There's Still Time to Get on It and Make Your Mark." (full-page advertisement, 1988 federal election.) *New Breed*, 20 October.

———. 1990. *Voting Statistics for the 1988 Federal Election.* Ottawa: Elections Canada.

Canada. Royal Commission on Electoral Reform and Party Financing. 1990. "Summary of Issues of Hearings from the Royal Commission on Electoral Reform." Ottawa.

Canadian Broadcasting Corporation (CBC). 1990. *CBC Northern Service.* Ottawa: CBC.

CBC Radio. 1982. *Yukon Territorial Election Coverage.* Whitehorse: CBC Northern Service. Tapes.

———. 1985. *Yukon Territorial Election Coverage.* Whitehorse: CBC Northern Service. Tapes.

Canadian Press. 1987a. "408 Voters Hold Key for NDP in Yukon." *Whitehorse Star*, 1 February.

———. 1987b. "Northern Schools Using Native Traditions to Win Back Students." *Whitehorse Star*, 5 December.

———. 1989. "Inuit Assembly Vote First Electoral Step on Road to Autonomy." *Globe and Mail*, 11 April.

———. 1990. "Saskatchewan Gov't Gives Former CBC Employees Money for Study." *Whitehorse Star*, 17 December.

———. 1991a. "Detroit TV Watched by Northern Residents." *Whitehorse Star*, 27 December.

———. 1991b. "Patterson Re-elected." *Whitehorse Star*, 16 October.

Canadian Radio-television and Telecommunications Commission. 1987. *Political Broadcasting – Complaints re: Free Time and Editorial Time Allocations.* CRTC Circular No. 334. Ottawa: CRTC.

———. 1988. *Federal General Election.* CRTC Circular No. 351. Ottawa: CRTC.

———. 1990a. "Notice: Native Broadcasting Policy." Ottawa: CRTC.

———. 1990b. "Notice." *News North,* 1 October.

———. 1991. *Public Hearing.* (TVNC). 8 July. Published in *Nunatsiaq News,* 31 May 1991.

Canadian Radio-television and Telecommunications Commission. Committee on Extension of Service to Northern and Remote Communities. 1980. *The 1980s: A Decade of Diversity – Broadcasting, Satellites, and Pay-TV.* Ottawa: Minister of Supply and Services Canada.

Cassidy, Frank, and Robert L. Bish. 1989. *Indian Government: Its Meaning and Practice.* Lantzville: Oolichan.

Charlie, Patricia. 1990. "Summary of Research Findings." In Valerie Alia et al., *Interviews.* London.

Chronicle-Herald (Halifax). 1984. "Native Vote Could Influence (24) Ridings." 18 August.

———. 1990. "Micmacs Seek Political Clout: NS Aboriginal Peoples' Liberal Association to Hold First Meeting Today." 16 February.

CKRW Radio. 1982. *Yukon Territorial Election Coverage.* Whitehorse: CKRW.

———. 1985. *Yukon Territorial Election Coverage.* Whitehorse: CKRW.

Coates, Ken S. (producer). 1989. *Audrey McLaughlin Campaign.* (Yukon, British Columbia and Ontario – campaign for leadership of federal New Democratic Party.) Whitehorse: NEDAA television, NNBY, 25 November.

Coates, Ken S., and William R. Morrison. 1988. *Land of the Midnight Sun – A History of the Yukon.* Edmonton: Hurtig.

Collin, Ken. 1990a. Submission to the Royal Commission on Electoral Reform and Party Financing. Ottawa.

———. 1990b. Testimony before the Royal Commission on Electoral Reform and Party Financing, 20 April, Thompson.

Coon Come, Matthew. 1990. Testimony before the Royal Commission on Electoral Reform and Party Financing, 13 March, Ottawa.

Cotterill, Ewan, and Linda Sorensen. 1990. Testimony before the Royal Commission on Electoral Reform and Party Financing, 24 May, Yellowknife.

Craven, Barbara. 1990. Testimony before the Royal Commission on Electoral Reform and Party Financing, 26 March, Victoria.

Crowfoot, Strater, Blackfoot Tribe Band Administration and Siksika Nation. 1990. Testimony before the Royal Commission on Electoral Reform and Party Financing, 16 May, Gleichen.

Dahl, Roy K. 1990a. "Money Trouble to Close Two Papers." *Native Press,* 17 August.

———. 1990b. "NACS Closes Doors in Ottawa." *Native Press,* 17 August.

Dakota-Ojibway Tribal Council. 1990. Testimony before the Royal Commission on Electoral Reform and Party Financing, 19 April, Winnipeg.

Fairman, Shayne. 1990. Testimony before the Royal Commission on Electoral Reform and Party Financing, 14 May, Whitehorse.

Fiddler-Berteig, Ona. 1990. "Update: Saskatchewan Native Communications Corporation." *New Breed,* 24 April.

Fisher, Matthew. 1989a. "Every Vote Counts in a Territorial Election." *Globe and Mail,* 20 February.

Ford, Neil. 1985. *Yukon Territorial Election Coverage.* Whitehorse: CBC Radio.

Fox, Ray. 1989. *Retrospective: Twenty Years of Aboriginal Communications in Canada.* Edmonton: National Aboriginal Communications Society.

Germain, Anthony. 1991. "Summary of Research Findings." In Valerie Alia et al., *Interviews.* London.

Glavin, Terry. 1990. "NDP Indian Land Strategy World Restructure BC Map." *Vancouver Sun,* 5 March.

Gould, Gary P. 1990. Testimony before the Royal Commission on Electoral Reform and Party Financing, 5 June, Sydney.

Hamelin, Louis-Edmond. 1978. *Canadian Nordicity.* Montreal: Harvest House.

Hamilton, David. 1990. Testimony before the Royal Commission on Electoral Reform and Party Financing, 24 May, Yellowknife.

Hardie, Garth. 1990. "Summary of Research Findings." In Valerie Alia et al., *Interviews.* London.

Holman, John. 1990. "Radio Stations Struggling." *Native Press,* 17 August.

Hutchison, David. 1990. "Broadcasting Policy in Canada and the United Kingdom: Politics, Technology and Ideology." *Canadian Journal of Communications* 15 (May): 76–95.

Inuit Circumpolar Conference. 1989. "Draft Principles and Elements on Communication and Information." In *Draft Principles for a Comprehensive Arctic Policy.* Lachine: ICC.

Kane, Ken, et al. 1990. *Television Northern Canada (TVNC).* Whitehorse: Northern Native Broadcasting Yukon.

Kenna, Kathleen. 1989. "A Frozen Yukon Election ... NDP, Tory Cliff-hanger Predicted in Yukon Vote." *Toronto Star*, 19 February.

Kinnear, Cheri. 1990. Testimony before the Royal Commission on Electoral Reform and Party Financing, 23 July, Iqaluit.

Klingle, Paul, et al. 1985. *The Costs of Choice: Report from the Task Force on Access to Television in Underserved Communities*. Ottawa: Minister of Supply and Services Canada.

Korbin, Kelley. 1990. "Summary of Research Findings." In Valerie Alia et al., *Interviews*. London.

Langford, Cooper. 1990. "Native Station Rules." *Native Press*, 28 September.

Lawrence, Guy. 1990. *40 Years on the Yukon Telegraph*. Quesnel: Caryall.

Levy, Gary, and Graham White, eds. 1989. *Provincial and Territorial Legislatures in Canada*. Toronto: University of Toronto Press.

McClellan, Catharine, et al. 1987. *Part of the Land, Part of the Water: A History of the Yukon Indians*. Vancouver: Douglas & McIntyre.

MacGregor, Roy. 1989. *Chief: The Fearless Vision of Billy Diamond*. Markham: Penguin.

Marchand, Len. 1990. "History of Aboriginal Participation within the Electoral System." Brief submitted to the Royal Commission on Electoral Reform and Party Financing, Ottawa.

Marchand, Len, and Marc Leclair. 1990. Testimony before the Royal Commission on Electoral Reform and Party Financing, 13 March, Ottawa.

Masten, E.R. 1990. Testimony before the Royal Commission on Electoral Reform and Party Financing, 19 March, Fredericton.

Mayer, Leona. 1990. Testimony before the Royal Commission on Electoral Reform and Party Financing, 20 April, Thompson.

Michael, Patrick L. 1987. *The Yukon Legislative Assembly: Parliamentary Tradition in a Small Legislature*. Whitehorse: Government of the Yukon.

Mitcham, Allison. 1989. *Atlin: The Last Utopia*. Hantsport: Lancelot.

Morin, Gerald, Clem Chartier and Ron Campone. 1990. Testimony before the Royal Commission on Electoral Reform and Party Financing, 17 April, Saskatoon.

Native Council of Canada. 1990. Testimony before the Royal Commission on Electoral Reform and Party Financing, 12 June, Ottawa.

Native Press. 1990. "Programs to Fill Education Gap." *Native Press*, 5 October.

Northwest Territories. *Official Languages Act*, S.N.W.T. 1984 (2), c. 2.

Northwest Territories Data Book 1990/91. Yellowknife: Outcrop.

Northwest Territories Legislative Assembly. 1990. "To Reach Your MLA During the Seventh Session of the Eleventh Legislative Assembly." Notice published in NWT newspapers. Yellowknife.

Peter, Saali. 1990. "Elijah Harper, the People's Hero." *Arctic Circle* (September/October).

Robinson, Viola M. 1990. Testimony before the Royal Commission on Electoral Reform and Party Financing, 5 June, Sydney.

Roth, Lorna. 1991a. "CBC Northern Service and the Federal Electoral Process: Problems and Strategies for Improvement." In *Election Broadcasting in Canada*, ed. Frederick J. Fletcher. Vol. 21 of the research studies of the Royal Commission on Electoral Reform and Party Financing. Ottawa and Toronto: RCERPF/Dundurn.

————. 1991b. "Interviews, Eastern Arctic." Conducted for the Royal Commission on Electoral Reform and Party Financing, Ottawa.

Roth, Lorna, and Gail Guthrie Valaskakis. 1989. "Aboriginal Broadcasting in Canada: A Case Study in Democratization." In *Communication for and Against Democracy*, ed. Marc Raboy and Peter A. Bruck. Montreal: Black Rose.

Schiller, Bill. 1987. "How They Made an Indian School a School for Indians." *Toronto Star*, 7 December.

Shiell, Les. 1990. "Native Renaissance." *Canadian Geographic* (August/September): 59–66.

Smellie, Janet. 1990a. "Allooloo Doesn't Want Constituency Split in Two." (Note: error in headline reverses meaning of story.) *Nunatsiaq News*, 2 November.

————. 1990b. "Inuktitut Becomes One of Eight NWT Official Languages." *Nunatsiaq News*, 12 April.

————. 1990c. "Kakfwi Says 2,000 Will Upgrade Literacy by 1993." *Nunatsiaq News*, 2 November.

Smythe, Daniel. 1990. "Summary of Research Findings." In Valerie Alia et al., *Interviews*. London.

Stamp, Robert M. 1974. "Schools on Wheels: The Railway Car Schools of Northern Ontario." *Canada: An Historical Magazine* 1 (Spring): 34–42.

Thorbes, Clare. 1990. "Summary of Research Findings." In Valerie Alia et al., *Interviews*. London.

Tobin, Chuck. 1990. "Reform Party Lures 100 to Meeting, Elects Executive." *Whitehorse Star*, 30 October.

Vancouver Sun. 1984. "Prince Rupert: Native Voters Hold the Key – If They Use It." 18 August.

Walsh, Lyle. 1990. Testimony before the Royal Commission on Electoral Reform and Party Financing, 20 April, Thompson.

Wattie, Chris. 1990. "Electoral Boundary Case Could Carry Aftershocks." *Whitehorse Star* (Opinion), 11 December.

Weller, Geoffrey R. 1983. "Provincial Ministries of Northern Affairs: A Comparative Analysis." In *Resources and Dynamics of the Boreal Zone,* ed. R.W. Wein, R.R. Riewe and I. Methuen. Ottawa: ACUNS.

Werezak, William, Joyce Brown and Peggy Woods. 1990. Testimony before the Royal Commission on Electoral Reform and Party Financing, 17 April, Saskatoon.

Whidden, Richard. 1990. Testimony before the Royal Commission on Electoral Reform and Party Financing, 20 April, Thompson.

Whipp, Stephen. 1990. Testimony before the Royal Commission on Electoral Reform and Party Financing, 24 May, Yellowknife.

Winnipeg Free Press. 1984. "NDP (Kenora–Rainy River) Winner Credits Heavy Native Support." 5 September.

Yukon. Chief Electoral Officer of the Yukon. 1989. *The Report of the Chief Electoral Officer of Yukon on the 1989 General Election.* Whitehorse: Government of the Yukon.

———. 1990. *Voting in Yukon Elections.* Whitehorse: Government of the Yukon.

Yukon. Government of the Yukon. 1987. *Yukon Elections Results.* Whitehorse: Government of the Yukon.

———. 1990. *Legislative Assembly of Yukon.* Whitehorse: Government of the Yukon.

Zebrinski, Jan. 1990. Testimony before the Royal Commission on Electoral Reform and Party Financing, 20 April, Thompson.

4

ELECTORAL REFORM AND CANADA'S ABORIGINAL POPULATION
An Assessment of Aboriginal Electoral Districts

~

Roger Gibbins

THIS STUDY DOES not address the moral weight or political priority which should be assigned to the aspirations of Canada's Aboriginal peoples. Rather it addresses the potential, and the potential problems, of using electoral reform as a means of addressing those aspirations. More specifically it asks the following question: to what extent can and should the electoral process be modified, so as to provide guaranteed Aboriginal representation in the House of Commons?

Since 1960, when legislation prohibiting residents of reserves from voting in federal elections was repealed, all Aboriginal Canadians have now been formally incorporated in the electoral processes of the Canadian state. Nonetheless, there is little question that the existing electoral system does not provide an effective bridge between Aboriginal communities and the broader political community. Voter participation rates are often low, sometimes very low, the system provides very limited opportunity for the election of Aboriginal members to the House of Commons and, more generally, it fails to enable Aboriginal communities to exercise significant leverage on the political process.

However, these shortcomings do not lead automatically to the conclusion that the electoral system should be fundamentally reformed so as to reflect the particular circumstances, problems and aspirations of Aboriginal peoples. Nor should they necessarily be taken as support for the creation of Aboriginal electoral districts (AEDs) embedded in the

Canadian electoral system. On the contrary, the following analysis suggests that AEDs would do little to enhance Aboriginal political power, would encounter serious logistical problems, and might well conflict with widely held values of the Canadian political community in general.

The main body of the study is introduced by a brief discussion of the role played by elections in democratic states. The primary analysis then begins to look at the representational problems which confront Canada's Aboriginal peoples. The focus then shifts to a possible solution: the creation of Aboriginal electoral districts (AEDs) within the electorate at large. A working model for AEDs is developed, and a number of issues surrounding such units are addressed in detail. In conclusion, provincial parallels are explored, and the linkage between electoral reform and Aboriginal self-determination is examined.

THE ROLE OF ELECTIONS IN DEMOCRATIC SOCIETIES

Elections perform a variety of roles that go beyond holding governments responsible for their actions and providing citizens with a minimal degree of influence on public policy. Elections also play an important symbolic role, and indeed this is why elections of sorts routinely take place in countries that make no pretence of being democratic. In all states, electoral participation symbolically reaffirms the relationship between citizens and the state. Thus we vote because we feel we should, not because we expect our vote to be decisive with respect either to specific outcomes – who wins in our local constituency – or to more general results, the fate of the Free Trade Agreement, for example. We use our vote both symbolically and affectively, although we may also convince ourselves that it has at least some instrumental value.

For these reasons, low rates of electoral participation are symptomatic of distress within the political process and/or political community. When particular groups stand apart in this way, a low rate of participation suggests a significant degree of alienation and disaffection. Even if such behaviour is construed as a specific protest against the electoral process itself, and not against the encompassing political system, it serves as an important danger signal, given the centrality of the electoral process to the existence of democratic states. Electoral participation thus serves as a measure of health for the political community, or at least for its electoral components. In the case of Canada's Aboriginal peoples, the vital signs are often distressingly weak.

The right to vote, to participate in the electoral process, is a basic right of Canadian citizenship, shared by the adult population and subject to a diminishing set of restrictions based on residency, mental capacity and incarceration. It should be noted, however, that the right to vote does not in any formal sense include a right to participate in an electoral process that is meaningful, that offers a "real choice," and that holds out a reasonable chance that candidates sharing one's own characteristics can and will be elected. Such electoral characteristics, while certainly desirable, cannot be constitutionally mandated or institutionally guaranteed. Indeed, the number of Canadians who feel that they are denied a "real choice," that their candidates are "outgunned" and the "rules are fixed," are legion; Aboriginal people may simply present an acute case of a more general and intractable problem. At the same time, this conclusion does not negate the possibility that Aboriginal peoples face unique barriers which abridge or even nullify the right to vote.

Here it should be stressed that contemporary democratic theorists place little emphasis on the outcome or impact of elections on *policy*. It is assumed that groups with particular policy axes to grind will use a variety of political means quite apart from the electoral process, means which could include the organization of interest groups, lobbying, mobilization of the media and civil disobedience. However, theorists do place considerable emphasis on the *representational* outcome of elections, that is to say on the composition of elected legislative assemblies which will in turn shape public policy. This latter aspect of elections plays a particularly important role in assessing the potential of electoral reform to address Aboriginal aspirations.

Legislative representation can be *direct* or *virtual*. *Direct* representation takes place when individuals from the group under discussion are present as elected members of the appropriate legislative assembly. Thus, for example, women and Aboriginal peoples enjoy direct representation in the House of Commons to the extent, and only to the extent, that there are women and Aboriginal MPs. It should, however, be noted that women (or Aboriginal) MPs are elected by constituents who are both female and male, they have a mandate to represent all constituents regardless of their gender, and no specific mandate to represent women (or Aboriginal people) at large. Thus representation is at present less direct than that which would be provided through the Aboriginal electoral districts discussed below.

Virtual representation is analogous to the way in which a lawyer represents the interests of clients. A skilful lawyer can represent his or her client without sharing any characteristics with that client; a woman can represent a man, an honest man a thief, and so forth. A white male MP might accordingly well be able to represent the interests of Aboriginal and female constituents; whether he would be inclined to do so could well depend upon the power of such groups at the ballot box. At the same time it is fair to say that in the political arena, virtual representation is seen as inferior to direct representation simply because it is virtual. In this sense, representative assemblies are judged by their membership and not by their deeds, although the latter clearly play a very important role as Aboriginal people (and women) assess the performance of parliamentary institutions over the past 20 years. As we shall see, proposals for electoral reform in response to Aboriginal aspirations primarily address the lack of *direct* Aboriginal representation in legislative assemblies; the shortcomings of *virtual* representation are assumed and are not dwelt upon at any length.

It should also be emphasized that the importance of direct minority-group representation within the House of Commons depends upon which "hat" voters happen to wear when making judgements about parliamentary institutions. For example, a young Indian mother living in Regina might be quite disturbed by the scarcity of Aboriginal and women MPs. The degree of her disturbance will, however, depend upon the political value that she attaches to her gender and/or ethnicity. If, in a political sense, she sees herself first and foremost as a Westerner, an environmentalist, a peace activist, supporter of the pro-life movement, New Democrat or continentalist, then her assessment of parliamentary representation may be quite different than if she sees herself politically first and foremost as an Aboriginal, a woman, or as both. This is an important point to which we will return later.

SHORTCOMINGS OF THE ELECTORAL SYSTEM FOR ABORIGINAL PEOPLES

The accusation that the electoral status quo is not working well for Canada's Aboriginal peoples rests on two principal points. First, with the notable exception of the Northwest Territories, Aboriginal candidates rarely run for election and are rarely elected to the House of Commons when they do. Second, rates of Aboriginal electoral participation are often, although not universally, very low. As a consequence, the electoral system fails to provide an effective vehicle of political interaction or influence for Aboriginal peoples. While one might argue that the current state of Aboriginal affairs in Canada also provides more tangible evidence that the political system, and by implication the electoral process, are not responsive to Aboriginal interests and aspirations, this argument is not pursued here.

ABORIGINAL REPRESENTATION IN THE HOUSE OF COMMONS

The existing electoral system erects substantial barriers to the direct representation of most minority groups in the Canadian House of

Commons. Although groups which enjoy substantial geographical concentration may exercise significant leverage in specific ridings, as do Aboriginal voters in the Northwest Territories, the population size of federal ridings (approximately 90 000 individuals) precludes minority-group control in most cases. (The obvious exception here is the francophone population which, while a national minority, forms a majority in most Quebec ridings.) In the 1986 census, for example, 262 865 Canadians were identified as Blacks, a number which is certainly significant in absolute terms. Yet when dispersed over 295 constituencies, Blacks made up less than one percent of the typical constituency.

As a consequence of geographical dispersion, and perhaps also of less structural and less savory aspects of the electorate, we find that the composition of the House of Commons does not reflect that of the Canadian electorate. MPs are far more likely to be male, white and middle-class than are Canadians as a whole. These disparities can in turn raise questions of political legitimacy. For example, when the House debates issues such as abortion or Aboriginal rights, the charge can be made that the outcome of the debate would be quite different if the membership of the House included greater representation from potentially affected groups. The composition of the House may also have an impact not only on the numerical outcome of the vote, but on the character of the debate leading up to it. Thus, while Aboriginal MPs, unlike women MPs, will never constitute a majority in the House, Aboriginal MPs may be able to shape the nature of parliamentary debate and, as a result, the nature of public policy.

We know, then, that the House of Commons serves at best as a flawed mirror of Canadian society, and that the scarcity of Aboriginal MPs reflects more general problems confronting all minority groups in the country; the problem is not simply the concern of Aboriginal people. The question is, what can and should be done? Can the electoral process be reformed, so as to ensure adequate or at least more proportionate Aboriginal membership in the House of Commons? Can an equally compelling case be made for a variety of other minority groups? In either case, should reform be pursued if at all possible, or are there important offsetting costs?

One response to such questions is simply to ignore the issue in the belief that other forms of political action, including the activity of interest groups, provide adequate minority-group leverage on the political process, and that the electoral weight of minorities is sufficient to ensure virtual, if not direct representation. This strategy would suggest that greater emphasis be placed on bolstering the other political resources of Aboriginal communities, a course of action very much in keeping with the pursuit of Aboriginal self-government.

A second approach is to assume that representational distortions in the House of Commons will diminish with the passage of time and changing social mores. Here we might note, for example, that a significant increase has occurred over the past few decades in the proportion of women MPs in the House, although that ratio is still well below the proportion of women in the electorate. (In the 1988 election, 13.2 percent of the elected candidates were women, an increase from 9.9 percent in 1984.) It is doubtful, however, that the example of women will be seen to hold out much hope for much smaller, ethnic communities. If women, who constitute more than 50 percent of the electorate, are still badly underrepresented in the House, what does this augur for minority groups?

A third way is to provide some mechanism by means of which direct representation can be guaranteed. Such mechanisms are routinely employed by the Liberals, New Democrats and Progressive Conservatives in the selection of convention delegates; selection rules guarantee that a specified minimum proportion of delegates will be women and will be under a certain age. In the recent national Liberal leadership convention, such instruments were further developed by the establishment of an Aboriginal Peoples' Commission within the party, and the election of more than 100 delegates through Aboriginal Liberal Clubs across the country. The issue at hand is whether such an approach should also be applied to the establishment of Aboriginal electoral districts within the electorate as a whole.

PARTICIPATION RATES

At the present time, Aboriginal rates of electoral participation appear to be relatively low, in some cases alarmingly so, although the empirical evidence is not without its ambiguities. Conventional measures of voter turnout are generated through survey data and, in the Canadian case, through the National Election Studies which have been run in conjunction with federal elections since 1965. However, Aboriginal respondents constitute a very small proportion of such national samples, in part because reserves are excluded from the sampling frame. As a result it is impossible, within the context of the National Election Studies, to compare Aboriginal turnout rates to those of other groups. More generally it is impossible to assess the participation rates of Métis and non-status Indians, because there is no comprehensive or consensual definition of either community. If the size and membership of these groups cannot be determined, participation rates cannot be calculated.

Table 4.1

Illustrative electoral participation rates for selected Aboriginal polling stations

(percentages)

	1984	1988
Yukon		
Old Crow	73.4	77.1
Teslin	65.5	82.1
Nunatsiaq		
Sachs Harbour	64.7	59.8
Baker Lake	57.8	68.1
Eskimo Point	75.4	69.6
Western Arctic		
Fort Good Hope	49.2	47.0
Fort Franklin	55.2	54.9
Snowdrift	70.0	63.2
Wetaskiwin (Alberta)		
Ermineskin Reserve	15.2	58.6
Louis Bull Reserve	10.2	53.6
Yellowhead (Alberta)		
Paul Reserve	3.1	13.4
Chateauguay (Quebec)		
Kahnawake	0.3	0.1
Lethbridge–Foothills (Alberta)		
Blood Reserve	5.7	25.9
Brandon–Souris (Manitoba)		
Oak Lake Reserve	71.1	35.2
Abitibi (Quebec)		
Lac-Simon	3.7	16.7
Waswanipi	52.3	49.2
Thunder Bay (Ontario)		
Fort William Reserve	53.5	54.2
Peterborough (Ontario)		
Otonabee Reserve	61.7	62.3
Cochrane–Superieur (Ontario)		
Heron Bay–Pic River Reserve	64.5	71.7
Calstock Reserve	65.6	54.9
Kenora–Rainy River (Ontario)		
Bearskin Lake Reserve	46.9	92.1
Muskrat Dam Lake Reserve	78.7	66.7
Grassy Narrows Reserve	27.0	41.5
Rat Portage Reserve	51.7	53.2
Cariboo–Chilcotin (BC)		
Anaham Band Reserve	51.5	67.0

The only empirical evidence on turnout rates is provided by the detailed poll by poll reports of the chief electoral officer. Even here, however, evidence can only be gleaned from polls with an exclusively Aboriginal population; Aboriginal voters who cast, or fail to cast, their vote in "mixed" polls cannot be traced. Thus it is impossible to determine turnout rates for the large urban Aboriginal population.

With these serious limitations as a backdrop, table 4.1 presents some fragmentary evidence from 1984 and 1988, collected in Aboriginal communities across Canada. The evidence, it must be stressed, is illustrative only; it is neither exhaustive nor conclusive. Nevertheless, the table does show a striking degree of variation across Aboriginal communities. In many cases, particularly in northern polls where, not coincidentally, Aboriginal candidates were present, turnout rates equal or surpass those of non-Aboriginal communities. In other cases, particularly in some of the larger, southern Aboriginal communities, turnout rates are very low, and certainly fall well below the Canadian norm of a 75 percent voter turnout in federal elections.

It is interesting to note the 1984/1988 difference in the two Wetaskiwin polls shown in table 4.1. In the 1988 election, the Progressive Conservative candidate and eventual MP, Willie Littlechild, was a Cree from the Ermineskin Reserve. His candidacy had a marked impact on the turnout rate, although in 1988 the Ermineskin and Louis Bull reserves still had rates slightly below the constituency average. The Wetaskiwin experience shows that turnout rates for Aboriginal communities could be significantly increased if the political parties would nominate more Aboriginal candidates, and if they would do so in circumstances where such candidates stood a reasonable chance of success.

To a degree, Aboriginal participation rates could be marginally increased by "fine-tuning" the existing electoral process. More effort could be made to cultivate the Aboriginal vote; more advertising could be done, and more use could be made of Aboriginal languages. In these respects, useful lessons can be drawn from the Australian experience, where the mandatory voting requirement has meant that state and federal authorities have had to make quite extraordinary efforts to make the ballot accessible to Aboriginal communities and their voters, efforts which include mobile polls, carried into Aboriginal communities by light aircraft and four-wheel drive vehicles, over a two-week period leading up to the election. Yet it is doubtful that even extensive "fine-tuning" would greatly increase the chances of Aboriginal candidates being elected or make federal elections more "meaningful" for Aboriginal communities and voters. As a consequence, it is also unlikely that such exercises would have a significant impact on participation rates. Thus other questions must be asked: Should more fundamental reform be contemplated? More specifically, should Aboriginal electoral districts be created within the Canadian electorate?

ABORIGINAL ELECTORAL DISTRICTS

Throughout the democratic world, electoral constituencies are usually based on geographical location (place of residence) rather than on the characteristics of the voter. In other words, the ballot that any specific voter uses is determined by where the voter lives rather than by who the voter is; all voters within the same geographical area use the same ballot. Exceptions are rare indeed. In Britain, special House of Commons constituencies for Oxford and Cambridge graduates lasted until 1950, and special Senate representation still persists for Dublin College graduates in Ireland. However, as the survey by Rudnicki and Dyck (1986) shows, only in New Zealand has a segmented electoral system been used to structure the relationship between Aboriginal communities and the national government. Whether the New Zealand model is even appropriate for that country, never mind one for export, is a matter of lively and ongoing debate (Fleras 1985).

Contrary to the general rule, an Aboriginal electoral district (AED) would be one in which the electors were identified first and foremost by their Aboriginal status, and only secondarily by their place of residence. In a geographical sense, AEDs would overlap with, or be superimposed upon, conventional electoral districts. For example, an Indian living in the district of Vancouver Quadra would have the option of voting with other Quadra residents in the conventional federal constituency, or in an Indian AED that might well encompass most, if not all, of British Columbia. Thus AEDs would not be territorial in the usual sense, although in some cases they might coincide with provincial boundaries; they would represent people, but not the land on which people happen to live.

Maori Seats in New Zealand

In New Zealand, people of Maori ancestry can vote for candidates in one of four Maori seats in the House of Representatives. These seats were established in 1867, and constitute one of the few examples in the democratic world of a franchise based on racial rather than universal or territorial grounds. However, the innovation was not completely unique in New Zealand itself, where special legislative representation had also been granted to a number of other groups, including gold miners in the South Island and pensioners in Auckland. Four Maori ridings provided legislative representation for 60 000 Maori, while 72 seats were provided for the 250 000 European settlers.

Until 1967, only full-blooded Maori could stand for election in the Maori seats, while Maori candidates were not allowed to run in general ridings. Since 1967, Maori candidates have run and have been elected in general ridings, but no non-Maori candidates have run in the Maori ridings. Prior to 1975, voters were assigned to the Maori or non-Maori rolls according to their degree of Maori blood; since 1975, people of Maori ancestry can choose to register on either roll.

The Maori seats were seen as a temporary measure; the expectation was that within five years, Maori voters would be absorbed into the general rolls. As a consequence, "Maori representatives were not regarded necessarily in the same light as their European counterparts. Rather, they were perceived as observers with speaking rights over issues of relevance only to Maoris" (Fleras 1985, 556). In recent times, Maori representatives have forged a close working relationship with the Labour Party, and as a consequence, several Maori members have served in the New Zealand cabinet.

In more general terms, it seems to be an open question whether Maori representatives and Maori people have been well served, either by this alliance or by the system of Maori seats. At present only about 40 percent of Maori voters are registered on the Maori roll, while 60 percent are listed on the general roll. Not coincidentally, the contemporary Maori population is overwhelmingly urban. The electoral system set up for them has been plagued by confusion, by low turnouts, by major discrepancies in the size of constituencies, by the opposition of the majority of the non-Maori electorate and by the ambivalent support of the Maori themselves (Fleras 1985).

CONSTRUCTING A MODEL

In order to construct a model by means of which the notion of Aboriginal electoral districts can be assessed, we must begin with the size and

Table 4.2
Canada's Aboriginal population

Aboriginal peoples	Single origin	Multiple origin	Total	Seat "entitlement"
Indian	286 230	262 730	548 960	6.14
Inuit	27 290	9 175	36 465	0.41
Métis	59 745	91 865	151 610	1.70

Source: 1986 census.

geographical distribution of the Aboriginal population. To this end, table 4.2 presents the 1986 census breakdown for Canada's Aboriginal population.

The seat "entitlement" is calculated according to the terms of the *Representation Act, 1985*, and using the 1986 census. The total 1986 provincial population (excluding the Yukon and Northwest Territories) is divided by 279 to produce a quotient of 89 414. The total respective Aboriginal populations are then divided by this quotient to determine the seat "entitlement."

In order to apply the information contained in table 4.2, two critically important caveats must be kept in mind. The first is that the census categorizations, and thus the size of the respective Aboriginal populations, are somewhat elastic and have been contested at times by Aboriginal organizations.[1] These issues are particularly acute with respect to the Métis. Given that the term "Métis" has constitutional status but no constitutional definition, the parameters and size of the population so described are inherently contentious, with census estimates tending to be much smaller than those provided by Métis organizations. If incentives existed for individuals to see themselves and be seen by others as Métis, then the size of this population could increase substantially. To a modest degree, AEDs could supply such incentives. Here it may also be noted that the refusal of some Aboriginal communities to participate in the national census also complicates estimates of the total Aboriginal population.

The second caveat arises from the census distinction between single-origin and multiple-origin ethnic identifications. A "single-origin" Indian would be an individual whose parents were both Indians; one of "multiple origin" would be an individual who declared only one parent to be of Indian, or partial Indian, descent. As the reader will – not surprisingly – note, the contribution of persons of "multiple origin" to the total Aboriginal population is substantial. This contribution constitutes in its turn a concern, in that there is no way of knowing what proportion of such individuals would opt into an Aboriginal electorate. (There is also no way of knowing what proportion of single-origin individuals would do so, but we can assume that the proportion would be both substantial and greater.) Accordingly, since it is not possible to assess the size of the Aboriginal electorate with any precision, it is equally difficult to estimate the appropriate number of Aboriginal electoral districts.

It should also be noted that people identified as multiple-origin Indians in the 1986 census may include a number of individuals of Asian origin. The understandable terminological confusion between

Asian and Aboriginal "Indians" creates further complications for any-one trying to use census figures to determine the potential size of Aboriginal electorates.

With these caveats in mind, how do we proceed? First we will assume that the Aboriginal electorates will be drawn from the total Aboriginal populations reported in table 4.2. This assumption undoubt-edly overestimates the proportion of multiple-origin individuals who would opt into the Aboriginal electorate and who are, indeed, of Aboriginal descent, but this error may be offset in part if the census estimates of the Aboriginal populations prove to be low. In the second place, we will assume that three distinct sets of AEDs would have to be created, one for each of the three constitutionally recognized Aboriginal peoples since general AEDs, rather than districts specifically for Indians, the Inuit and Métis, would be difficult to implement; they would blur distinctions among Aboriginal peoples that have been both strongly defended and constitutionally entrenched, would swamp the Inuit, and would amalgamate quite disparate Aboriginal interests. Our third assumption will be that the number of AEDs would be determined by dividing the respective Aboriginal populations by the same denominator used to establish the number of seats for each province. While an argu-ment could certainly be made for using a smaller denominator, per-haps one that was 75 percent of the standard quotient, this option would not seem to be justified, given that the Aboriginal numerator has already been inflated, both by the assumption that all Aboriginal peoples of multiple origin would opt into the AEDs, and by the demonstrably false hypothesis that all multiple-origin Indians are of Aboriginal descent. However, it must be stressed that the size of the denominator is largely a political decision, albeit one that is constrained by the courts. Arguments based on Aboriginal rights would certainly be made that a different denominator should be used in the construction of AEDs. Given that the Supreme Court of Canada has endorsed significant dif-ferences in constituency populations within provinces, and that sig-nificant interprovincial differences persist in Canada (most notably with respect to Prince Edward Island and the northern Territories), it is certainly conceivable that smaller AEDs than those envisioned here could be created.

If, however, we assume a rough equivalency in constituency size, table 4.2 generates an estimate of six Indian AEDs, two for the Métis population and one for the Inuit, for a total of nine. These estimates will be utilized throughout the analysis that follows.

Two issues remain: how would such AEDs affect the provincial dis-tribution of parliamentary seats, and how would AEDs be distributed

Table 4.3
Total Aboriginal population by province

	Indian	Métis	Inuit	Total	Estimated seat loss*
Newfoundland	4 695	1 440	4 125	10 260	0.11
Prince Edward Island	1 120	160	30	1 310	0.01
Nova Scotia	13 060	1 105	310	14 475	0.16
New Brunswick	8 700	745	190	9 635	0.11
Quebec	63 590	11 440	7 360	82 390	0.92
Ontario	150 720	18 280	2 965	171 965	1.92
Manitoba	55 950	33 285	700	89 935	1.01
Saskatchewan	55 215	25 695	195	81 105	0.91
Alberta	68 965	40 130	1 130	110 225	1.23
British Columbia	112 795	15 295	1 030	129 120	1.44

Source: 1986 census.

*Calculated by dividing the total Aboriginal population in each province by the electoral quotient (89 414). It should be noted that the total figures are slightly less than the sum of the Indian, Métis and Inuit figures; this discrepancy results from a small number of individuals having multiple origins which spanned two or more Aboriginal categories. For example, the same individual could show up as a multiple-origin Indian *and* as a multiple-origin Inuit.

on a geographical basis? To answer these questions we must turn first to table 4.3, which presents the provincial breakdown of the *total* Aboriginal population, i.e., Aboriginal people of single and multiple origin. The two northern Territories are not included in this table, but are dealt with at greater length below.

Table 4.3 shows that the creation of AEDs would have no appreciable impact on the representation of the four Atlantic provinces in the House of Commons. However, the "shrinkage" in the size of provincial electorates that would result from their creation could lead to the loss or "reassignment" of one seat each for Quebec, Manitoba, Saskatchewan, Alberta and British Columbia, and of two seats for Ontario. (The question of seat loss for the northern Territories is discussed below.) The extent of the shrinkage, and thus the possibility of seat loss, would depend upon the proportion of Aboriginal voters who elected to vote in AEDs. Given that this proportion would not be known initially and might well vary from one province to the next, carving out AEDs from provincial electorates would be a difficult and contentious undertaking.

It could well be the case, of course, that new Aboriginal seats would be added to the existing provincial allocation of seats, so that the process of creating AEDs would neither create losers nor call for reassignment. Certainly there would be strong political incentives for this approach, but it would ignore the fact that AEDs *would* reduce the size of the non-Aboriginal electorate, and thus *should* reduce parliamentary representation. Their creation would also require constitutional amendment. Here it should be noted that if AEDs were simply added to the existing constituencies, then the parliamentary weight of the Atlantic provinces would be marginally reduced, and that of the West would be significantly increased by four to five seats at a minimum.

The final matter to be determined in this model is the geographical distribution of the AEDs. The simplest case would be the electoral district for the Inuit, for there would only be one. Therefore, Inuit across the country would all have the opportunity to vote in a single constituency. It should, however, be borne in mind that just over 50 percent of the potential Inuit constituency would live in the northern Territories, with the great bulk of them living in the eastern Arctic. We may therefore ask whether the Inuit AED would be seen as a meaningful electoral vehicle for the remaining, relative handful of Inuit scattered across the 10 provinces. (Of particular concern would be the Inuit communities in northern Quebec, Northern Ontario and Labrador.) In all likelihood, the relatively assimilated "southern" Inuit would be the least inclined to opt into their AED, even though, in theory, an Inuit electoral district would have more to offer them than to the Inuit who already control the eastern Arctic constituency of Nunatsiaq.

The provincial distributions in table 4.3 suggest that the six Indian AEDs would be distributed so that there would be one for British Columbia, one for Alberta, one spanning Manitoba and Saskatchewan, two in Ontario and one spanning the five eastern provinces. The two Métis constituencies would likely be divided at the Saskatchewan-Manitoba border. Although it would not be essential that AEDs coincide with provincial boundaries, the provincial imperative in Canadian life would predicate such an outcome, one that might also facilitate campaign activities in what would be huge ridings. Even if constituency boundaries were set by other criteria, such as treaty boundaries, the problems associated with size would remain, though the AEDs might be more homogeneous in other respects.

THE ABORIGINAL FRANCHISE

If AEDs were created, individual citizens of Aboriginal status would face a choice, or, more realistically, an ongoing series of choices. Should they vote in their appropriate Aboriginal district? Should they exercise their franchise as an Indian or as a Métis? Or should they vote in the conventional district in which they live – Calgary Centre, North York, or wherever? In the latter case, individuals would be implicitly choosing to cast their vote in a non-Aboriginal role; by not opting for the Aboriginal ballot, they would be voting first and foremost as Albertans, as Liberals, as concerned mothers, as environmentalists, but not as Aboriginal people per se.

This element of choice raises both some interesting conceptual issues and some operational problems. First, Aboriginal citizens would have the freedom to choose, at each and every federal election, whether to vote in the AEDs or in the regular district. While this freedom of choice would be essential, it would present enumerators with considerable logistical problems; it could also be a difficult choice to make time and time again. Second, given freedom of choice, the population size of the AEDs would always be indeterminate. The number of citizens represented by any one such district would depend upon the number of voters who, in a given election, decided to opt for the Aboriginal ballot. This indeterminacy would, in turn, make it very difficult to calculate initially how many AEDs would be required to provide adequate, but not excessive, representation for the respective Aboriginal populations. It would also raise the possibility, although not necessarily the probability, that some Aboriginal MPs might be elected by a relative handful of voters. Third, it would be necessary to have all Aboriginal people entered simultaneously on two voting lists, one for the appropriate AED and the other for the conventional district. If this dual listing was not done, then it would prove difficult for Aboriginal citizens to exercise their vote. Fourth, there would have to be some system to prevent Aboriginal voters from voting in both districts, if double counting were to be avoided.

SPECIFIC ISSUES, PROBLEMS AND CONCERNS

Does the Constitutional Recognition of Aboriginal Peoples Provide a Sufficient or Compelling Rationale for Particularistic Electoral Representation?

The *Constitution Act, 1982* recognizes Aboriginal Canadians in a number of important ways. Section 25 states, in part, that "the guarantee in this Charter of certain rights and freedoms shall not be construed so as to abrogate or derogate from any Aboriginal, treaty or other rights or freedoms that pertain to the Aboriginal peoples of Canada ..." Section 35(1) states that "the existing aboriginal and treaty rights of the aboriginal peoples of Canada are hereby recognized and affirmed," while section 35(2) states, "in this Act, 'aboriginal peoples of Canada' includes the Indian, Inuit and Métis peoples of Canada." At issue here is whether this constitutional recognition per se supports a particularistic form of electoral representation for Aboriginal peoples. Can one argue that it creates the legal framework or rationale for Aboriginal electoral districts? The likely answer is no.

It should also be noted that the Charter recognizes and gives constitutional expression to a number of other groups. Is it possible, then, that the particularistic electoral recognition of one group could lead to demands for similar recognition of others? Should we consider, or would we be forced to consider, special electoral districts for the disabled? For multicultural communities? For pensioners? Conversely, is it possible that the Charter, instead of offering support for the principle of AEDs, may in fact prohibit creating electoral districts along racial or indigenous rather than territorial lines? Simply put, is an electorate segmented on the basis of groups reflective of or compatible with the *Canadian Charter of Rights and Freedoms?* Does section 25, which shields Aboriginal rights from other sections of the Charter, open the door to AEDs without doing the same for analogous claims by other groups? While this is likely the case, and though it is far from clear that other groups would try to extend the principle of AEDs to themselves, neither conclusion is certain.

The questions here go beyond constitutional and legal technicalities to raise more fundamental questions of principle. What values should the electoral system express? Should it declare the basic equality of individuals or provide expression for collective differences? Should all individuals participate in a single electoral forum, or should participation be segmented by race, gender or other characteristics? To date, Canadian practice has opted for the first solution proposed for each of these questions. The creation of AEDs would follow the choice of the second answer, and would in turn necessitate a significant shift in Canadian political values.

Who Would Determine the Aboriginal Roll?

At the present time, individuals are entered on the voting list by enumerators hired at the time of federal elections. These enumerators are required to determine a relatively simple set of facts: is the individual 18 years of age or over, is he or she a Canadian citizen, and does he or she live in the district being enumerated? In virtually all cases, such information is provided by the individual being enumerated, or by another person living in the same household. The enumerator is not required to test the statements made, to determine, for example, whether or not the individual is really a Canadian citizen. Legal sanctions backstop the enumerator.

It is not clear, however, if conventional enumerators would or should be able to enumerate Aboriginal electoral districts. Would they be required to ask each and every potential voter whether he or she is of Aboriginal descent? How far back could such descent go? Would individuals have to prove Aboriginal descent? Could there be a workable set of guidelines that enumerators *and* potential voters could use to determine who is and who is not qualified for the various AEDs? Or should the matter simply be left in the hands of the individual, with all Canadians having the choice of opting into Aboriginal districts, should they choose to do so?

In this last respect, it is interesting to note the Australian provisions for determining whether or not an individual should be counted as an Aboriginal in the national census. For this to happen, three conditions must be met:

- the individual must be of Aboriginal descent;
- the individual must elect to describe himself or herself as an Aborigine; and
- the individual must be recognized as an Aborigine by the community.

In other words, individuals have the right to declare, or not declare, themselves as Aborigines, but this right is conditional on both Aboriginal descent and community acceptance. At least hypothetically, then, Aboriginal communities have some control over their own formal membership; individuals cannot opt into the community of their own volition.

In this context one could ask if Aboriginal communities in Canada should also have some control over the composition of the Aboriginal electorates. Should the matter be left entirely in the hands of the individual, confronted at his or her door by the federal enumerator, or should the individual's choice be subject to community approval? To put it mildly, the second option would raise a host of bewildering operational difficulties. At the very least it would require an independent process for the construction of voting lists for AEDs, one that could not be completed within the existing confines of an election campaign.

Here it is also important to stress another point. One of the rationales of AEDs would be to provide a form of electoral expression for Aboriginal citizens who do not live within clearly identified Aboriginal communities. At least conceptually, an Indian AED would enable a young Indian couple living in a North York highrise to vote as Indians in an Indian district. However, identifying such individuals, and thus providing them with the opportunity to opt into the Aboriginal electorate, would require that every Canadian be enumerated with that possibility in mind. Moreover, in the case of the hypothetical highrise couple, it would be extraordinarily difficult to exercise any degree of community control over the composition of the voting list. Who could or should determine whether the individuals involved were recognized by the community – what community? – as Indians, Métis or other?

The conceptual and operational problems would be most acute for those individuals living outside recognized Aboriginal communities, for those individuals with a complex rather than single ethnicity, and for those persons experiencing some ambivalence about the electoral relevance of their ethnicity. Ironically, it is for just such individuals that AEDs have the greatest theoretical appeal. Conversely, AEDs might have the greatest practical appeal and utility for the reserve-based Indian communities, those that also have the most to gain from the implementation of Aboriginal self-government. And while Indian AEDs would not be easy to create or to sustain, the problems they would encounter would surely pale beside those faced by AEDs for the Métis.

Are AEDs a Necessary Condition for Aboriginal Representation in the House of Commons?

Although the creation of AEDs would guarantee that a significant number of Aboriginal members would sit in the House of Commons, AEDs are not a necessary condition for the election of Aboriginal MPs. Aboriginal MPs have been elected under the existing system, although admittedly very infrequently, and have been elected in constituencies where the great majority of the electorate was not of Aboriginal descent. Len Marchand, for example, was elected in an interior British Columbia riding in which Aboriginal people formed a small minority. More recently, in the 1988 federal election, Willie Littlechild was elected as the Progressive Conservative candidate in the Alberta riding of Wetaskiwin. Littlechild received 20 090 votes, or 50 percent of the 40 147 total votes cast, for a margin of victory which was close to the norm for Conservative candidates in Alberta in that election. Although Wetaskiwin contains the high-profile Hobbema Reserve, Aboriginal people constitute only a small proportion of the population; of the 46 080 people in the riding who declared a single ethnic origin in the 1986 census, 44.8% were of British, 20.2% of German, 6.1% of Ukrainian, 5.8% of Dutch, 4.2% of French and only 2.9% of Aboriginal descent. While the Aboriginal proportion of the electorate may have been somewhat larger than the census figures suggest, given that some of the Hobbema bands did not participate in the 1986 census, it was nonetheless small.

The Wetaskiwin example, of course, may only prove that exceptional Aboriginal candidates can win in exceptional circumstances. Thus it may offer little support for a more general argument that the election of Aboriginal MPs is not contingent upon the existence of AEDs. It may also demonstrate that the critical variable is the influence of Aboriginal people within party organizations. In the Wetaskiwin case, the Progressive Conservative candidate went into the 1988 election with a formidable advantage, the Conservatives having won every seat in the province since 1972. In a sense, then, the election was decided in the intraparty contest to determine who would be the Conservative candidate; the election was a formality that Conservative candidates passed through en route to the House of Commons. Therefore, the prospects of direct minority-group representation in the House may be determined more by the processes by which candidates are chosen than by the electoral process itself. Such intraparty procedures, however, are less open to public regulation than is the electoral process per se. Legislation may be able to provide prompts and incentives, but the critical factor may well be evolutionary changes in Canadian public opinion.

This discussion raises in turn a number of important questions. Would the establishment of AEDs make it even more difficult for Aboriginal candidates to come forward and, if nominated, to win in conventional districts? Would their existence mean that Aboriginal people would be seen by party organizations and/or voters as inappropriate candidates in non-Aboriginal ridings? Certainly such segregation would be an unfortunate development, although just how unfortunate would depend upon the extent to which a Willie Littlechild and a Len Marchand are exceptions to the Canadian rule. If the odds against Aboriginal candidates are at present in fact very long, then the price may not be significant.

One might also ask whether AEDs would reduce the incentives for other MPs to concern themselves with Aboriginal issues. In an important sense, Aboriginal people living within their riding would not be their constituents. The member from Smokey River would not have to concern himself or herself with Aboriginal people within the district, because they would be the responsibility of the MPs from the relevant AEDs. Thus, while AEDs might enhance the sensitivity of ordinary MPs to Aboriginal issues by injecting more Aboriginal MPs into parliamentary debate and caucuses, they would also take away Aboriginal constituents, and therefore Aboriginal pressure, from the vast majority of MPs.

There is a more general concern here that extends beyond the recruitment and possible election of Aboriginal candidates. Would AEDs promote the more active participation of Aboriginal peoples in the political process? Would they encourage political integration? While a definitive answer is not possible, it is important to note Rudnicki and Dyck's observation on the New Zealand experience: "Rather than assisting the Maori to be full and integrated partners in New Zealand society, separate representation has in fact contributed to a considerable amount of Maori withdrawal from the political process" (1986, 384).

How Could AEDs Be Squared with the Parliamentary Norms and Conventions of Party Discipline?

The creation of AEDs would ensure that a significant minimal number of Aboriginal candidates (nine in the case of the model under discussion here) would be elected to the House of Commons. However, the creation of AEDs per se predicts nothing about what would happen to Aboriginal MPs once elected, and does not determine what role they would play in the House of Commons. The matter at issue here is whether Aboriginal MPs would belong to the regular party caucuses, or whether they would sit as one or more independent blocs. This, in turn, would depend on whether Aboriginal candidates ran as Liberals, New Democrats, Progressive Conservatives, Bloc québécois, or Reformers, whether they ran as candidates for Aboriginal parties or as Independents.

At first blush it may appear self-evident that Aboriginal MPs should sit as independents in the House of Commons; the very creation of AEDs would seem to presuppose some independence for Aboriginal MPs, once elected. Would it make sense to go to the length of creating AEDs, only to have Aboriginal MPs bound by the constraints of party discipline, to have such a handful dispersed among and swallowed up by the various caucuses?

The norms of party discipline would certainly restrict the ability of Aboriginal MPs to speak up in public about the Aboriginal concerns of their constituents. (The private pursuit of constituency interests is not constrained by party discipline, although a successful outcome may well be influenced by whether the MP sits on the government or opposition side of the House.) Note, for example, the following Canadian Press story describing the predicament of Progressive Conservative MP Willie Littlechild:

'Indians Suspicious About Littlechild's Silence on Dispute'
Ottawa (CP) – Where is Willie Littlechild?

Natives across Canada want to know why Prime Minister Brian Mulroney has failed to call on the one member of his caucus best-qualified to defuse the confrontation that has erupted in Oka, Que.

Littlechild, a lawyer, is a Cree who represents the Alberta riding of Wetaskiwin.

Littlechild has made no public statements during a number of recent crises: the land dispute at Oka, the gambling controversy at Akewasasne and the native opposition to the Meech Lake accord. Critics charge the government has muzzled him but Littlechild said nobody has told him to keep mum. He prefers to remain behind-the-scenes rather than make public pronouncements.

Liberal MP Ethel Blondin, a Dene from the western Arctic, believes Littlechild has probably tried to intercede, only to be stifled by the government.

"I think they said: 'Don't bother us. This is our position. You'll have to suffer like everybody else. Keep your mouth shut and you'll get your just reward,'" said Blondin, who considers Littlechild a good friend.

"I think they've abused him severely. It's embarrassing for a person of that stature essentially to be neutered."

Littlechild was mowing the lawn of his home in Hobbema, Alta., about halfway between Edmonton and Red Deer, when he reluctantly spoke to The Ottawa Citizen by telephone Friday.

He said he has kept out of the limelight on purpose.

"It's easier for me because I'm an obvious focus of attack from both sides on any of those major Indian issues. I don't want to deal with that kind of stuff in public in the media," he said.

Littlechild was in Geneva, Switzerland last week at a meeting of the United Nations Working Group on Indigenous Peoples when trouble erupted at Oka. He said no one from the government, including Indian Affairs, consulted him on the matter.

Lawrence Courtoreille, vice-chief of the Assembly of First Nations and a fellow Cree from Alberta, said natives are disappointed that Littlechild has not spoken out on their behalf.

"Willie is more intelligent, has more principles and more decency than the Prime Minister or (Indian Affairs minister) Tom Siddon. We're kind of appalled that he hasn't come forward and proven it, regardless if he's a PC member or not," said Courtoreille. (*Calgary Herald* 1990, A8)

Here it should be stressed that the writer is not endorsing the assessments of Mr. Littlechild, or those of other politicians, embedded within the Canadian Press story. At the same time the story captures the very real dilemma that party discipline can pose, a dilemma that is particularly acute for MPs within the government caucus. While such MPs can exert private influence, their actions are circumscribed in the public sphere.

If Aboriginal MPs were to sit as independents, they would be isolated from the real levers of parliamentary and ministerial power. Parliamentary government in Canada is party government, and independent MPs have little opportunity to exercise any significant influence, much less power. Certainly independent Aboriginal MPs would have no chance of a cabinet position, the golden ring of Canadian politics. Therefore, Aboriginal MPs elected through AEDs would face the difficult choice of operating within the constraints of party discipline, choosing private influence over freedom of public action or of acting as independents in the House of Commons, locked out of the party and ministerial mechanisms through which effective political influence and power are exercised in Ottawa. The choice is a difficult one in that both options raise doubts about the practical utility of AEDs. The bottom line is that effective parliamentary power is exercised collectively through party organizations; the circumstances are exceptional, indeed, when a single representative can wield the degree of power employed by Manitoba MLA Elijah Harper during Manitoba's ratification debate on the Meech Lake Accord.

A position midway between independent MPs and conventional party caucuses could emerge if Aboriginal MPs sat as and acted as an Aboriginal bloc. Such a strategy might enhance the collective influence of these MPs and, with a slight alteration of existing rules, might win party status for the bloc, along with the accompanying parliamentary privileges and resources. In a minority government situation, something by no means rare in Canada, an Aboriginal bloc could exercise considerable power. It should be stressed, however, that an effective bloc presupposes a common set of Aboriginal interests that would cut across the various Indian, Inuit and Métis constituencies.

In a more general sense, AEDs may create an awkward problem of role definition for the MPs elected to represent the voters in those constituencies. Take, for example, the case of a typical MP, say a woman from London, Ontario. She is expected to bring her constituency's preferences into play when debating the issues on the parliamentary agenda, subject, of course, to the constraints of party discipline. However, there are also many issues – gun control, abortion or foreign aid to Ethiopia – for which the fact that she is from London, Ontario may be of little, if any, relevance. But what about the case of an Aboriginal MP? Is he or she expected to cast every issue in an Aboriginal mould? An MP would not only be expected to represent the Aboriginal interests of his or her constituents, but also a wide array of constituents' other interests, interests that could not be neatly labelled "Aboriginal." How would the Aboriginal MP operate in those situations? Would the MP have an electoral "mandate" for the myriad issues on the parliamentary agenda that have little, if anything, to do with Aboriginal affairs? While both Aboriginal MPs and constituents would clearly have an interest in the non-Aboriginal agenda, the format of AED elections may muzzle the expression of this interest.

How Would Election Campaigns Be Organized within AEDs?

The parliamentary dilemma that would face Aboriginal MPs (the frustration of party discipline versus the impotence of independence) is directly related to the manner in which election campaigns would be organized in AEDs. Under the best of circumstances, AEDs would be huge in terms of geography, although not in terms of the number of voters. Aboriginal voters would be hard to identify and would be thinly spread over quite literally hundreds, if not thousands, of cities, towns and rural communities. Reaching such voters could be called a Herculean task, yet even such a description would underestimate the problems that Aboriginal candidates would confront. The costs of television, radio and newspaper advertising might be prohibitive, yet it is not clear that the Aboriginal electorate could be sufficiently well identified to permit direct mail campaigns. If, on the other hand, the Aboriginal TV, radio and print media were to provide effective ways of reaching the Aboriginal electorate, then public funding for this purpose could both address the advertising problem and provide badly needed financial support to the media outlets.

At the very least, Aboriginal candidates would have to receive levels of public subsidization that would exceed – appropriately exceed – that received by other candidates. Even then it is difficult to imagine how Aboriginal candidates could run an effective campaign. Nor would problems end with the campaign. Once elected, Aboriginal MPs would face an equally daunting logistical task in trying to keep in touch with their constituents. Rather than being relatively close to their constituents, Aboriginal MPs would be far more remote from them than conventional MPs, and while the problems would be particularly acute for Métis MPs, given the larger geographical size of their constituencies, they would be formidable for all Aboriginal MPs.

The situation would be eased if the candidates in AEDs ran under conventional party labels. In that case, normal party advertising would suffice, so long as Aboriginal voters cast their votes along conventional party lines. If, however, voters wanted to choose among Aboriginal candidates according to their stand on Aboriginal issues, voters would still be completely in the dark.

The choice here is both stark and damning. If AEDs were not rolled into the conventional party campaigns, Aboriginal candidates would face an extremely difficult task during the election campaign, and Aboriginal MPs would face an equally difficult communications task, once elected. On the other hand, if AEDs were rolled into the conventional party campaigns, the whole rationale for having AEDs in the first place would be called in question. Aboriginal voters already have the opportunity to choose among competing national parties; what they lack is an effective electoral mechanism for addressing Aboriginal interests, aspirations and concerns. Yet practical campaign difficulties make it uncertain, perhaps even unlikely, that AEDs could provide such a mechanism.

What Impact Would AEDs Have on Parliamentary Representation for the Canadian North?

The creation of AEDs would pose particularly acute problems for political representation in the Canadian North. The first question to be asked is what would happen to Aboriginal voters living there. Would they be rolled into larger AEDs spanning Aboriginal communities in the South? If not, then the AEDs would seem to be somewhat peculiar and exclusive creatures, taking no account of the substantial and politically influential Aboriginal communities in the North. However, if AEDs were expanded north of 60°, further difficulties would result.

Table 4.4
Aboriginal population of the northern territories

	Yukon		N.W.T.	
	Total	%	Total	%
Indian*	4 770	20.4	9 370	18.0
Inuit*	65	0.3	18 355	35.3
Métis	220	0.9	3 815	7.3
Other	18 305	78.4	20 480	39.4

Source: 1986 census.

*Includes both single- and multiple- Aboriginal origin.

The Northwest Territories span two federal ridings: Nunatsiaq in the east, and Western Arctic in the Mackenzie Valley. The great bulk of the Inuit population lives in Nunatsiaq, where Inuit voters form the overwhelming majority of the electorate. (Not coincidentally, the three major parties ran Inuit candidates in Nunatsiaq in the 1988 election.) The majority of the Indian and Métis population lives in the Western Arctic, where Aboriginal voters constitute a very substantial minority of the electorate, as table 4.4 shows.

Dislocation would be least acute, although not insignificant, in the Yukon. Inuit and Métis voters have little leverage within the existing riding, and, therefore, might welcome the opportunity to vote in AEDs. However, Yukon Indians would go from being a minority with some influence in the small Yukon riding (population 23 360 in 1986) to playing a much smaller and less influential role in a new Indian AED (population 80 000 to 90 000), one that would most likely encompass British Columbia as well as the Yukon. More importantly, the Yukon MP, the individual who spoke for and symbolically represented the Territory in the national Parliament, would be answerable to an electorate that was exclusively non-Aboriginal in composition. In this important sense, the political voice of the Yukon would be that of non-Aboriginal people; its own Aboriginal nuances and inflections absorbed into an AED dominated by a southern-oriented Aboriginal electorate.

The Western Arctic would also be transformed from a dynamic balance of Indian, Métis, Inuit and non-Aboriginal voices and interests into a wholly non-Aboriginal constituency. The North would speak with a non-Aboriginal voice, its northern Aboriginal voices less audible in larger, southern-dominated AEDs. In addition, it might well be necessary to reduce the number of existing northern ridings if AEDs took away a sizable proportion of the northern electorate. (The combined non-Aboriginal population in the Yukon and NWT amounts to less than 40 000 people, or well under half the population of a typical southern constituency.)

If anything, the situation in the eastern Arctic, or Nunatsiaq, would be even more difficult. An Inuit AED would encompass the existing Nunatsiaq riding, but there would also be additional voters from the Yukon and Western Arctic, from Northern Ontario and Quebec, from Labrador and from communities scattered across Canada. Would the Inuit voters then control the *territory* of the eastern Arctic, or would the Inuit AED be a more ephemeral concept, one linked to people, but not to land? And what about non-Inuit voters (Indians, Métis and non-Aboriginal people) who live in the existing riding of Nunatsiaq? For whom would they vote? Who would speak for their interests as northern Canadians with a particular set of concerns? Would the Inuit MP be able to speak for all Inuit, or be the de facto member for the eastern Arctic?

What Would Be the Operational Problems Associated with AEDs?

The creation of Aboriginal electoral districts would present a host of operational problems for those charged with the administration of federal elections. Polling stations across the country would have to have a constituency ballot, plus ballots and voting lists for each of the AEDs (normally three) which overlapped the riding. It would be impossible, pending extensive technological change, to use Aboriginal voting lists to determine if an individual had already voted, because the same lists would be in use across all the AEDs. As discussed above, enumerators and returning officers would have to have some way to determine whether or not individuals were entitled to vote in the AEDs. Mechanisms would have to be in place to enable individuals to move onto or off the Aboriginal roll.

It should also be noted that results for the AEDs would not be available at the same time as those from other ridings; it could take several days to aggregate and count Aboriginal ballots cast in the very large AEDs. Thus, on election night Canadians would have only partial returns; they would know the outcome in only roughly 97 percent of the seats. This in turn could have two possible effects. In a very close election, the final outcome would depend on the vote in the AEDs; the country would be kept on tenterhooks while the Aboriginal vote was counted. It is, however, more likely that the election would be decided before the Aboriginal vote was counted. In this case, it would appear as if, and to a degree in fact would be the case, that the Aboriginal vote was irrelevant to the election outcome.

Could Aboriginal Representation Be Enhanced through Senate Reform?

The proposed model of AEDs for the House of Commons would not necessarily apply to such districts within a reformed and elected Upper House. (The smaller number of Senate seats, and thus the smaller number and even larger geographical area of AEDs, would further compound the campaign problems discussed above.) At the same time, if AEDs are to be considered in any proposals for electoral reform, it seems inevitable that the concept will form part of the constitutional debate on Senate reform. For example, a reformed Senate could be seen as a vehicle, not only for more effective regional representation, but also for the representation of non-territorially defined groups. Thus Senate reform might provide the opportunity for some institutionally defined form of Aboriginal representation, although this might be more feasible in a *non-elected* but reformed Senate. It should be stressed, however, that the primary dynamics of Senate reform are to be found outside the Aboriginal arena. Moreover, any attempt to yoke Aboriginal aspirations to Senate reform might be seen by Aboriginal people as procrastination, if not the kiss of death, and as yet another impediment by the proponents of Senate reform.

What Is the Anticipated Level of Public Support for Electoral Reform in General, and for AEDs in Particular?

Proposals for electoral reform have been common features of the Canadian political landscape since Alan Cairns's (1968) ground-breaking analysis of the impact of the electoral system on regional conflict. Yet, despite the appeal of electoral reform to some segments of the academic community, there is little evidence that reform has captured a significant constituency among political élites or the general public. The status quo, warts and all, appears to have enduring appeal; the impulse of Canadians to reform has found a more congenial home in movements for Senate and intraparty reform.

What, then, are the prospects for a supportive public response to the creation of AEDs? In New Zealand, where Maori seats have been an innocuous part of the political landscape for 123 years, a substantial majority of the population would support their abolition (Fleras 1985, 564ff.). In Canada, the proposals for the creation of AEDs could spark opposition among components of the multicultural community, and quite possibly within the general electorate. This opposition would probably not be based on a generalized opposition to Aboriginal aspirations, but rather on a specific attachment to an electoral process based on universal values. The success of any proposals for AEDs would likely depend upon the existence of a much more comprehensive reform package, within which a proposal for AEDs would be embedded. Success would also require vigorous and consensual support from Aboriginal communities themselves. Such support may be unlikely to emerge in the short run, if only because the aspirations and energies of Aboriginal leaders are primarily directed toward constitutional reform and Aboriginal self-government.

The Provincial Analogue

Throughout this document, references to the electoral system refer specifically to the system used in federal elections. Nevertheless, much of the underlying analysis could also be applied in principle to questions of Aboriginal electoral representation in the provincial realm. In that case, AEDs would be smaller geographical units; this fact would reduce, although by no means eliminate, the campaign problems discussed above. In some provinces, of course, the size of the Aboriginal communities would not warrant AEDs, or would do so for only one or two Aboriginal groups. Given, however, that provincial constituencies tend to include much smaller populations than their federal counterparts, AEDs would be viable in most provinces. Certainly any federal electoral reform which embraced AEDs would exert considerable pressure for corresponding provincial reform.

Linkage of AEDs to Aboriginal Self-Government

The pre-eminent political and constitutional aspiration of Canada's Aboriginal peoples is captured by the term "self-determination" which, in an operational sense, boils down to "Aboriginal self-government." In essence, Aboriginal self-government refers to a greater degree of autonomous political control over Aboriginal land, over economic development of that land, and over the social, cultural and political institutions which shape Aboriginal communities. In limited models of Aboriginal self-government, such communities would exercise a range of powers and responsibilities analogous to those of local governments in Canada. In more expansive models, the range of powers and responsibilities would approximate those exercised by provincial governments and, in some cases, be analogous to those exercised by sovereign states.

This study does not provide an appropriate opportunity to present a detailed conceptual discussion of the various models of Aboriginal self-government, or any assessment of whether self-government would provide a viable solution to the manifold problems confronting Aboriginal communities.[2] Instead, the present inquiry addresses two more limited, yet important questions. First, would the creation of AEDs facilitate the achievement of Aboriginal self-government, and thus self-determination? Second, would the achievement of Aboriginal self-government imply or necessitate the creation of AEDs?

In addressing these two interrelated questions, I will assume a rather expansive model of Aboriginal self-government, one in which such governments would exercise powers approximating those of provincial governments. While this assumption brings out some of the central conceptual issues in bold relief, the analysis which follows can also be applied to less expansive models.

Perhaps the first point to stress is that existing models of Aboriginal self-government are almost exclusively based on local communities; they are attached, for example, to particular bands and reserves, and not to Indians or Aboriginal people as a whole. Self-governing communities would accordingly tend to be both numerous and small. They could also not be easily integrated into existing Canadian political institutions, not being large enough to constitute an AED for parliamentary elections, and being too numerous to be readily incorporated into existing patterns of Canadian executive federalism (Ponting and Gibbins 1984; Gibbins and Ponting 1986). It would therefore be essential to have some form of Aboriginal political representation over and above that provided by Aboriginal governments. In this sense, AEDs would not be precluded by the development of Aboriginal self-government.

It should also be noted that even in the most optimistic scenarios, Aboriginal self-government would exclude large segments of the Aboriginal population, specifically most individuals living in urban areas, and those living in Aboriginal communities for which self-government was neither possible nor desirable. Therefore the question of political representation of those excluded, a number that may well encompass the majority of the Aboriginal population, must still be addressed. Here again, the creation of AEDs is not precluded.

Enclave Aboriginal populations – communities which are overwhelmingly of Aboriginal descent and enjoy a secure land base – are potentially well served by Aboriginal self-government, although even in this case, important legislative responsibilities will continue to reside with the federal and provincial governments, and thus effective forms of legislative representation are still required. It is the population not living in enclaves, the people dispersed across Canadian cities and towns, who lack any land base and cannot be reached by Aboriginal governments, who are potentially best served by the creation of AEDs. However, this population is also the one that may be least likely to attach a high priority to Aboriginal status when voting, and that would be the most difficult to enumerate for the purpose of establishing AEDs. Ironically, then, AEDs may make the most sense for Aboriginal peoples who are both the least interested and the most difficult to reach.

If we contemplate Aboriginal governments whose legislative scope approximates that of provincial governments, there will still be an important role for the provincial and federal governments in the lives of community residents. At the very least, the federal and provincial governments will continue to legislate in areas having a substantive impact on Aboriginal communities – environmental policy, post-secondary education, health care and so forth. As a consequence, residents would still need to have a provincial and federal franchise. The important question is whether that franchise should be exercised through AEDs or through conventional districts. If Aboriginal governments in fact handled the primary Aboriginal concerns of their constituents, then AEDs would not make sense. The provincial and federal franchises should be used to give expression to political interests which extend beyond an Aboriginal identification. To combine Aboriginal self-government with AEDs would potentially limit the definition of the political personality of Aboriginal Canadians coming under the jurisdiction of Aboriginal governments. Thus, AEDs may be wrong in principle for enclave Aboriginal populations and impractical for those not in enclaves. The corollary to this argument is that AEDs gain in appeal to the extent that Aboriginal governments exercise a limited legislative scope and autonomy.

CONCLUSION

In bringing this study to a close, it is useful to return to the opening question: to what extent can and should the electoral process be modified, so as to provide guaranteed Aboriginal representation in the House of Commons?

The primary advantage of Aboriginal electoral districts would undoubtedly be *guaranteed* and *direct* Aboriginal political representation within the House of Commons. Although the impact of such representation would depend upon the number or proportion of AEDs, and the extent to which Aboriginal members operated within conventional party caucuses and were subject to the normal constraints of those caucuses, there is little question that AEDs would help inject a more forceful Aboriginal perspective into parliamentary debate. It is also likely that the electoral process would become more meaningful for many, although by no means all, Aboriginal voters. *If* the candidates for the AEDs were to run on conventional party tickets, say, as Liberals or Progressive Conservatives, national party organizations would be forced to develop more detailed Aboriginal policies, both in order to recruit Aboriginal candidates and to appeal to the Aboriginal electorates. On balance, AEDs would likely increase the electoral impact and thus the parliamentary influence of Aboriginal communities, in part because their impact and influence are so minimal at the present time. Of course, a good deal would depend upon the number of AEDs. It is possible, however, that the number of seats suggested in the above model would be seen as little more than tokenism by Aboriginal leaders, and also that the notion of a substantially larger number of seats would be rejected by the larger political community.

An underlying issue in all of the foregoing discussion is the potential impact of AEDs on the citizenship of Canada's Aboriginal population. Electoral participation is the *sine qua non*, the symbolic expression of citizenship. What, then, would AEDs have to say about the citizenship of Canada's Aboriginal peoples? Would we be reverting to the days before the Bill of Rights, when Indians had to choose to be either Indians and not vote or Canadians and vote, but in so doing lose status as Indians? Would we be forcing a similar choice upon Aboriginal peoples today? Are you a Canadian, and thus a voter in regular constituency elections, or are you an Indian, Métis or Inuit, and therefore required or encouraged to use a separate ballot?

The values of that larger community come into play in a number of ways. The belief in the political equality of individuals lies at the very core of Canadian political culture. While deviations from the size of the electoral quotient are tolerated to accommodate the special cases of the northern Territories, Prince Edward Island, and sparsely populated rural regions, it is not clear that such tolerance would stretch far enough to permit a sufficient number of AEDs, sufficient, that is, to meet the expectations of Aboriginal leaders and to produce some real measure of parliamentary influence. The limits to tolerance spring from a cultural commitment to the neutral ballot and to the use of the same ballot by all voters regardless of their income, religion, gender or race.

In short, selling the merits of a racially segmented electoral system to Canadians would be a difficult task. It could only be accomplished if the proposal had the strong, vigorous and unanimous support of Aboriginal leaders, if the operational problems could be solved, if the proposal could be rooted in the existing constitutional recognition of Aboriginal rights, and if it could be shown that AEDs were a necessary condition for the achievement of Aboriginal aspirations and the protection of Aboriginal interests.

ABBREVIATIONS

c.   chapter

S.C.   Statutes of Canada

s(s).   section(s)

NOTES

This study was completed in July 1991.

1. The first caveat is of least concern with respect to the Inuit population.

2. For readers wishing to pursue such issues, a voluminous literature now exists. For examples, see: Asch (1984); Boldt and Long (1985); Canada, House of Commons (1983); Ponting (1986).

REFERENCES

Asch, Michael. 1984. *Home and Native Land: Aboriginal Rights and the Canadian Constitution.* Agincourt: Methuen.

Boldt, Menno, and J.A. Long. 1985. *The Quest for Justice: Aboriginal Peoples and Aboriginal Rights.* Toronto: University of Toronto Press.

Cairns, Alan C. 1968. "The Electoral System and the Party System in Canada, 1921–1965." *Canadian Journal of Political Science* 1:55–80.

Calgary Herald. 1990. "Indians Suspicious About Littlechild's Silence on Dispute." 22 July, A8.

Canada. *Constitution Act, 1982,* being Schedule B of the *Canada Act 1982* (U.K.), 1982, c. 11, ss. 25, 35.

——. *Representation Act, 1985,* S.C. 1986, c. 8, Part I.

Canada. House of Commons. Special Committee on Indian Self-Government. 1983. *Indian Self-Government in Canada.* Ottawa: Minister of Supply and Services Canada.

Fleras, Augie. 1985. "From Social Control Towards Political Self-Determination? Maori Seats and the Politics of Separate Maori Representation in New Zealand." *Canadian Journal of Political Science* 18:551–76.

Gibbins, Roger. 1988. *Federalism in the Northern Territory: Statehood and Aboriginal Development.* Canberra and Darwin: Australian National University, North Australia Research Unit.

Gibbins, Roger, and J. Rick Ponting. 1986. "An Assessment of the Probable Impact of Aboriginal Self-Government in Canada." In *The Politics of Gender, Ethnicity and Language in Canada,* Vol. 34 of the research studies of the Royal Commission on the Economic Union and Development Prospects for Canada, ed. Alan Cairns and Cynthia Williams. Toronto: University of Toronto Press.

Ponting, J. Rick, ed. 1986. *Arduous Journey: Canadian Indians and Decolonization.* Toronto: McClelland and Stewart.

Ponting, J. Rick, and Roger Gibbins. 1984. "Thorns in the Bed of Roses: A Socio-Political View of the Problems of Indian Government." In *Pathways to Self-Determination: Canadian Indians and the Canadian State,* ed. Leroy Little Bear, Menno Boldt and J. Anthony Long. Toronto: University of Toronto Press.

Rudnicki, Walter, and Harold Dyck. 1986. "The Government of Aboriginal Peoples in Other Countries." In *Arduous Journey: Canadian Indians and Decolonization,* ed. J. Rick Ponting. Toronto: McClelland and Stewart.

CONTRIBUTORS TO VOLUME 9

Valeria Alia   University of Western Ontario
Augie Fleras   University of Waterloo
Roger Gibbins   University of Calgary
Robert A. Milen   Research Coordinator, RCERPF

ACKNOWLEDGEMENTS

The Royal Commission on Electoral Reform and Party Financing and the publishers wish to acknowledge with gratitude the permission of the following to reprint and translate material:

Calgary Herald; Harry W. Daniels; University of Ottawa Press.

Care has been taken to trace the ownership of copyright material used in the text, including the tables and figures. The authors and publishers welcome any information enabling them to rectify any reference or credit in subsequent editions.

~

Consistent with the Commission's objective of promoting full participation in the electoral system by all segments of Canadian society, gender neutrality has been used wherever possible in the editing of the research studies.

THE COLLECTED RESEARCH STUDIES*

---

* The titles of studies may not be final in all cases.

COMMISSION ORGANIZATION

CHAIRMAN
Pierre Lortie

COMMISSIONERS
Pierre Fortier
Robert Gabor
William Knight
Lucie Pépin

SENIOR OFFICERS

Executive Director
Guy Goulard

Director of Research
Peter Aucoin

Special Adviser to the Chairman
Jean-Marc Hamel

Research
F. Leslie Seidle,
  Senior Research Coordinator

Legislation
Jules Brière, Senior Adviser
Gérard Bertrand
Patrick Orr

Coordinators
Herman Bakvis
Michael Cassidy
Frederick J. Fletcher
Janet Hiebert
Kathy Megyery
Robert A. Milen
David Small

Communications and Publishing
Richard Rochefort, Director
Hélène Papineau, Assistant
  Director
Paul Morisset, Editor
Kathryn Randle, Editor

Assistant Coordinators
David Mac Donald
Cheryl D. Mitchell

Finance and Administration
Maurice R. Lacasse, Director

Contracts and Personnel
Thérèse Lacasse, Chief

EDITORIAL, DESIGN AND PRODUCTION SERVICES

www.ingramcontent.com/pod-product-compliance
Lightning Source LLC
Chambersburg PA
CBHW070910270326
41927CB00011B/2514